Praise for *Leveraging Data in Healthcare*

Ms. Saltiel Busch powerfully and succinctly reflects the current role and challenges of the modern CIO. In her cogent analysis, she alludes to the demands of the evolving healthcare business and technology, projecting that the more innovative and forward-thinking CIOs are better equipped to manage change and ultimately thrive in their professional roles.

—Lac Van Tran
Senior Vice President, CIO, and Associate Dean, Rush University Medical Center, Chicago

Organizations aspiring to meet the challenges of the future would be prudent to consider the frameworks and processes outlined by Ms. Saltiel Busch in evaluating the state of their healthcare data. Her book outlines the people, processes, assumptions/constraints and technology competencies that should be considered in conducting effective gap analysis management. Kudos for developing a roadmap for this complex body of work!

—Michelle Currie
CDO, CETA Performance Services LLC, San Francisco

Technological advances in healthcare including EHR implementation and related technologically incentivized revenue streams present a double-edged sword to the healthcare industry. Ms. Saltiel Busch identifies many of these risks and challenges, most notably the evolution of new but necessary hybrid management roles that join clinical and financial technology in a new and different way.

—Kevin Flynn
Vice President Finance/CFO, Associates in Nephrology, SC, Chicago

As Ms. Saltiel Busch aptly points out, the executive leadership roles are becoming increasingly integrated. As healthcare embraces the challenges of the Triple Aim, the collaboration of the information executive team is critical.

—James Brenza
CDO, InXite Health, Delaware, OH

Ms. Saltiel Busch provides great insights as to the changing dynamic in leadership teams at hospitals and health systems.

—Scott Becker
CEO and Publisher, Beckers Hospital Review, Chicago

Leveraging Data in Healthcare

Best Practices for Controlling,
Analyzing, and Using Data

Leveraging Data in Healthcare

Best Practices for Controlling, Analyzing, and Using Data

Rebecca Mendoza Saltiel Busch

CRC Press
Taylor & Francis Group
Boca Raton   London   New York

CRC Press is an imprint of the
Taylor & Francis Group, an **informa** business

A PRODUCTIVITY PRESS BOOK

CRC Press
Taylor & Francis Group
6000 Broken Sound Parkway NW, Suite 300
Boca Raton, FL 33487-2742

© 2016 by HIMSS
CRC Press is an imprint of Taylor & Francis Group, an Informa business

No claim to original U.S. Government works

Printed on acid-free paper
Version Date: 20151102

International Standard Book Number-13: 978-1-938904-84-4 (Paperback)

Visit the Taylor & Francis Web site at
http://www.taylorandfrancis.com

and the CRC Press Web site at
http://www.crcpress.com

De oppressor liber (Free the oppressed)

Motto of the U.S. Army Special Forces (Green Beret)

All my best to the silent soldiers who have quietly dedicated,

and some given, their lives with valor, courage, and dignity in service to our country.

Thank you for defending the face of freedom.

Contents

List of Figures

List of Tables

Acknowledgments

Several interviews facilitated the writing of this book. They include folks in the roles of chief information officer (CIO), chief data officer (CDO), patient financial services (PFS), and medical data auditor. A gracious thank you to several individuals in particular for their time, insight, and sharing of experiences: anonymous; Jamie McPeek-Johnson, PFS Director, Cook County Health and Hospitals System; Bruce Smith, CIO, Advocate Medical Center; Mary Stanley, PFS Director, retired; Lac V. Tran, Senior Vice President and CIO, Rush Medical Center; and Dr. Eugene Kolker, CDO, Seattle Children's Research Institute.

Contributing chapter commentaries: Scott Becker, Andre Boucher, James Brenza, Michelle Currie, Kevin Flynn, Thomas Hornburg, David Kolb, Eugene Kolker, Duane Lisowski, Nicolas Marko, Susan K. Newbold, and Lac V. Tran.

A big thank you to MBA team members who whipped out the red pen, listened to my banter, and tolerated my whiteboard drawings: Alberto Busch, Andrew Busch, Samantha Busch, Gokulnaveen Deivasigamani, Marianne Devo-Green, Elizabeth Foley, Annie Glynn, Jarrett Kreger, Cristina Malushel, Gretchen Manthei, Nicole McManus, Tara McManus, Jonathan Smith, Lynna Smith.

Thanks also to the very very patient folks at HIMSS and CRC Press: Matt Schlossberg and Kristine Mednansky.

A special thank you to my final cut editor—"BJ" Secretarial Forces Extraordinaire—for those platinum words and verbs that bring most debaters to one knee.

Author

Rebecca Mendoza Saltiel Busch, RN, MBA, CCM, CFE, CPC, CHS-IV, CRMA, CICA, FIALCP, FHFMA, is the founder and chief executive officer of Medical Business Associates, Inc. (MBA), established in 1991 as a minority, woman-owned medical data auditing and healthcare consulting firm. The author attributes her company's success to the development and implementation of a unique analytical workflow process—interactive and iterative behavioral model, system, and method for detecting fraud, waste, and abuse—that identifies all critical tasks, conditions, and standards that promote a stable, dynamic, and scalable healthcare business.

In addition to authoring three books (*Healthcare Fraud: Audit & Detection Guidebook*, *Electronic Health Records: An Audit and Internal Control Guide*, and *Personal Healthcare Portfolio: Your Health & Wellness Record*), Rebecca has been granted seven U.S. data analytic design patents (pharmaceutical applications), one U.S. patent pertaining to electronic health record case management systems, and patents pending on an anomaly tracking system and an interactive and iterative behavioral model, system, and method for detecting fraud, waste, and abuse. Rebecca has authored 52 articles and delivered more than 100 presentations to consumers, government, corporate, and professional entities, has prepared academic course work, and serves as an adjunct professor for a healthcare fraud, examination, risk management, and compliance certificate program.

Recognized as an expert in her field, Rebecca has developed data management practice standards for emerging chief data officers, medical data scientists, and auditors that ultimately support and defend complex issues impacting the bottom line. She currently provides technical investigative, audit, and review expertise to various government agencies and expert testimony on health-related issues in both state and federal courts (see Appendix III for a professional workflow or visit www.rebeccabusch.com).

Introduction

I have been tracking healthcare data (information) in medical environments since I was a child standing guard next to someone special. My introduction to healthcare information started at the age of 12, when I spent the summer sitting beside my grandmother in an acute care facility. At the time, I recall telling the doctor (my father) that the only people working around the hospital were the nurses. In high school and college, I worked in various healthcare facilities, and after graduation, I joined the healthcare profession as a registered nurse.

Later, these clinical experiences proved to be invaluable in developing a 30-year career managing a consulting practice. At first, my consulting business focused on auditing medical bills and helping hospitals correct their internal processes to minimize future errors. My client list grew from hospitals to include other providers, payers, insurance companies, regulatory government agencies, self-insured corporations, attorneys, and others who needed help in navigating healthcare data.

I found myself teaching classes, writing books, providing expert testimony, and advocating for patients. After 30 years of analyzing details, I can summarize in one sentence why most medical and billing errors occur in the healthcare industry: the root cause of all errors, gaps, and failed milestones at some point circles back to a data point that was unknown, misunderstood, misplaced, ignored, and/or just simply not processed.

Before I ever heard the term *big data*, I knew the answer to solving problems for my clients existed in the details (aka data). Leveraging technology, my internal processes started to shift to using more data mining and data analysis. Whatever question I was asked, the answer could always be found in the data. I couldn't help myself from wondering, what if the healthcare industry could manage its data better? How would this impact the bottom line and patient care?

In the year 2015, we now know that the big data revolution in healthcare is upon us. The takeaway from this book is to identify how the C-suite revolution is impacting the chief information officer (CIO), the emerging chief information roles, the need for data intelligence, and the importance of sharing data across the organization. The data has always been there. However, as these roles emerge, it is becoming increasingly apparent that the market lacks a clear, patient-centric data policy. What is needed are new processes and people who are empowered to utilize actionable data to solve problems, increase profitability, and improve quality of care. Take this one step farther by asking your organization these simple questions: Do we have a data policy? Who is being served by the data policy? Is the policy in the best interest of the patient or the organization? I would respectfully introduce the notion that organizations need to operationalize a data policy that is patient holistic. When it comes to getting at the right data to make the right decision, simply stop, look, and think.

Thank you for reading!

Rebecca

Chapter 1

Current Operational State of Managing Health Information

To some physicists, chaos is a science of process rather than state, of becoming rather than being.

—**James Gleick**
American author

This book explores issues and strategies impacting a market in transition. A market that is transitional at an accelerated pace will keep any chief information officer (CIO) up at night. Difficulties may arise for an organization in its ability to operationalize the management of government mandates within the needs of the facility. Other organizations would feel challenged by the proliferation of data and its mechanism of assimilation, access, use, and security management issues, for example, the ability to accurately match the list of data-related items to the individual patient.

Recent surveys report the top 10 challenges faced by electronic health record (EHR) users: slowed productivity; integration with other systems; customization; importing existing records; learning to use; instability, bugs, and latency; costs; deficient functionality; end-user adoption; and achieving meaningful use.

Lending background to some of these challenges, this chapter begins with a bit of history on the policy, governance, and evolution of our public health system and the management of data in the delivery of healthcare services. Data is collected and analyzed to create information that is suitable for making decisions and has become the driving force behind numerous technology initiatives. Orchestrating this data collection, to meet the challenges faced by EHR users, carries its own challenge.

This book examines the impact of data, its respective technology, the increasing use of data scientists, and other management roles to provide user end support on deriving aggregated intelligence. These "information" roles include the chief information officer (CIO), the chief financial officer (CFO), the chief medical information officer (CMIO), the chief technology officer (CTO), the chief nursing information officer (CNIO), and the chief data officer (CDO), in addition to other hybrid information officer roles and their various departmental support functions. The financial side of healthcare and information utilization is discussed in the following chapters. That discussion reviews the parallel routes of information and revenue functions, the areas where they overlap, and the need to achieve true information integration within the generated data.

A Bit of History

Chaos—the mindset of healthcare. Without question, effective information management requires those in leadership roles to be focused, productive, and remain calm. I like James Gleick's quote on chaos as it relates to healthcare: "Those of us entrenched in the healthcare industry can better appreciate the operational state of healthcare as an ongoing operational process that is constantly changing and ever moving."

In other words, expect the unexpected because no day will be like any other. Those who choose to remain stagnant will fail. If you are one of those barely surviving by keeping your head just above water, know that not much has changed since the days of the Roman Empire. Today's commonly known third-party system (payers, providers, patients, and the respective fragmented relationships of accountability) dates back to the politics of Roman emperor Constantine (306 AD). Emperor Constantine funded public health initiatives and directed contemporary state religious institutions to care for the sick. This was one of the first public healthcare models that directed care for the poor by various volunteer, religious, civic, or philanthropic organizations. The provision of public healthcare has been a process ever since.

The next fundamental shift in the systematic delivery of public healthcare occurred outside of the United States in the late 1800s, as world governments centralized control of their territories by region and the system of public healthcare established its roots in the form of mandated government-sponsored programs. From their inception, these non-U.S. government public health programs were centralized from both a policy and a process perspective. Over time, they evolved as public health–initiated compulsory government initiatives. These non-U.S. public health insurance-type programs date back to 1883 in Germany, followed by Sweden in 1891 and Denmark in 1892. Similar programs were sponsored in Austria, France, Hungary, Norway, Britain, Russia, and the Netherlands through 1912. Throughout these countries, the centralization of policy and process became a common framework for public healthcare governance. In essence, the risk of managing healthcare started as a government-sponsored program conceptually similar to U.S. Medicare and Medicaid government-sponsored programs.

So now let's ask ourselves, comparatively, what was happening in the United States during this time, and were we different?

The task of developing the mechanics to refine the Constitution and the Bill of Rights and the mechanisms to execute them took about 25 years; during that time, the subject of healthcare management (at that time for a population of merely 10,000) was left to the states. This tone was consistent with other governmental matters in which control or enforcement of specific laws was shifted to the state level. From the onset, the infrastructure of healthcare in the United States was fragmented in its policy, process, and governance. Keep this in mind as we discuss the Affordable Care Act or any future federally legislated mandate versus current attempts to operationalize centralized public policy considering a widely diverse U.S. population of 316 million people dispersed among

50 states that implement their own diverse public policies, excluding the processes, policies, and standards of private healthcare programs and other subgroups that cross state lines.

The ultimate goal set forth by the Centers for Medicare and Medicaid Services (CMS), Division of CMS Innovation Center, is to become a data-driven organization by relying on strategically defined "information resources" (data) to achieve their current mission of "better healthcare," "better health," and "lower costs through systems improvement" (modernization, software, and training). This centralized policy focuses on the use of technology to leverage information to achieve their goal. Readers will be reminded of this policy as they venture through the various role descriptions that define the emergence and application of technological innovation relevant to the new healthcare landscape.

Public and private programs further subdivide the attributes of process, policy, and governance within the United States, and then once again by public and private employees, in addition to those individuals who are not unemployed. This fragmented approach is how we differ from other countries with established healthcare systems. If you understand the fundamental basis or foundation of U.S. governance—the sharing of power between the federal and state governments—you will better understand the current quagmire that has emerged in attempts to reform and manage healthcare in the United States. The driving force behind this country's core governing principles was the preservation of individual liberty and the need for controls to prevent any one entity, agency, or government initiative from limiting or denying individual liberty.

This gave rise to federalism—the division of power and responsibilities between the federal government and individual states. Federalism as a whole ensured that no single government could exert too much power over any governmental body, thereby maintaining the balance between government control and personal liberty. In terms of healthcare, this process created 50 separate regulatory systems, as each state decided for itself how to handle the healthcare demands of a growing population. While this may appear to be a big leap in the discussion, it provides some perspective as to why we have U.S. public health policies subdivided at both the federal and state levels, in addition to further subdivisions by category based on patients and the providers of healthcare.

Public Policy's Shift to the State

Much of our current private healthcare system evolved from the provision of employee health benefit plans. The employer-sponsored health benefit originated from a need to resolve employee injuries in order to get the employee back to work. The employer took on the risk of managing employee health in order for its workforce to thrive. Today this culture is evolving into healthcare coverage, merging health benefit programs with developing wellness programs. This employer-sponsored healthcare coverage system functions side by side with another of the nation's oldest types of healthcare coverage—provisions for injuries resulting from occupations. (Private employers principally drove the policies and standards in the current healthcare market.) These healthcare "policies" varied by employer and were for the most part shaped by market standards and legislative mandates on both the state and federal levels. Regardless, the cost of benefit coverage for an employee injury is the same; who is managing the risk of injury is what changes, allowing provisions for occupational injuries to influence group health. The notion of compensating employees for job-related bodily injury has a much longer history than the organized public health system that exists today.[1] The Nippur Tablet No. 3191, from the ancient civilization of Samaria dating back to 2050 BC, defines a law that provided "monetary compensation for specific injury to workers' body parts, including fractures."[2] World history on benefits to injured workers is extensive and continues to change even today. Provisions for work-related injuries in the United States were germinated by various events. An illustrative example is the Federal Employers Liability Act (FELA) enacted in 1908. The history behind this initiative is captured in an 1889 speech by President Benjamin Harrison to the U.S. Congress, which defined the working conditions for a railroad worker as being similar to those of soldiers at war:

> It is a reproach to our civilization that any class of American workmen, should in the pursuit of a necessary and useful vocation, be subjected to a peril of life and limb as great as that of a soldier in time of war.[3]

Federal statutes continue to define various work-related injuries, including but not limited to the Federal Employees' Compensation Act (5 USC §§ 8101–8193), the Federal Employment Liability Act (FELA) (45 USC §§ 51–60), the Merchant Marine Act (the Jones Act) (46 USC § 688), the Longshore and Harbor Workers' Compensation Act (LHWCA) (33 USC §§ 901–950), and the Black Lung Benefits Act (30 USC §§ 901–945). (This list does not include state-level workers' compensation programs.)

A deeper dive into the history of health benefits to U.S. citizenry can be summarized by various historical events documented in Table 1.1. Each program has its own history that is fragmented by process, policy, and governance. Take note of the incremental dollars from an industry perspective and from a civil monetary perspective for noncompliance activity.

The brief discussion on workers' compensation and the parallel track of the development of the organized public health system simply revolves around the notion and need to manage the health of a specified population. In addition, the repair of a work-related injury is analogous to the illness model that evolved in the private sector of group health. The patient would go see the doctor for illness, unlike the current movement encouraging an individual to seek healthcare to stay healthy.

The illness model of managing health was sponsored by the health strategies, which incorporate policy, governance of a program, and the need to get an injured or sick individual back to a baseline of functionality.

Systems and Subsystems

The point is simple if one can understand process and both anticipate and appreciate the complexity of federal and state policies and the implementation processes and governance of what we attempt to define as our new healthcare system. Our country's founding fathers focused their attention on the preservation of liberty above all costs and created the legislative framework that prevents any person, agency, or branch of government—federal or state—from suppressing personal liberty.

The Affordable Care Act of 2010 (ACA) challenges more than 100 years of fragmented public versus private health policies, governance, politics, and deeply rooted processes.[4] The challenge of creating one highly centralized public health system dictating policy, administrative processes, and procedures from each participating faction delivering healthcare services has become overwhelmingly apparent.

Table 1.1 Timeline for the Development of For-Profit Movement and Other Healthcare Market Activities

Payer Activity	Growth Rate	National Healthcare Spending (in Millions)[a]	Year	Major Healthcare Market Events by Year	Event (Fraud) Penalties (in millions)[a]	Yearly Penalties (in millions)[a]
			1789	Congress establishes the U.S. Marine Hospital Service. The service was funded by compulsory contributions from seamen's wages.		
			1847	The Massachusetts Health Insurance Company of Boston becomes the first insurer to issue sickness insurance.		
			1849	New York passes the first general insurance law.		
			1853	The French mutual aid society, La Societe Francaise de Bienfaisance Mutuelle, establishes a prepaid hospital care plan in San Francisco.		
			1863	The Travelers Insurance Company of Hartford, Connecticut, offers accident insurance for railway mishaps (followed by other forms of accident insurance). Travelers was the first to issue insurance resembling today's policies.		
			1870s	Railroad, mining, and other industries begin to provide company doctors funded by deductions from workers' wages.		
			1877	Granite Cutters Union establishes the first national sick benefit program.		
			1910	Montgomery Ward & Co. enters into one of the earliest group insurance contracts.		

(Continued)

Table 1.1 (Continued)   Timeline for the Development of For-Profit Movement and Other Healthcare Market Activities

Payer Activity	Growth Rate	National Healthcare Spending (in Millions)[a]	Year	Major Healthcare Market Events by Year	Event (Fraud) Penalties (in millions)[a]	Yearly Penalties (in millions)[a]
			1910s	Physician service and industrial health plans are established in the Northwest and remote areas.		
			1912	The National Convention of Insurance Commissioners (now the National Association of Insurance Commissioners) develops the first model for state law, the standard provisions law, for regulating health insurance.		
			1913	The International Ladies Garment Workers Union (ILGWU) begins the first union medical services.		
			1915–1920s	Efforts to establish compulsory health insurance programs fail in 16 states.		
			1929	Baylor Hospital contracts with local teachers to prepay hospital services.		
			1930	Blue Cross adopts community-based pricing for health insurance.		
			1937	The Blue Cross Commission is established.		
			1930–1940	Private payers emerge with risk-based models, targeting low-risk insureds.		
			1939	The Revenue Act of 1939 (Section 104) establishes employee tax exclusion for compensation for injuries, sickness, or both received under workers' compensation, accident, or health insurance.		

(Continued)

Table 1.1 (Continued) Timeline for the Development of For-Profit Movement and Other Healthcare Market Activities

Payer Activity	Growth Rate	National Healthcare Spending (in Millions[a])	Year	Major Healthcare Market Events by Year	Event (Fraud) Penalties (in millions[a])	Yearly Penalties (in millions)[a]
			1940	Blue Cross joins private risk-based pricing models, targeting low-risk insureds.		
			1943	The War Labor Board rules the wage freeze does not apply to fringe benefits.		
			1945	Truman tells Congress he wants a nationalized healthcare plan.		
$12.90		$117	1950	Payer market; research expenditures hit $117 million.		
			1954	The Revenue Act of 1954 (Section 106) excludes from taxation employers' contributions to accident and health plans benefiting employees and clarifies that such contributions had always been deductible as business expenses.		
			1956	MedLabs, Inc. (later known as American Medical International [AMI]) is incorporated.		
			1956	The not-for-profit Parkview Hospital is built in Nashville, Tennessee, a project led by Dr. Thomas Frist.		
	"Year 1"	$27,534	1960	Partnerships between lawyer Richard Eamer and lawyers Leonard Cohen and John Bedrosian form National Medical Enterprises (NME).		
			1960	MedLabs buys its first hospital.		

(Continued)

Table 1.1 (Continued) Timeline for the Development of For-Profit Movement and Other Healthcare Market Activities

Payer Activity	Growth Rate	National Healthcare Spending (in Millions)[a]	Year	Major Healthcare Market Events by Year	Event (Fraud) Penalties (in millions)[a]	Yearly Penalties (in millions)[a]
			1960	There is a public outcry over the lack of insurance for elderly and other outcast high-risk individuals.		
			1965	Medicare and Medicaid legislation passes as Titles XVIII and XIX of the Social Security Act.		
			1965	Medicare and Medicaid are implemented.		
$40.70			1965	MedLabs changes its name to American.Medical Enterprises (AME).		
		$42,174	1965	Government research expenditures hit $1.5 billion, up 1,824%.		
		$52,062	1967	AME makes a hospital purchase in London—the first European hospital management company.		
			1968	Firestone Tire and Rubber Co. begins to self-fund health benefits.		
		$59,012	1968	Dr. Frist and Jack Massey form a for-profit hospital management company (Hospital Corporation of America [HCA]).		
			1968	National Medical Enterprises (NME) is incorporated in California.		
		$66,396	1969	The for-profit NME purchases several not-for-profit hospitals.		

(Continued)

Table 1.1 (Continued)   Timeline for the Development of For-Profit Movement and Other Healthcare Market Activities

Payer Activity	Growth Rate	National Healthcare Spending (in Millions[a])	Year	Major Healthcare Market Events by Year	Event (Fraud) Penalties (in millions[a])	Yearly Penalties (in millions)[a]
	6-year span, +25%	$83,266	1971	AME purchases Chanco Medical Industries (owner of 24 hospitals).		
		$92,975	1972	AME changes its name to AMI.		
			1973	The Health Maintenance Organization (HMO) Act of 1973 establishes benefit, administrative, financial, and contractual requirements for entities seeking designation as federally qualified HMOs. The act also requires most employers who offer an HMO to offer a federally qualified HMO.		
			1974	The Employee Retirement Income Security Act of 1974 (ERISA) establishes uniform standards that employee benefit plans must follow to obtain and maintain their tax-favored status. ERISA supersedes or preempts all state law otherwise applicable to pension and welfare plans covered by ERISA. ERISA still recognizes the states' role in regulating insurance.		
			1978	The Pregnancy Discrimination Act amends Title VII of the Civil Rights Act of 1964. It requires that employers treat disabilities and medical conditions associated with pregnancy and childbirth the same as other disabilities or medical conditions.		
		$220,444	1979	HCA owns 140 hospitals.		

(Continued)

Table 1.1 (Continued) Timeline for the Development of For-Profit Movement and Other Healthcare Market Activities

Payer Activity	Growth Rate	National Healthcare Spending (in Millions)[a]	Year	Major Healthcare Market Events by Year	Event (Fraud) Penalties (in millions)[a]	Yearly Penalties (in millions)[a]
		$253,916	1980	AMI buys Hyatt Medical Enterprises (owner of 8 hospitals).		
	10-year span, +253%	$294,182	1981	AMI purchases Brookwood Health Services (owner of 11 hospitals).		
		$330,736	1982	The Tax Equity and Fiscal Responsibility Act (TEFRA) mandates development of an inpatient paid provider system (PPS).		
		$365,333	1983	The Medicare Prospective Payment System covering diagnosis-related groups (DRGs) becomes effective for 1,500 hospitals.		
		$402,282	1984	HealthSouth is incorporated in Delaware as Amcare by founder Richard Scrushy.		
			1984	AMI purchases Lifemark Corporation (owner of 25 hospitals).		
			1984	The Deficit Reduction Act of 1984 (DEFRA) changes the tax treatment and contribution limits of voluntary employee beneficiary associations (VEBAs) and imposes new nondiscrimination rules for VEBAs similar to those for tax-qualified pension and profit-sharing plans. DEFRA makes Medicare the secondary payer for covered health expenses of workers ages 65–69 who are covered by an employer plan.		

(Continued)

Table 1.1 (Continued) Timeline for the Development of For-Profit Movement and Other Healthcare Market Activities

Payer Activity	Growth Rate	National Healthcare Spending (in Millions)[a]	Year	Major Healthcare Market Events by Year	Event (Fraud) Penalties (in millions)[a]	Yearly Penalties (in millions)[a]
		$439,876	1985	Amcare changes its name to HealthSouth.		
			1986	The Consolidated Omnibus Budget Reconciliation Act of 1985 (COBRA) requires employers with 20 or more employees to offer continued health coverage to terminated employees and dependents for a specified period (18 or 36 months).		
		$573,990	1988	AMI sells 104 hospitals in response to declining revenues.		
		$714,019	1990	AMI merges with American Medical Holdings (AMH).		
		$714,019	1990	The Omnibus Budget Reconciliation Acts of 1986 and 1990 mandate an outpatient PPS system.		
	10-year span, +166%	$781,611	1991	NME owns 150 hospitals; it agrees to pay a $1 billion settlement for fraudulent billing practices, with $132 million in settlements with patients.	$1,000	
		$962,196	1994	NME owns hospitals in Singapore, Australia, Malaysia, Thailand, Indonesia, United Kingdom, Spain, and Switzerland.		
		$1,016,503	1995	NME merges with American Medical International (AMI) and renames itself Tenet Healthcare.		
			1995	Australia restricts NME activities; eventually, NME sells its international interests.		

(Continued)

Table 1.1 (Continued) Timeline for the Development of For-Profit Movement and Other Healthcare Market Activities

Payer Activity	Growth Rate	National Healthcare Spending (in Millions[a])	Year	Major Healthcare Market Events by Year	Event (Fraud) Penalties (in millions[a])	Yearly Penalties (in millions)[a]
			1996	The Health Insurance Portability and Accountability Act of 1996 (HIPAA) sets national nondiscrimination and "portability" standards for individual health insurance coverage, HMOs, and group health plans; it establishes tax-favored treatment of long-term care insurance. The administrative simplification section of the act calls for regulations on standard electronic formats and for the privacy of personal health information. The act institutes a pilot medical savings account (MSA) program, limited to 750,000 individuals by the year 2000. See the Consolidated Appropriations Act of 2001, enacted in 2000, for an extension of the MSA pilot program.		
			1996	The Mental Health Parity Act requires group plans that offer mental health benefits to provide the same level of coverage for such benefits that they provide for medical and surgical benefits. The act does not apply to groups of fewer than 50 and substance abuse or chemical dependency treatment. The act provides an escape clause in the event plan costs increase more than 1% due to the act. The provisions of this act expired on September 30, 2001, and have not been extended.		

(Continued)

Table 1.1 (Continued)   Timeline for the Development of For-Profit Movement and Other Healthcare Market Activities

Payer Activity	Growth Rate	National Healthcare Spending (in Millions)[a]	Year	Major Healthcare Market Events by Year	Event (Fraud) Penalties (in millions)[a]	Yearly Penalties (in millions)[a]
			1996	The Newborns' and Mothers' Health Protection Act requires plans that provide coverage for maternity benefits to provide coverage for a minimum 48-hour (for normal vaginal birth) or 96-hour (for caesarean delivery) inpatient length of stay for a mother and her newborn following delivery. The act also mandates timely postdelivery care when the mother and newborn are discharged prior to the expiration of these minimum lengths of stay.		
			1997	The Balanced Budget Act of 1997 (BBA) provides several health benefits–related provisions. It creates Medicare+Choice program. It establishes new guarantee opportunities for Medicare supplement policies in conjunction with the expansion of private plan options. It creates the Children's Health Insurance Program (CHIP), a new state children's health program, modifies Medicaid to increase state flexibility in administering the program, and provides $24 billion in federal funds over 5 years to support the program.		
		$1,125,381	1997	Tenet Healthcare merges with OrNda for $3.2 billion.		
			1997	Blue Shield of California pays $12 million to settle allegations that it filed false claims for payment under its contract with the government to process and pay Medicare claims.	$12	
		$1,190,890	1998	Tenet Healthcare pays $12 million in fraud settlement charges on behalf of OrNda's past conduct.	$12	

(Continued)

Table 1.1 (Continued) Timeline for the Development of For-Profit Movement and Other Healthcare Market Activities

Payer Activity	Growth Rate	National Healthcare Spending (in Millions)[a]	Year	Major Healthcare Market Events by Year	Event (Fraud) Penalties (in millions)[a]	Yearly Penalties (in millions)[a]
			1998	Blue Cross and Blue Shield of Illinois (BCBSIL) pleads guilty to Medicare fraud charges for the years 1985–1994 and agrees to pay $144 million in fines to the federal government, the largest penalty assessed against a Medicare claim processor for fraud.	$144	
			1998	The Canadian for-profit LifeMark Health is founded.		
			1998	HIPAA update: National Provider Identifier transactions and code sets are published; National Employer Identifier Registry is published.		
			1998	The Omnibus Consolidated and Emergency Supplemental Appropriations Act requires plans to provide coverage for reconstructive surgery after mastectomies.		
			1999	The Financial Services Modernization Act of 1999 restricts financial institutions' disclosure of "nonpublic personal information." It limits the ability of financial institutions to disclose (1) certain information about consumers to nonaffiliated third parties and (2) certain information the institutions receive from nonaffiliated third parties. It requires financial institutions to disclose to consumers their policies and practices with respect to information sharing among both affiliated and nonaffiliated entities. It requires that in certain circumstances, consumers be notified prior to disclosure and given the opportunity to prevent the disclosure of personal information.		

(Continued)

Table 1.1 (Continued) Timeline for the Development of For-Profit Movement and Other Healthcare Market Activities

Payer Activity	Growth Rate	National Healthcare Spending (in Millions)[a]	Year	Major Healthcare Market Events by Year	Event (Fraud) Penalties (in millions)[a]	Yearly Penalties (in millions)[a]
			2000	The Electronic Signatures in Global and National Commerce Act of 2000 gives electronic signatures and records the same weight as written signatures and records, which should lead to easier administration of electronic benefits, compensation, and human resources systems.		
			2000	HIPAA update: Transaction and Code Sets Final Rule is published.		
		$1,353,256	2000	HCA pays $840 million settlement for Medicare fraud.	$844	
			2000	Ambulatory Payment Classification codes (APCs) take effect.		
			2000	The Consolidated Appropriations Act of 2001 extends the pilot MSA program by 2 years to December 31, 2002, and renames the program Archer MSAs.		
	12-year span, +122%	$1,733,436	2003	For-profit HealthSouth is accused of a $1.4 billion accounting scandal of value inflation.		
			2005	Founder Scrushy of HealthSouth is acquitted.		
		$2,021,000	2005	AmeriChoice of Pennsylvania agrees to settle false claim processing activity for $1.6 million.	$1.6	
			2006	Founder Scrushy of HealthSouth is convicted of bribery.		

(Continued)

Table 1.1 (Continued)   Timeline for the Development of For-Profit Movement and Other Healthcare Market Activities

Payer Activity	Growth Rate	National Healthcare Spending (in Millions)[a]	Year	Major Healthcare Market Events by Year	Event (Fraud) Penalties (in millions)[a]	Yearly Penalties (in millions)[a]
			2006	Tenet pays $725 million settlement for Medicare fraud.	$725	
			2006	HealthSouth agrees to pay $445 million to settle investor lawsuits.	$445	
		$2,152,100	2006	A Texas physician is ordered to pay for a motorized wheelchair scheme and is given a 10-year prison sentence.	$13	
			2007	HIPAA update: National Provider Identifier compliance deadline.		
			2008	Condell Health Network and Medical Center (MC) pay for self-reporting possible Healthcare fraud.	$36	
			2008	Jackson Madison General Hospital pays to settle false claim allegations.	$2.567	
			2008	Cepalon pays to resolve allegations of off-label marketing.	$425	
			2008	Walgreens pays to settle Medicaid prescription drug allegations.	$9.9	
			2008	New Jersey hospital pays to resolve allegations of inflating charges.	$3.85	

(Continued)

Table 1.1 (Continued)   Timeline for the Development of For-Profit Movement and Other Healthcare Market Activities

Payer Activity	Growth Rate	National Healthcare Spending (in Millions[a])	Year	Major Healthcare Market Events by Year	Event (Fraud) Penalties (in millions[a])	Yearly Penalties (in millions)[a]
			2008	HealthEssentials Solutions, Inc. pays restitution for submitting false statements relating to healthcare matters.	$3.105	
			2008	New Orleans hospital pays to resolve Medicaid fraud allegations.	$3.3	
			2008	Grant Park Center pays United States and Washington, D.C., to settle allegations of fraudulent Medicare and Medicaid billing.	$2	
			2008	Bayer Healthcare pays United States to settle allegations of paying kickbacks to diabetic suppliers.	$97.5	
			2008	MedQuist pays to settle false claim allegations.	$6.6	
	5-year span, +38%	$2,391,400	2008	Yale University pays to resolve Claims Act and common-law allegations.	$7.6	$597.422
			2009	Eli Lilly pays to resolve allegations of off-label promotion of Zyprexa.	$1,415	
			2009	University of Medicine and Dentistry of New Jersey pays to settle kickback cases related to cardiology program.	$8	

(Continued)

Table 1.1 (Continued)   Timeline for the Development of For-Profit Movement and Other Healthcare Market Activities

Payer Activity	Growth Rate	National Healthcare Spending (in Millions)[a]	Year	Major Healthcare Market Events by Year	Event (Fraud) Penalties (in millions)[a]	Yearly Penalties (in millions)[a]
			2009	HIPAA updates: See the American Recovery and Reinvestment Act of 2009 (enacted February 16, 2009) for the following section references. Application of new tiered civil penalties based on the nature of HIPAA violations, up to $50,000 per violation and an annual maximum of $1.5 million. (Section 13410). Enforcement by state attorneys general for offenses occurring postenactment (Section 13410e). State attorneys general may now bring suits seeking statutory damages and attorney's fees for HIPAA violations. Previously, such enforcement was exclusively limited to the Office of Civil Rights (OCR) within the federal Department of Health and Human Services (HHS).		
			2009	Oklahoma hospital group pays to resolve False Claims Act allegations.	$13	
			2009	HIPAA update: HHS and the Federal Trade Commission (FTC) will promulgate interim final regulations on notification of breaches. The FTC rules will apply to breach notification by personal health records (PHRs) that are not covered by HIPAA or business associate agreements (Sections 13402 and 13407).		
			2009	The parent company of two New Jersey hospitals pays to settle false claim allegations.	$7.95	
			2009	Kerlan-Jobe Orthopaedic Clinic settles kickback allegations.	$3	

(Continued)

Table 1.1 (Continued) Timeline for the Development of For-Profit Movement and Other Healthcare Market Activities

Payer Activity	Growth Rate	National Healthcare Spending (in Millions)[a]	Year	Major Healthcare Market Events by Year	Event (Fraud) Penalties (in millions)[a]	Yearly Penalties (in millions)[a]
	1-year span, +3.96%	$2,486,000	2009	Other 2009 Office of Inspector General (OIG) cases.	$2,462.143	$3,909.093
			2010	Two Atlanta-based nursing home chains pay to settle False Claims Act case.	$14	
			2010	Brookhaven Memorial Hospital Medical Center pays to resolve fraud allegations.	$2.9	
			2010	Eon Labs pays United States to settle allegations of submitting false claims to Medicaid.	$3.5	
			2010	New Jersey Hospital pays to resolve allegations of inflating charges.	$6.35	
			2010	Alpharma pays to resolve False Claims Act allegations in connection to drug Kadian.	$42.5	
			2010	Schwarz Pharma pays to settle False Claims Act allegations concerning reimbursement claims for unapproved drugs.	$22	
			2010	Novartis Vaccine & Diagnostics pays to resolve False Claims Act allegations.	$72	
			2010	Medicare Fraud Strike Force charges 94 doctors and healthcare company owners for alleged false billings.	$251	
			2010	National Cardio Labs settles civil allegations that it defrauded federal health programs.	$3.6	

(Continued)

Table 1.1 (Continued)   Timeline for the Development of For-Profit Movement and Other Healthcare Market Activities

Payer Activity	Growth Rate	National Healthcare Spending (in Millions[a])	Year	Major Healthcare Market Events by Year	Event (Fraud) Penalties (in millions[a])	Yearly Penalties (in millions)[a]
			2010	Novartis Pharmaceuticals pays to resolve off-label promotion and kickback allegations.	$420	
			2010	Healthcare reform legislation: Affordable Care Act.		
			2010	GlaxoSmithKline pays to resolve criminal and civil liability regarding manufacturing deficiencies in a Puerto Rico plant.	$750	
			2010	HIPAA updates: HHS and the Office of Civil Rights clarify application of criminal penalties for noncovered entities (Section 13409). HHS secretary is required to conduct periodic audits of entities covered by HIPAA (Section 13411). The right to electronic access of records by patients takes effect (Section 13405e).		
			2010	Manhattan U.S. attorney charges 44 members of the Armenian American organized crime enterprise with a Medicare fraud scheme.	$100	
			2010	73 members of an organized crime enterprise are indicted for a healthcare fraud scheme.	$163	

(Continued)

Table 1.1 (Continued)   Timeline for the Development of For-Profit Movement and Other Healthcare Market Activities

Payer Activity	Growth Rate	National Healthcare Spending (in Millions)[a]	Year	Major Healthcare Market Events by Year	Event (Fraud) Penalties (in millions)[a]	Yearly Penalties (in millions)[a]
			2010	Dey Pharma, L.P. pays to resolve False Claims Act allegations.	$280	
			2010	Ameriton, Ltd. pays to resolve kickback claim associated with laboratory testing services.	$16.3	
			2010	St. Joseph Medical Center pays to resolve False Claims Act allegations in connection with kickbacks.	$22	
			2010	Detroit Medical Center pays to settle False Claims Act allegations.	$30	
			2010	Pharmaceutical manufacturers pay to settle False Claims Act cases.	$421.2	
			2010	Pharmaceutical manufacturers pay to resolve allegations of off-label promotion of epilepsy drug.	$214.5	$2,834.85
	1-year span, +4.59%[b]	$2,600,000[b]	2010	Other 2010 OIG cases.		

(Continued)

Table 1.1 (Continued)   Timeline for the Development of For-Profit Movement and Other Healthcare Market Activities

Payer Activity	Growth Rate	National Healthcare Spending (in Millions)[a]	Year	Major Healthcare Market Events by Year	Event (Fraud) Penalties (in millions)[a]	Yearly Penalties (in millions)[a]
			2010	HIPAA update: 18 USC § 1347: "Health care fraud. (a) Whoever knowingly and willfully executes, or attempts to execute, a scheme or artifice (1) to defraud any health care benefit program; or (2) to obtain, by means of false or fraudulent pretenses, representations, or promises, any of the money or property owned by, or under the custody or control of, any health care benefit program, in connection with the delivery of or payment for health care benefits, items, or services, shall be fined under this title or imprisoned not more than 10 years, or both. If the violation results in serious bodily injury (as defined in section 1365 of this title), such person shall be fined under this title or imprisoned not more than 20 years, or both; and if the violation results in death, such person shall be fined under this title, or imprisoned for any term of years or for life, or both. (b) With respect to violations of this section, a person need not have actual knowledge of this section or specific intent to commit a violation of this section."		
			2011	St. Jude Medical Center pays to settle claim that company paid kickbacks to physicians.	$16	
			2011	HIPAA updates: Clarification of ability to pursue civil penalties when criminal penalties are not pursued (Section 13405).		

(Continued)

Table 1.1 (Continued)   Timeline for the Development of For-Profit Movement and Other Healthcare Market Activities

Payer Activity	Growth Rate	National Healthcare Spending (in Millions)[a]	Year	Major Healthcare Market Events by Year	Event (Fraud) Penalties (in millions)[a]	Yearly Penalties (in millions)[a]
			2011	Caresource pays to resolve false claim allegations.	$26	
			2011	Catholic Healthcare West agrees to pay to settle False Claims Act allegations.	$9	
			2011	APS Healthcare pays to settle investigation into false Medicaid claims.	$13	
			2011	Forest Pharmaceuticals pays to settle criminal violations.	$164	
			2011	CVS Pharmacy agrees to pay to resolve false prescription billing cases.	$17.5	
			2011	Serono pays to settle False Claims Act case.	$44.3	
	1-year span, +3.70%[b]	2,700,000	2011	Renal Care Group pays United States to settle whistle-blower case for disregard to federal law when billing Medicare.	$82.642	
			2012	HIPAA update: Regulations for methodology for distributing penalties or settlement money to harmed individuals (Section 13410). HIPAA X12 standards, version 5010, compliance date. These standards are for the electronic transmission of certain healthcare transactions. Healthcare providers, health plans, and clearinghouses are required to conform. These standards are necessary to prepare for the implementation of ICD-10-CM scheduled for October 1, 2013.		

(Continued)

Table 1.1 (Continued) Timeline for the Development of For-Profit Movement and Other Healthcare Market Activities

Payer Activity	Growth Rate	National Healthcare Spending (in Millions[a])	Year	Major Healthcare Market Events by Year	Event (Fraud) Penalties (in millions[a])	Yearly Penalties (in millions[a])
			2013	HIPAA update: Extended deadline for complying with new accounting and disclosure rules for information kept in EHRs acquired after January 1, 2009 (Section 13405c).		
			2014	HIPAA update: GAO will report on the impact of American Recovery and Reinvestment Act of 2009 (ARRA) (Section 13424). Initial deadline for complying with new accounting and disclosure rules for information kept in EHRs acquired before January 1, 2009 (Section 13405c).		
			2016	HIPAA update: Extended deadline for complying with new accounting and disclosure rules for information kept in EHRs acquired before January 1, 2009 (Section 13405c).		

Source: Statistics are from the Centers for Medicare and Medicaid Services (CMS), www.cms.hhs.gov; http://oig.hhs.gov/reports-and-publications/archives/enforcement/criminal_archive.asp#2006; Employee Benefit Research Institute (EBRI), *EBRI Health Benefits Databook*, 1st ed., EBRI, Washington, DC, 1999; Employee Benefit Research Institute (EBRI), *EBRI Databook on Employee Benefits*, 4th ed., EBRI, Washington, DC, 1997; Field, M.J., and Shapiro, H.T., eds., *A Connection at Risk*, National Academy Press, Washington, DC, 1993.

Note: Penalties from fraud are about a $2.8 billion market. Penalties noted are not inclusive of all dollars recovered.

[a] CMS statistics. https://www.cms.gov/statistics
[b] CMS projections. https://www.cms.gov/predictions

The ACA themes include an overall provision to expand coverage to individuals. The ACA further breaks down into several sections:

- Individual mandate
- Employer requirements
- Expansion of public programs
- Premium and cost-sharing subsidies to individuals
- Premium subsidies to employers
- Tax changes related to health insurance or financing health reform
- Health insurance exchanges
- Benefit design
- State roles
- Cost containment
- Improving quality and health system performance
- Prevention and wellness
- Long-term care
- Other investments

Every section within the ACA impacts a current operational process or creates a new process in healthcare. The processes will require new defined data points. The ACA has several new processes, for example, the individual mandate to have insurance. If an individual doesn't have a policy, then the individual may be subject to a tax penalty. Further, the entire process of managing subsidies to individuals requires infrastructure to track and validate the required data points. This now requires a process for the Internal Revenue Service (IRS) to track subsidies provided and respective individuals to document the subsidy or penalty on their tax return. Employers will require an infrastructure to manage small business tax credits or incorporate a reinsurance program.

Other provisions of the ACA may impact current established organizations by amending current procedures. The "other investments" category (examples include improvements to the Medicare program) improves workforce training and development and reauthorizes and amends the Indian Health Care Improvement Act. A current operational process (examples may include additional reporting requirements, skilled nursing facilities under Medicare, and nursing facilities under Medicaid) must disclose information regarding ownership and provide accountability requirements and expenditures.

Imagine the extraordinary challenge and difficulty that exists in assimilating, organizing, prioritizing, recording, and integrating all the diverse state and federal databases (assuming they exist) to include their respective policies, procedures, and standards that encompass everything from existing private health plans and employer-sponsored health plans to the diverse and continually evolving hybrid programs managed by private entities.

In an attempt to set a national standards for healthcare, the Affordable Care Act presumes to unify 50 separate (state) entities—all of which approach healthcare policy with different priorities—into one centralized system. State healthcare programs exercise varying degrees of independence, diversity, and regulatory independence and approach the starting line from different positions with respect to policy and care implementation plans. Some states will comply with the provisions of the Affordable Care Act, and other states will reject the notion of a centralized body determining what will or will not constitute healthcare and services provided to their citizens.

Despite the many arguments over health system pros and cons, the establishment of a successful centralized healthcare system without incorporating the basic needs of all stakeholders representing the U.S. healthcare system would prove futile.

The Provider Perspective and Core Challenge

Throughout U.S. history, providers of healthcare services have had one assembly line–type process that has been subjected to a multitude of policies, procedures, and standards. Any given federal program, state program, or privately managed program will have components that are implemented on parallel processes; however, it can and will display contradictory processes, policies, procedures, and standards. Furthermore, health plans vary in payment models, delivery standards, and defined mechanisms of delivery (an accepted delivery model, and defined methods and procedures, respectively), as well as the fundamental basis for healthcare services.

For example, some programs may pay for the brand name of a drug; others may only pay for a generic version regardless of the recommendation of the primary physician. The increasing narrow networks with the current plans being provided via the exchanges will require individuals to take an increasing role in validating whether their chosen provider is actually participating within the plan selected. Providers will need to aggregate new and emerging payer rules in order to effectively communicate them to prospective individuals seeking services.

The gathering of data by patients has been limited and siloed by the entity. It germinates between and among organizations that were touched by the patient for a specified time period. For example, take a patient with BCBS of Illinois who has received treatment for a 1-year period with Dr. Smith. Now the patient changes his benefit plan to Aetna. The patient now replaces Dr. Smith with Dr. Jones, who is an Aetna network provider. The data exchanged and maintained between BCBS of Illinois and Dr. Smith will not follow the patient in his relationship between Aetna and Dr. Jones. This pattern has resulted in just one example of a data silo. Data silos are pervasive throughout healthcare. A significant disruptor of the ACA is the centralizing of healthcare from the perspective of the individual patient versus a limited defined set of organizations involved in treating the patient. The ACA requires a patient-centric library of all-inclusive health information. The need for a personal health record is similar to that for an individual's credit report. In theory, the credit report is a central feed of all financial information on an individual. A personal health record is a central data feed of all health information related to the individual.

The U.S. market has been reactive and fragmented since its inception. Retrievable data generated from this fragmented healthcare delivery system is further complicated and mystified due to the fact that information relevant to specific individuals or organizations (public and private) may be buried in data silos. Nongovernment healthcare systems that exist outside defined, dedicated, and organized providers such as the Veterans Administration (VA) or Department of Defense (DOD) hospital installations are in essence one long chaotic assembly line of hospital emergency rooms that receive patients regardless of physical condition, medical history, citizenry, or intent or ability to pay for services rendered.

One Patient, One Condition: Different Benefit Plan Rules

Considering that individuals admitted to the emergency room may be associated with any one of the plans listed in Table 1.1, the provider still has only one assembly line process in which to treat patients relative to their condition. Now imagine this ingrained and established physician (provider)-centric assembly line process having to integrate the constantly evolving requirements of the Affordable Care Act (any legislated centralized policy) in addition to other established operating processes and procedures respective to local policies, procedures, standards, and reimbursement models. The bottom line is that there are countless data points to identify, accurately capture, assemble, organize, analyze, record, and store in order to effectively manage healthcare initiatives based on this critical data.

The current U.S. healthcare system is overwhelmed with trillions of individual patient health data records and continues to accumulate information at exponential rates. The challenge in developing a comprehensive patient-centric health data library is to recover data accumulated in "storage silos" (files not typically accessible or made readily available) that is not readily identifiable, accessible, or retrievable by providers requiring this information to effectively treat patients.

Health data (contemporary or historical) is interlinked by a variety of fragmented, contradictory, overlapping, and noncooperative systems that do not effectively or efficiently speak to each other. In a typical healthcare setting, fragmented patient data can ultimately document only a fraction of what a comprehensive patient's medical health record should specifically document. Decentralized and segregated medical record sets that reside inside a specific clinical domain that is part of a larger medical system may never be transmitted to the facility's central medical records department. Within any given hospital system's case management arena, a typical data point may resemble a patient with a documented heart condition who is informed that Medicare does not approve the service ordered by his physician, due to insufficient severity of his condition. However, a Medicaid program would indeed pay for it independent of severity attributes, assuming the medical necessity data points of the procedure are documented correctly.

The roles of the data scientist, data librarian, and data strategist are emerging concurrently with the need for technological tools to effectively mine, map, record, and store the emerging arena of complex and fragmented health data produced by millions of provider systems. Efficient and effective data mining is required to advance the management of health systems regardless of whether the patient is from a public, private, or independent domain. Now is the time to progress from the current fragmented, reactive, compartmented (silo) data-driven decision tree methodology to a much more responsive, comprehensive metric data-driven system.

The Easiest Route to Population Management

Going Forward

Recall the days when the information technology (IT) department was simply the department that managed access. The day-to-day job functions of the typical IT department included responding to user requests for system access, new passwords, software updates, technical support, and hardware management. New missions in healthcare are inspiring the creation of new roles. The contemporary IT landscape has developed into a system where the roles of chief information officer (CIO), chief medical information officer (CMIO), chief nursing information officer (CNIO), chief technology officer (CTO), chief data officer (CDO), chief population health manager (CPHM) (discussed in Chapter 8), and chief revenue officer (CRO) (discussed in Chapter 8), and various hybrid information roles, have integrated, diverged, expanded, contracted, and evolved—pick a straw.

Information technology strategies must now include the ever-increasing need to service complex data requirements that effectively support the population health management mission, in addition to critical revenue integrity initiatives. Revenue integrity has historically resided as a function confined within the domain of a corporate financial department; however, as recent healthcare trends indicate, this most critical function of collecting vital, reliable, and timely data has been tasked or outsourced to highly knowledgeable subject matter experts (SMEs) that are efficient, thorough, and cost-effective in the methodology of medical information data collection and management of field intelligence collection and analysis.

Comprehensive data security initiatives may be the sole domain of and managed by a chief information security officer (CISO), resulting in the emergence of CIO, CMIO, CTO, CDO, CRO, and CISO functions that incorporate requirements to manage nonsecurity data such as business and clinical intelligence. Separate roles are required to effectively manage, maintain, and update infrastructure. The intensity and scope or magnitude of the contemporary data environment requires niche technical roles in the management and provision of data and associated analytics. Resource identification and task allocation to achieve the goal of producing and providing actionable information from data collection (intelligence gathering) and analysis have dramatically shifted from simple data entry to full-circle quality assurance (QA) and quality control (QC) validation (the difference between profit and loss).

The days of "I just provide whatever it is they [departments] want or ask for" are gone. The sophistication of data management and data mining has resulted in an increased utilization of data scientists and technicians to facilitate the enablement of data end users to extract pertinent information and further facilitate an intelligence-driven enterprise. Furthermore, heavy reliance on data that supports revenue management initiatives has created additional revenue cycle overlaps into the CIO function through its necessity in the evolving discipline of revenue integrity management. This book will demonstrate the evolving best practices and standards necessary throughout the healthcare continuum to develop and manage data within and among all business functions, including revenue integrity management. Although these functions have been developed under the role of a CIO—ultimately to manage big data in healthcare—the newest chief on the block is the CDO. Throughout this book, specific case examples of medical audit teams working throughout the healthcare enterprise system to facilitate these endeavors will enable a deeper understanding of the importance of these efforts.

Somebody Has to Pay the Bill
Roadblocks in Technological Revolution

In today's healthcare market, technological revolution has been difficult to achieve as providers seek to maximize available intelligence derived from internal information systems and resident analytic data mining tools. Unfortunately, the reality of the situation is that much of IT spending is currently directed toward managing compliance-driven data requests and moving, storing, and protecting data, as opposed to mining database reservoirs for critically valuable information. In one scenario, the corporation CFO requests "intelligent data" to better enable an understanding of the costs associated with the delivery of care.

In another, the CMIO requests intelligent data to measure substantive patient outcomes in order to bracket and implement clinical direction to ultimately improve the organization's medical management of patient outcome benchmarks. The CNIO requires intelligent data to effectively evaluate the efficiencies of patient care to better manage operating costs, as well as the respective delivery of quality nursing care. The CISO is concerned with maintaining the security of the data.

Ultimately, all players within an organization will gain from a data strategy (discussed in Chapter 5). Therefore, a critical role is the ability to dismantle current roadblocks one layer at a time, all the while moving beyond the status quo. The question is, does your organization have a formal data strategy, and should your organization develop a chief data officer to take ownership of this niche need?

Throughout this book, discussions on data management will take place in the context of its traditional reporting route through the CIO. However, with respect to data, the issues and practice standards raised would also fall within the context of a CDO.

A Review of the Status Quo

The status quo of the healthcare provider market is marked by information that is unstructured, proprietary, and fragmented into silos that are not accessible to all parties who have a legitimate need for the information. Furthermore, the operational state of the healthcare market is decidedly transitional.

CMS offers monetary incentives to Medicare and Medicaid providers to develop and utilize electronic health record (EHR) systems. These monetary incentives include performance incentive goals to help implement or encourage the use of these systems. An illustrative EHR metric is the adoption of meaningful use criteria (standardized data points for future analysis), which has spurred significant investment among all provider types in the purchase of EHRs that have varying levels of functional capability. The facts, however, spell out a different scenario: organizations that simply lack the resources for competent and costly IT support are being left in the dust.

That being said, the majority of these smaller providers see the value of health IT, but they can't come up with a clear solution to the question "What should we be doing?"[5] So as we step back and analyze the landscape of health organizations that are progressively moving forward, the key driver of progress will be CIOs that embrace the transition from hard-copy paper records to full use of EHRs and other supporting health IT solutions that focus on data aggregation in one homogeneous state that supports efficient and effective analysis.

Health provider systems have health data waiting to be extracted or disseminated from a variety of sources. In addition to EHR systems, data exists in imaging systems, electronic prescribing software, healthcare claims from insurance companies, public health reports, and the burgeoning market of wellness apps and mobile health devices.[6] Again, the goal of today's CIO is to identify and unify these disparate information resources into one cohesive tool that will simultaneously cut costs, improve efficiency, and ultimately provide better care to patients.

As it stands, most healthcare organizations' data emanates from clinical, financial, or operational applications divested into systems that may or may not speak to each other. When used effectively, clinical data improves care quality and supports population health management. Financial data assists hospitals in analyzing costs and determining issues affecting the bottom line. Operational data examines facilities management and resource utilization.

In the current landscape, the majority of providers collect this information across different system platforms that lack fluidity and interconnectedness. For example, providers glean clinical data not only from EHRs, but also from insurance claim forms and health information exchanges (HIEs) with other local providers. Although this is not a fluid practice, providers need to refine the ability to share information among different providers within the same medical system, in addition to providers who operate in different medical systems. This is our biggest challenge. A provider may glean clinical data from an EHR, which may or may not provide a complete picture, from the patient or the patient's caregiver or representative, and sometimes by requesting medical records from other providers who may have been involved in the patient's care. In terms of financial and operational data, most providers have separate systems that handle financial data and allow for varying levels of data analysis. "Health data which is diverse in nature consists of structured and unstructured patient data and business information in varying fragmented formats that rarely adheres to any standard or format. This information/data is typically generated via legacy IT systems and distributed across hard-to-penetrate vertical information 'silos' potentially owned or controlled by any number of stakeholders that have different and possibly competing interests and business incentives."[7]

While some organizations have acquired integrated information systems that cover hospital and ambulatory care, the bulk of available clinical data is in silos within disparate storage systems that cannot communicate with one another or limit the exchange of information to subsets of data. Moreover, hospitals and healthcare systems have been slow to develop the clinical data warehouses required to effectively aggregate and normalize available information from multiple clinical and administrative systems within their own organizations. The data problems are really threefold:

- The failure of providers to collect health data in a standardized format
- The existence of unstructured health data that is difficult to assimilate and analyze
- Diminished access to business and clinical intelligence

An Evolving System and the CIO's Role

Keeping these challenges in mind, it is important to identify the needs of an evolving healthcare system to better understand the emerging role(s) of the CIO. To put it succinctly, providers must use analytics to turn IT inside out. Providers, along with all healthcare market players, must develop a data-centric approach that considers data a critical asset for research, clinical, and business sustainment and development requirements. This mindset of analytics should also materialize in consumer-centric tools for individuals to make informed data-driven decisions about their own health. In fact, the data points for clinical and financial data-driven management of one's health often overlap. A single data point could result in and facilitate a distinct clinical or financial decision.

According to Dr. Shafiq Rab, vice president and CIO of Hackensack University Medical Center in New Jersey, "it is important to keep an eye on business objectives when trying to implement new IT infrastructure."[8] Not only that, but health IT systems should strive for "total connectivity," giving real power to the doctors and nurses on the ground who are making the decisions in real-time.[9]

Moving from Data Storage to Utilization of Data

What it all boils down to is a requirement for CIOs to properly align IT and business objectives in a way that is conducive to supporting informatics (information science) and data mining to support modern-day business intelligence goals and objectives. In doing so, providers must eliminate redundant data warehouses in favor of a unified approach that will lead to a system that better supports a clinical decision, increased business efficiency, and most importantly, the unification of health information available to providers, situating them in the best possible position to formulate sound operational policy and execute quality care. It will be the CIO's top priority to facilitate these changes for the betterment of his or her organization in terms of performance on the clinical and business levels. The CIO should work in collaboration with other chiefs in the organization, such as the CFO, CDO, CRO, and CMIO, to articulate the data strategy and a detailed operational process to achieve the organizational goals and objectives.

Benefits from a Data-Driven Environment

Before we can accomplish these tasks, let's break down the two forms of intelligence: clinical and business. Clinical intelligence (CI) supports activities such as quality improvement, care management, and population health management. Ideally, organizations will be able to automatically feed EHR, other independent integrated devices or cloud-based tools, and administrative and claim data warehouses in near real time, and start running analytics against constantly updated information. This kind of approach enables healthcare systems to provide actionable information for clinical decision support and care management while automating routine aspects of population health management.[10] Some of the more commonly agreed upon purposes of clinical intelligence include

- Assess population health needs in order to identify emerging issues and develop an appropriate medical and public safety response
- Stratify populations by the level of health risk
- Predict which individuals are likely to become seriously ill
- Identify individual care gaps; distinguish between social, socioeconomic, ethnic group, or benefit plan provision
- Measure intermediate and long-term outcomes
- Evaluate provider performance and organization based on quality measures
- Drive quality improvement programs
- Measure and analyze reasons for variations in care
- Assess effectiveness of new forms of treatment
- Create more individualized plans of treatment that will lead to better healthcare outcomes

Taking this list into consideration, the functionality of these programs depends almost exclusively on our healthcare system's ability to actuate the movement of data from stagnant paper records to EHRs (if not already there), and then proceed to fluid data analysis that only becomes possible when all pertinent clinical information is electronically maintained in such a way as to avoid segmentation. Another element of clinical intelligence, as mentioned earlier, is population health management.

Population health management has been defined as "the technical field of endeavor which utilizes a variety of individual, organizational and cultural interventions to help improve the morbidity patterns and the healthcare use behavior of defined populations."[11] The emergence of accountable care organizations (ACOs) places a strong emphasis on population health management. As healthcare systems and physician groups form ACOs, they are discovering the need for entirely new forms of clinical (and business) intelligence that link the provision of quality care data with the costs of delivering that care. Furthermore, population health management requires analytics for everything from identifying care gaps and providing clinical decision support to predictive modeling, risk stratification, and outcomes and performance measurement. Most EHR vendors fail to supply analytics suitable to effectively conduct population health management, making it difficult for ACOs to measure the activities they are required to measure or reach their overarching goal of achieving better healthcare outcomes at a lower cost of care.

On the other hand, other health IT vendors, including some big data firms, offer a wide range of analytics that can be integrated with EHRs and other supporting data resources. "Among these are applications for patient attribution, patient registries, prebuilt clinical protocols, risk stratification, predictive modeling, care gap identification, utilization management, benchmarking, clinical dashboards and automated work queues. Some companies claim that they can predict who will require future hospitalizations and will have the ability to measure the relationship between patient outcomes and cost."[12] ACOs are focused on managing all aspects of a patient's care. The ACO is intended to provide a complete picture of clinical information. ACOs are an evolving system that is characterized by a healthcare delivery model receiving payments based on quality metrics and reductions for treating a defined population. The ACO risk model requires the ability to leverage electronic health record information and the ability to synthesize information in a timely fashion for dynamic metric analysis.

Business Intelligence: Integration and Deployment

Now we examine business intelligence (BI). Business intelligence addresses the financial and operational aspects of healthcare systems, including contract negotiations, facility management, measurement of resource allocation, and cost analysis. The goals of BI are as follows:

- Develop ability to identify and analyze financial gaps
- Compare costs of delivering care and maintaining facilities with reimbursement levels
- Allocate reimbursements to providers
- Avoid referral leakages out of network
- Stratify risk from a cost standpoint
- Enable utilization management
- Manage charity care
- Ensure patient financial responsibility met
- Ensure reimbursement levels are commensurate with care
- Determine staffing and operational needs

In today's market, most healthcare organizations either own or outsource revenue cycle management applications, which improves their billing and collection services. Being able to efficiently, effectively, and rapidly mine data for both cost analysis and performance measurement is the ultimate goal of any enterprise in terms of the business intelligence process.

Note that the majority of healthcare organizations employ BI software and programs that are primarily used in the greater business community and are not health data–centric. This software and related programs tend to be tailored for traditional business use, with only a few specifically customized for applications that support healthcare organizations. To summarize, a market gap exists for programs that are specifically engineered for healthcare organizations and providers. Healthcare providers (clinical and financial) must have the ability to analyze information that consists of clinical, financial, and operational intelligence data. Revenue and delivery models are changing with respect to incentives and reimbursement for these organizations. If they do not adapt, they will not survive.

Today, the clinical intelligence and business intelligence field is very fluid and continues to rapidly evolve. Healthcare organizations are creating opportunities for transparency of select data points within their respective organizations. For example, health insurers are now allowing selected data point access for analytics, such as predictive modeling applications. Providers are creating opportunities for transparency of outcome and quality metrics within their organization. Health data management is the emerging target of clinical and financial information systems to operationalize CI and BI among all healthcare participants.

Taking Necessary Steps

Looking to the future, we start to piece together the steps that must be taken by hospital CIOs with regard to emerging information technologies and their applicability to the business of running a group of healthcare providers. The first step is to inventory all data points within the organization. This is followed by seeking the information user and understanding its use, relevancy, and impact on the organization. A process should be established to properly tag what data is relevant and necessary. The CIO should ensure that a process is in place for the collection of all relevant and necessary data as defined by the organization. Before organizations can use clinical or business intelligence, they must identify, acquire, and convert it to a homogeneous form that can be analyzed on a standard platform.[13] In the case of claim data, it must be "cleaned" by professional subject matter experts before physicians can maximize its potential or, for that matter, before the data can be useful for any purpose. For example, a doctor may order a test to rule out a stroke diagnosis, and there may be some coding in the available insurance information that relates to stroke, but it may require an SME to clean the file to identify that the code was just an exclusionary test, as opposed to treatment based, as documented in the patient's medical history.

Since healthcare data is already unstructured, one of the major barriers to developing real information integration is the requirement for compiling health information into one homogeneous state, as mentioned above. The information is all there, but the need to get it in one place and in one form is the true challenge of IT professionals who are trying to seamlessly coordinate with a wide field of providers. The ultimate goal is to bring big data to the healthcare community. In doing so, the most important implication is obviously the ability to coordinate data on a level and with a speed that could save lives day in and day out. Opportunities to improve the quality and effectiveness of care, and the ability to combine information gained from big data and genomic research bode well for a world of individualized treatment of illness and disease, as opposed to the one-size-fits-all approach historically used. This holds great promise for more cost-effective treatment of ailments such as cancer and depression, and better clinical outcomes—both of which are points of interest for the CIO and CFO. The benefits of big data are endless—from reduced hospital admissions to better medication management to improved strategic planning and even heightened fraud protection.

Once the available data is identified, collected, and assembled from internal clinical and financial information systems, health organizations can focus on integrating external data (from, say, patients themselves via mobile health applications) to assist with such things as predictive analytics and the utilization of emerging data analysis to drive clinical and operational change.[14]

Hospitals and health insurers are currently applying big data to clinical care in three principal ways:

1. Improving care of chronic diseases
2. Uncovering the clinical effectiveness of treatments
3. Reducing readmissions

Medicare is imposing penalties on hospitals that fail to improve care in three critical areas:

1. The 30-day readmission rate of patients with acute myocardial infarction, health failure, or pneumonia.
2. The meaningful use of EHR systems. By not incorporating meaningful use data points, the ability to data mine one provider or condition to another would be compromised.
3. Hospital-acquired conditions.

The costs related to these issues are projected to increase dramatically if the treatment of widespread age-related chronic conditions such as diabetes, obesity, and heart disease is not brought under control. These are the real-life business situations that drive the need for increased effectiveness in IT solutions and systems that are being implemented by CIOs.

Other Noteworthy Operational State-of-Healthcare Delivery Market Information

Current literature is inundated with topics concerning research on the critical attributes of analytics and the need to transition from a traditional CIO model to a data intelligent CIO model. This cannot be done without the integration of analytics. The level of analytic integration correlates directly with and provides for a fully enabled health IT (HIT) environment.[15] Research supports the savings and leverage that the IT-enabled environment provides. A 2011 McKinsey report states, "The healthcare industry can potentially realize $300 billion in annual value by leveraging patient and clinical data."[16] However, the healthcare industry is still in the very early stages of using analytics. It is still common to find preformatted Excel spreadsheets and the use of cumbersome importing and labor-intensive manipulation of data in MySQL. Other natural language processing applications and crystal report-type functions with limited user adaption continue to be extracted by the user. Active clinician query into defined data warehouses or registries is still in its infancy.

Attainment of interoperability is expected to be achieved with the use of health information exchanges (HIEs); however, the widespread use of community-wide HIEs is not expected in the near future. When community-wide HIEs are used today, they are rarely comprehensive of all providers' respective data points; this lack of comprehension by design limits the analytics derived. This book focuses on using data analytics to achieve and maintain revenue integrity within the provider setting. An effective strategy will include data input from home monitoring devices and mobile health applications, as well as patients in transport or in transition. In addition, an effective healthcare delivery data strategy will include the assimilation of various data registries with a clinical focus on chronic conditions. At some point, all of the data representing the health of one individual will need to be aggregated to support effective clinical decisions.

Another area that will continue to be modified is managing risk within the patient population. Therefore, risk stratification and predictive modeling must remain on the radar. How will we classify a patient by health risk? Will that classification determine how we assign that individual to a particular health intervention program? How will we associate costs by this assignment and assess our quantifiable metrics?

Author's Note: What keeps you up at night? Your reaction to this question may direct internal discussions within your organization. At the C-suite level, the discussion may involve initiating a vulnerability assessment. Within internal audit, a discussion may involve a review of the current audit charter. Regardless of the need, start the conversation within your organization to mitigate areas of vulnerability for it.

Final Thought

What keeps the average CIO up at night? As discussed in the beginning of the chapter, some would say the management of government mandates within the needs of the facility. Some would say the proliferation of data and its mechanism of assimilation, access, use, and security management issues. The themes of challenges presented by electronic health system users, decreased productivity, and inefficient use of technology provided integration with other systems; ongoing customization; end-user adoption; and incorporating CMS's criteria for meaningful use. Chapter 2 reviews the evolving leadership roles within the healthcare organization.

CEO Perspective

I believe we are coming back quickly to the provider's assumption of risk. It will start with medical homes for primary care and expand to include the rest of the healthcare delivery system through the ACO. Therefore, an integrated EMR is the underpinnings that will eliminate duplication and ineffective care. It must also allow for the new "apps" that will monitor patient health on a concurrent basis. So, population health is built from the bottom up and not from the top down or the community to the individual. This means healthcare for each member will be concurrent and interactive, not retrospective. Those that can't do this will fail just like they did in the old IPAs.

David Kolb
FACHE Chief Executive Officer, Directed Knowledge, and
Former Chief Executive Officer, Founder, HFN, Inc., Oak Brook, Illinois

Endnotes

1. Guyton, G.P., A Brief History of Workers' Compensation, *Iowa Orthopaedic Journal* 19: 106–110, 1999.
2. Ibid.
3. About FELA, Wettermark Keith Personal Injury Lawyers, http://www.railroadinjurylawyers.org/about-fela/ (accessed August 2014).
4. Summary of the Affordable Care Act, April 2013, http://kff.org/health-reform/fact-sheet/summary-of-the-affordable-care-act/ (accessed August 2014).

5. Eastwood, B., Can Healthcare Big Data Reality Live Up to Its Promise? August 2013, http://www.itworld.com/article/2829722/big-data/can-healthcare-big-data-reality-live-up-to-its-promise-.html (accessed August 2014).

6. Eastwood, B., Can Healthcare Big Data Reality Live Up to Its Promise? August 2013, http://www.cio.com/article/2383299/healthcare/healthcare-can-healthcare-big-data-reality-live-up-to-its-promise.html (accessed August 2014).

7. Terry, K., 2007, http://himss.files.cms-plus.com/FileDownloads/2014-09-30%20NetApp%20Analytics_The%20Nervous%20System%20of%20IT-Enabled%20Healthcare.pdf (accessed December 2014).

8. Guerra, A., Shafiq Rab, MD, VP & CIO, Hackensack University Medical Center, Chapter 2, June 2013, http://healthsystemcio.com/2013/06/19/shafiq-rab-md-vp-cio-hackensack-university-medical-center-chapter-2/ (accessed August 2014).

9. Eastwood, B., Being a Successful Healthcare CIO Requires Vision, March 2014, http://www.cio.com/article/2377842/healthcare/being-a-successful-healthcare-cio-requires-vision.html (accessed August 2014).

10. Terry.

11. Hillman, M., Testimony before the Subcommittee on Health of the House Committee on Ways and Means, April 2002, http://waysandmeans.house.gov/legacy/health/107cong/4-16-02/4-16hill.htm (accessed October 2014).

12. Terry.

13. Terry.

14. Bernard, A., Healthcare Industry Sees Big Data as More Than a Bandage, August 2013, http://www.cio.com/article/2383577/data-management/healthcare-industry-sees-big-data-as-more-than-a-bandage.html (accessed August 2014).

15. Terry.

16. Pennic, F., Infographic: Analytics Is the Nervous System of IT-Enabled Healthcare, May 2013, http://hitconsultant.net/2013/05/16/infographic-analytics-is-the-nervous-system-of-it-enabled-healthcare/ (accessed August 2014).

Chapter 2

The Role of the CIO and Hybrid Chiefs in Charge

Information is not knowledge.

—Albert Einstein
Theoretical physicist

Chief Information Officer

The chief information officer's (CIO) role is to provide vision and leadership for developing and implementing information technology initiatives. The CIO directs the planning, implementation, maintenance, and upgrades of enterprise IT systems in support of day-to-day business operations and to support initiatives aimed at improving cost effectiveness and service quality and informing business development strategies. The CIO proposes budgets for programs and projects, purchases and upgrades equipment, supervises computer specialists and IT workers, and presides over IT-related projects. This individual is responsible for all aspects of the organization's information technology and systems (Table 2.1).

The CIO is typically involved in directing the information and data integrity of an organization and providing assurance that information technology functions are aligned to the mission and objectives of the enterprise. These functions often include staffing data centers, technical service centers, and help desks, and developing and maintaining production scheduling functions, communication networks (voice and data), computer program development, and computer system operations.

The CIO is often responsible for maintaining the integrity of all electronic and optical books and records of the enterprise. Currently, those in leadership roles are often pulled into day-to-day operations of the information technology services functions. The future for IT is not only in providing direction as the enterprise grows through internal organic growth and external acquisition, but also in managing data intelligence within the organization. In recent years, the industry has also seen the emergence of hybrid information officer roles, in particular that of chief data officer

Table 2.1 Primary Responsibilities of the CIO

Provide technological guidance within an organization
Supervise information system and communications network
Develop and implement customer service platforms to serve the organization in every aspect
Design, establish, and maintain a network infrastructure for local and wide area connectivity and remote access
Consult with administration, department managers, and manufacturing representatives to exchange information, present new approaches, and discuss equipment and system changes
Participate in vendor contract negotiations for all new computer equipment and software purchased for the corporation
Create a cost–benefit analysis as well as support a detailed definition of data requirements and departmental workflows
Oversee Internet and computer operations
Manage the day-to-day operations of the information technology department, including directing staff who support administrative computing, networking, user services, telecommunications, and other information technology functions
Assess and anticipate technology projects and recommend appropriate action and resources
Establish and direct the strategic and tactical goals, policies, and procedures for the information technology department
Propose hardware and software solutions to accomplish the company's business objectives
Identify user needs and solve problems

(CDO), which have evolved as a result of specific healthcare market demands for the meaningful use of data.

A Bit of History

The complexity of information generated within the contemporary U.S. healthcare system has prompted a rapidly emerging attitude of "divide and conquer." Lack of information or data continuity across the U.S. healthcare continuum has resulted in targeted or niche areas of expertise that are further segmented by diverse information types.

Historically, the roles, responsibilities, and title of the information or data subject matter expert (SME) were defined by a job analysis (JA) that, in most cases, narrowly defined the scope of work. The information or IT specialist existed within a narrowly defined box demarked by expertise. That expertise was limited to designing methods to collect and retrieve data. The CIO is involved in managing the overall information technology for the entire organization.

The application of information utilized by the IT specialist to achieve predetermined goals and desired outcomes has become very complex. The need for expertise when dealing with complex healthcare data, coupled with the sheer volume of unstructured data available to the SME, can present enormous challenges in our attempt to effectively analyze data. How do we ensure the analytical maximization of all this data? Reflecting on Einstein's quote, "information is not knowledge," one could infer that the gathering of information in and of itself does not equate to knowledge; in a vacuum, simply knowing is not useful.

Essentially, information is data that is captured, retained, and aggregated; knowledge is what one derives from the information. That knowledge then provides the building blocks for analysis and problem solving. Current healthcare and legislative demands are revolutionizing the burgeoning number of data silos that exist in today's market. Technology initiatives or products are constantly being introduced into the healthcare market in attempts to address this massive cauldron of unstructured and underutilized data. Increasing demand to include formal information strategies at the C-suite level has formalized the role of the CIO. The sophistication of information technology is driving the changing roles in the market. History will demonstrate the impact of technology and the roles required to manage that technology.

Constantly evolving technology has highlighted the development of very specialized professional disciplines, starting with the mainframe era giving way to the personal computer (PC), coupled with the emergence of the Internet, intranet, and extranet systems. The mainframe era takes us back to the late 1960s, 1970s, and 1980s. The typical roles of the IT professional involved electronic data processing (EDP) managers, data processing (DP) managers, and automatic data processing (ADP) managers. In essence, mainframe computers operated as super calculators. Electronic data processing managers typically oversaw the activities of the organization's mainframe computer, its client–server network, and any peripheral equipment. Data processing managers tended to focus on the overall direction, coordination, and planning of the operations data center to support business decision requirements and further segmented responsibilities by more job subtitles as additional functions became automated. The introduction of personal computers was sparse during the early 1980s but gained near full "white-collar" penetration by the end of the decade.[1]

The role of management of information systems (MIS) emerged in the late 1980s and continued into the 1990s. Job functions for MIS managers were typically categorized into five areas: hardware maintenance, software installation, data management required to support planning and decision making, developing and managing procedures for design development, and documentation and administration of organizational requirements.

According to Graeme Philipson, an IT industry veteran and analyst, "the term CIO came into existence in America in the late 1980s, early 1990s."[2] "The idea was that it [CIO] was a C-level position, the same as the CFOs or COOs, and was meant to reflect the fact that the CIO or senior IT person should be on the board with the same level of influence and seniority as other C-level executives."[3]

However, early on the role of CIO tended to be viewed as commensurate with MIS or the IT departmental managers. Philipson further comments, "The role of MIS was being defined in terms of providing information systems to management. It really did not take into account the concept of the end user."[4] Times have clearly changed.

Hybrid Roles of Information Officers

The breadth and scope of functions associated with data have expanded into multiple diverse core competencies. Due to the increasing need to integrate new technology initiatives with the requirement to provide maximum value from data, a different type of expert (hybrid) was born.

This new "expert" was required to respond to legislated initiatives regardless of where the provider was positioned in the adoption and use of available technology. The need to efficiently and effectively manage healthcare reform by leveraging available technology required the development of several expert niche (hybrid) roles.

The first type is the chief medical information officer (CMIO), who typically manages the implementation of clinical information systems utilized by physicians, providers, and hospitals.[5] An illustrative market shift has been the introduction of computerized provider order entry (CPOE), where physicians electronically submit patient care instructions to other medical professionals and staff that require physicians themselves to have some basic technical system knowledge.

Another emerging hybrid role is the chief nursing information officer (CNIO). This role tends to focus on "heavy clinical involvement in all aspects of HIT implementation and subsequent workflow optimization and clinical transformation."[6] The CNIO is the senior informatics nurse who guides the implementation and optimization of health information technology (HIT) systems for an organization. The word *nurse* has been transformed from the traditional definition and expanded to include experience and education in informatics.

The proliferation of technology and data invited the creation of another very important function—security; thus, the chief information security officer (CISO) was born. With security being a major concern, it is critical to be able to accumulate, exchange, and manage data without compromising the information through unauthorized access, theft, or sabotage.

Last, but not least, we have another emerging hybrid role in the form of chief technology officer (CTO). An illustrative example of this new discipline in the healthcare industry is characterized by the U.S. Department of Health and Human Services (HHS), which provides a definition that highlights the importance of this new role: "The CTO oversees the opportunities to leverage underutilized assets—initially identified as data and our human capital—to maximize productivity."[7]

The message is loud and clear: the healthcare industry wants and needs innovation to achieve current market and legislative demands. As articulated in the Centers for Medicare and Medicaid Services Innovation Center statement:

> The CMS Innovation Center fosters healthcare transformation by finding new ways to pay for and deliver care that can lower costs and improve care. The Innovation Center identifies tests and spreads new ways to pay for and deliver better care and better health at reduced costs through improvement for all Americans.
>
> The Innovation Center has the resources and flexibility to identify, develop, rapidly test and encourage widespread adoption of innovative care and payment models, laying the groundwork for a broader transformation of our healthcare system to one that delivers better healthcare at lower costs.
>
> Better healthcare: Improve individual patient experiences of care along the Institute of Medicine's six domains of quality: Safety, Effectiveness, Patient-Centeredness, Timeliness, Efficiency, and Equity.
>
> Better health: Encourage better health for entire populations by addressing underlying causes of poor health, such as physical inactivity, behavioral risk factors, lack of preventive care and poor nutrition.
>
> Lower costs through improvement: Lower the total cost of care resulting in reduced monthly expenditures for each Medicare, Medicaid or CHIP beneficiary by improving care.[8]

Another evolving crosscutting industry role is that of the chief data officer (CDO). The increasing requirement for data collection and data management has introduced this role. The CDO focuses attention on organizational data strategy, data governance, including collaboration with internal and external partners, data space, and the impact value of data.

According to Wikipedia, a CDO "is a corporate officer responsible for enterprise-wide governance and utilization of information as an asset, via data processing, analysis, data mining, information trading and other means."[9]

Leading organizations realize that data problems are business problems and reflect weakness in a business strategy and resultant operations. Organizations typically address data issues or problems by tasking a resolution to a small IT cell within the department. If the IT department fails to resolve an organization's data problems, the enterprise may choose to appoint data managers to develop data governance mechanisms, committees, councils, and work groups that successfully identify and solve data-related issues, problems, and conflicts.

The CIO, together with the hybrid roles mentioned above, is evolving in response to the complexity of leveraging technology throughout all healthcare operations. In addition, many developing core niche competencies, such as clinical experts, infrastructure experts, and security experts, require the ability to manage, develop, and derive intelligence from the collection of enterprise data points through the use of niche experts.

Author's Note: Does your data strategy include analytics on how to measure and manage "new ways" to receive payment for services rendered, new ways to measure the delivery of care that reduces costs, and new ways to improve quality of care? These are the triple aim components of CMS's mission: better healthcare, better health, and lower costs through improvement.[10]

The CIO Today

Today's healthcare CIO role is rapidly evolving as technological and legislative changes drive dynamic change throughout the industry. In our capitalist economy, the healthcare industry is unique in the sense that it responds very directly to and is oftentimes driven by legislative reform, rather than market trends and demands. In today's market, meaningful use is driving the biggest changes in the health system and is forcing organizations to reexamine their use of medical technologies. This places the CIO directly in the cross fire of transformative change at an organizational level.

According to Brian Eastwood, managing editor of CIO.com's healthcare site, meaningful use (MU) is "the granddaddy of all healthcare IT challenges."[11] Compliance issues related to meaningful use are forcing hospital executives to adopt electronic health records (EHRs) in different stages, with incentives for programs that successfully implement the changes and penalties for those that lag behind.

The financial incentives for change (such as monies received for MU) are a major bargaining chip for CIOs who desperately try to prove their value to executives. This is an opportunity to distance themselves from the stereotype of "one-trick-pony" IT geeks who merely support business functions, as opposed to acting as drivers of innovation and generating profit themselves. Passed in 2009, the HITECH Act was part of the stimulus package (tax rebates and financial incentives) and mandates that providers verify their use of EHRs in varying stages. HITECH has galvanized healthcare businesses to examine the adoption, maintenance, integration, and analysis of EHRs and other clinical software, which continues to be the focus for many hospital CIOs.

The Balancing Act

Balancing EHR adoption and unprecedented accessibility requirements with HIPAA security protocols is another main concern for CIOs and chief information security officers (CISOs). For companies with a wider range of IT positions, the CISO is responsible for maintaining data security in an environment where doctors need to remotely access various types of patient information.

According to Gaylon Stockman, CISO of Lifespan in Providence, Rhode Island, the biggest challenge facing information security specialists is "finding the balance between protecting data and ensuring physicians have access to information they need." Stockman further discusses how "physicians and other caregivers are increasingly accessing patient data to make diagnoses and develop treatment plans. At the same time, stricter HIPAA requirements and new security threats introduced by mobile devices and other technologies are necessitating more controlled access to providers' data troves."[12]

In short, CIOs and their staff are facing a difficult balancing act in trying to make patient data available while simultaneously protecting that same data from unauthorized access and themselves from the increasingly harsh penalties of HIPAA's security requirements.

Ongoing Pressures

Another outside pressure facing CIOs is the electronic exchange of data associated with HIEs. HIE participants may include providers, payers, pharmacists, public health organizations, labs, diagnostic entities, and individual patients themselves.

According to HealthIT.gov, "The demand for electronic health information exchange from one health care professional to another is growing along with nationwide efforts to improve the quality, safety and efficiency of health care delivery. Meaningful use requirements, new payment approaches that stress care coordination, and federal financial incentives are all driving the interest and demand for health information exchange."[13]

Dr. William Yasnoff, president of the Health Record Banking Alliance, indicates that up to this point, it is unfortunate that HIEs haven't experienced any significant amount of information exchange success. He characterized the state of HIE as an "unmitigated disaster" as a result of technological, regulatory, and administrative barriers.

In an article titled "What Are the Top Barriers to Health Information Exchange?" readers' responses were aggregated in an attempt to identify barriers. The first obstacle identified was data ownership, with one respondent commenting,

> If Big Government controls the data everybody is afraid of how that power might be used. Legitimate fear. If institutions control the data the balkanization that makes the present system unworkable takes over. The present mess is obvious. If the patient controls the data the patient can and will selectively amend or release the data to serve his or her personal interests. This is the least workable and useful alternative.[14]

Another response to the obstacle of data ownership reads

> The greatest barrier to achieving success is the desire of individual health systems to control the data on the patients in their service areas. And in turn to mine that data, and control patient flow. It is clearly visible in every regional HIE I have personally been involved with. The providers don't like it, and the patients don't like it, and you can't blame them.[15]

The article continues to discuss patient access and participation as another barrier: "Giving patients control over their health information seems like the logical solution to the problem of ownership, but the reality is that patient control necessitates active participation by these individuals who may or may not care about HIE."[16]

The problem faced by many healthcare solutions, whether it be HIEs or mobile applications, is that patient participation is an absolute must for these programs to be successful, and it remains unclear whether populations of people can change their daily routines to incorporate the level of participation necessary for these types of solutions to be helpful across an entire landscape. The final two barriers mentioned in the article are sustainability and operability standards. Some responses from these sections are as follows:

> I'm concerned this could create a need for all patients to have access to technology for storage and for those that don't the government could step in and offer to provide basic access, but at what cost?

> At the end of the day, HIE costs money. And as it stands right now, no one is really sure who should pay for it. Without a means of supporting its operations, the organizations facilitating HIE won't be able to begin searching for solutions to the above problems.

> Getting information to move successfully between provider as well as state and federal agencies represents the top challenge to health information organizations (HIOs). Although these organizations have proven the ability to receive information, they have realized that a lack of consensus in terms of standards prevents them from pushing data effectively and economically.[17]

> It may be time to start over to achieve a standard without a lot of legacy baggage.

The literature is very consistent with concerns and questions raised. The debate is far from over on how the goals of better healthcare, better health, and lower costs through improvement are going to be realized.

Key Market Barriers for CIOs to Overcome

The article "What Are the Top Barriers to Health Information Exchange?" identified the main barriers for a CIO to consider when managing HIEs:[18] data ownership, patient involvement, sustainability, and operability and standards. These barriers arise from a healthcare system that is extremely fragmented with hundreds of different types of organizations nationwide involved in the exchange of information. In addition, the market has two operational barriers. They include conflicting state laws and multiple HIEs in each state. It may be time to consider an overhaul of the system in favor of a new approach that uniformly tackles the issue of data exchange and makes sense for all parties involved: providers, payers, and most importantly, patients.[19]

Author's Note: Within your data strategy, have controls in place to provide assurance of what data sources are authoritative.

Health Information Exchanges

Despite the identified barriers to HIEs, many remain optimistic that a successfully implemented and universally accessible system of HIE is right around the corner. In his article "Are We on the Cusp of Compatibility for Health Information Exchanges?" Dan Verel writes:

> We're always going to have multiple health information exchanges. HIEs are not a one-size-fits all.... As a policy matter, let us hope that as we build these technologies, our state governments allow such issues as to send data to a public health registry, school nurses, etc. Patients who are uncomfortable with sharing too much can be given a chance to opt out, but such privacy concerns shouldn't prevent the basic concept of data sharing or make it illegal or overly difficult.[20]

Robert Cothren, executive director of California Association of Health Information Exchanges (CAHIE), made the case for a regional exchange that melds components of some 30-odd HIEs in California and other western states, but noted that "it would be difficult."[21] A framework that allows unaffiliated organizations to trust each other for the purpose of exchanging health information needs to be established and fulfill the requirement to scale across multiple states and the nation. Whatever is developed in the near future needs to "reduce the cost of data sharing," he added.[22]

The HITECH Act also funded the creation of state HIEs. These groups have the unenviable task of helping healthcare organizations share data contained in thousands of proprietary EHR systems through the Nationwide Health Information Network Exchange initiative and are tasked with developing national standards and uniform policies for data exchange. For example, the Illinois Office of Health Information Technology (OHIT) was created by executive order to direct and coordinate state health IT and health information exchange initiatives.

In addition, there are close to 300 HIE organizations (most of which predate the HITECH Act) that represent their own geographic areas, set their own policies, and have matured more rapidly than state groups. "CIOs looking to get started with HIE will likely face more questions than answers and find it a highly political process."[23]

Accountable Care Organizations

In addition to meaningful use and HIEs, accountable care organizations (ACOs) are also becoming a consideration for CIOs as they attempt to align themselves with the operating structures of these expanding institutions. An ACO is a healthcare organization characterized by a payment and care delivery model that seeks to tie provider reimbursements to quality metrics and reductions in the total cost of care for an assigned population of patients. This issue, of course, is bigger than ACOs—it's a core principle of payment reform. CIOs must find a way to analyze data for ACOs, medical homes, and bundled payment models, as well as pay-for-performance, Medicare five-star programs, and so forth.

A group of coordinated healthcare providers form an ACO, which then provides care to patient groups. The ACO may use a range of payment models (capitation, fee-for-service with asymmetric or symmetric shared savings, etc.). The ACO is accountable to the patients and the third-party payer for the quality, appropriateness, and efficiency of the healthcare provided. The goals of the ACO model are to provide a more coordinated care experience for the patient, improve communication between multiple providers involved in an individual's plan of care, reduce duplication of services, and improve the quality of care an individual receives while at the same time reducing the cost of that care.

According to the Centers for Medicare and Medicaid Services (CMS), an ACO is "an organization of healthcare providers that agrees to be accountable for the quality, cost, and overall care of Medicare beneficiaries who are enrolled in the traditional fee-for-service program who are assigned to it."[24] ACOs serve about 10%, or 5.3 million, of all Medicare beneficiaries and currently serve approximately 33 million non-Medicare patients.[25]

Nationwide, ACOs continue to grow and are becoming a more consistent staple of the healthcare landscape as providers adapt to a marketplace based more on efficiency than volume, which was the system of the prior decade. As of April 2014, there were more than 150 non-Medicare ACOs, and combined Medicare and non-Medicare ACOs serve between 46 million and 52 million, or roughly 15%–18%, of the population.[26]

"The rapid growth of ACOs is very encouraging," says Niyum Gandhi, a partner in Oliver Wyman's Health & Life Sciences consulting practice. "But no one should be deceived: The process of shifting American healthcare to a new sustainable model is nowhere near the finish line. On the other hand, these numbers mean we have a critical mass lined up at the starting gate."[27]

The role of the CIO as it pertains to ACOs centers on the ability to augment the existing provider mechanisms with additional technological solutions that improve efficiency in the following ways:

- Reduced hospital readmissions
- Better medication management
- Improved strategic planning (clinical intelligence and business intelligence)
- Heightened fraud protection
- Reduced costs of care *and* business operations

In summary, ACOs and the ACO model are starting to shift health provider priorities in terms of how they deliver services. Nationwide, CIOs must determine the landscape of their own individual market when deciding how to react to ACOs with innovative technological solutions aimed at efficiency—the main focus of ACOs. Later chapters in this book discuss data strategies, methodologies, and considerations in evolving into a data-driven organization.

Author's Note: Do you see the CMS Innovation Center mission statement embedded in these efforts? The mission is better healthcare, better health, and lower costs through improvement.

Key Internal Barriers for CIOs to Overcome

Moving on, we must examine the internal issues facing CIOs, specifically IT infrastructure, C-suite interactions, data flow, big data itself, and system implementation and digitization, among others. "Under Pressure: The Changing Role of the Healthcare CIO," a report from the Economist Intelligence Unit (EIU), surveyed 100 senior IT executives across a range of U.S. healthcare providers. The EIU also conducted in-depth interviews with many healthcare technology leaders to gain their views on the most pressing issues facing them during this crucial time for healthcare IT.[28]

According to the EIU report, the CIO is taking on additional responsibilities and characteristics:

Strategist: CIOs are expected to become increasingly more strategic as the healthcare revolution rolls on. They must have a vision and a plan for balancing the needs for patient safety with the need for appropriate information sharing.

One EIU interviewee explains, "We create solutions that speak to key business issues as competitiveness and patient safety—many more areas that we previously did not get actively involved in. The survey reported over half of the respondents (53%) said they spend 75% of their time on operations and just 25% on strategy. But a majority (62%) said their role will become increasingly crucial to their organization as the IT revolution gathers pace."

Communicator: A need for effective communication requires CIOs to possess a solid understanding of their businesses' overall goals and to present the "art of the possible" when explaining how new technology may benefit the business.[29]

CIOs' communication skills—their ability to negotiate, build consensus, engage stakeholders, and make business cases—have improved dramatically since the days when they were in charge of data processing. A whole new communication skill set is needed for an audience that includes both clinicians and a staff of high-level "techies." CIOs must know their audience and cater to their unique knowledge and skill sets. The report explains that 60% of CIOs found that placing technology in terms of solving customer or partner problems helped them to better communicate the benefits to their business. To do this, CIOs need to check in with their staff and their business and ask questions in order to understand the existing, pressing needs of the customers and the business itself. CIOs need to tell a story about their strategic plan, presenting more than one potential solution, with all the pros and cons delineated so that their audience can make an informed decision about the technology.

Educator: As physicians and hospitalists accept the inevitable presence of ongoing market changes, such as meaningful use and the increase in ACOs, CIOs must take the lead in educating senior management on the best options available to move their healthcare entity in the best cost-effective direction. They need to be well versed on the benefits inherent in their strategic plan. "Successful CIOs are going to have to go out there and educate senior management on what they are doing and what the benefits are."[30]

Collaborator: It is one thing to have a great plan in place to steer your hospital entity through the IT storm. It is quite another to get the rest of the team to power the boat.

Per the report by the Economist Intelligence Unit, "CIOs also need to secure the buy-in of clinical staff when planning and rolling out new IT. Changing the behavior of those who use the technology—doctors, nurses, and other staff—may be a greater challenge than managing board-level expectations. CIOs need to secure clinical buy-in for new technologies, for instance by using senior physicians to champion technology among clinical teams and by demonstrating improved outcomes."

CIOs will have to engage stakeholders in order to help justify the investments. They will need to bring business experts in to evaluate the trade-offs, and they will need to manage clinical teams and practitioners to ensure effective implementation.

The Economist Intelligence Unit report continues:

> CIOs report that in order to be successful, they are having to get more directly involved in what clinicians do, and making sure clinicians are involved in IT department decisions by seeking their active participation

in developing and implementing technology solutions.... For most CIOs, this means not only promoting new technology to those who will use it, but also getting clinicians involved in developing the solutions—most especially nurses, physicians, and others who have direct contact with patients and are collecting the data.... Convincing doctors who are used to completing paper forms to start using far more complex digital devices is one of the bigger challenges—especially if using digital devices requires hours of training that they could otherwise devote to their practices.

Optimist: CIOs must have faith. Once they convince their board or organizational decision makers to support their strategies, they must strive to meet the objectives of meaningful use and qualify for their portion of incentives set aside (and avoidance of future penalties) to offset introducing EHRs and other money-saving technologies. CIOs will need to remember the end goal established by their organization when they are working toward developing and selling their ideas.

Innovator: An innovator is someone who introduces something that is *better* than what existed before. "CIOs have been pulled much more deeply into areas such as performance improvement, patient safety, and quality of care—and many more areas that once were the exclusive domain of clinicians and others outside the field of information technology.... We are now innovators; we create solutions that speak to key business issues such as competitiveness, patient safety—and many more areas that we previously did not get actively involved in."

CIOs must be willing to apply their ideas in areas outside of their comfort zone, and they must be relentless in gathering the knowledge they need to better understand how to improve their business.

Process change leader: Process change management refers to the idea of managing a set of basic tools or structures intended to keep any process of change under control. A process change leader provides the driving forces, visions, and processes that fuel large-scale transformation.

Process change leadership is an engine. It's about big visions and empowering people to make something happen. Change leadership is about making the big leaps, even as windows of opportunity come at us more quickly and close faster than ever before. Meaningful use is a huge opportunity, yet our window does not stay open for long. Today's CIO must take the leap and succeed in galvanizing individuals and segmented groups within his or her organization in order to qualify for the incentives. (Change management versus change leadership—what's the difference?) "You have to be a diplomat, you have to be a persuader, you have to be visionary, and you have to get outside the organization to understand what is going on in the outside world, and then bring that knowledge back. You also need a deep understanding of the business, on top of managing all the regulatory issues."[31]

Big data specialist: One role of the CIO that is not fully touched on in the report is that of big data specialist. As we know, big data is continuing to drive healthcare operations on the clinical side by integrating data systems for a synthesized repository of actionable data. The role of the CIO is to actively pursue ways to integrate available information from a variety of sources, including the following: electronic health records, revenue cycle management, imaging systems, electronic prescribing software, healthcare claims, public health records, and the burgeoning market of wellness apps and mobile health devices and other new technologies.

For more information on the specific technologies and methods utilized by big data, refer to Chapter 1, Table 1.1 where these processes are detailed in full. Eventually the role in managing data should be considered under the management of a chief data officer. Organizations will require a formal data strategy to effectively embrace a data-driven organization.

Categorically, the current IT roles in the market manage information through segmented functions: CIO, CMIO, CNIO, CTO, CDO, CISO, and their respective hybrids (collectively CIO et al.). The role of the CIO is to facilitate the secure flow of information to the people who need it when they need it. The overall goal of providers is to have the ability to make real-time healthcare decisions and gather actionable data that can improve clinical patient outcomes.

To meet these goals, healthcare entities need to utilize their IT specialists to their full potential. Is the CIO team actively involved at the C-suite level? Is the current market quagmire and transitional state distracting from the active mission? It is important not to lose sight of the primary mission—better healthcare, better health, and lower costs through improvement—currently being mandated through ongoing legislation. Do we know what it looks like and how to measure it? This goal cannot possibly be achieved without a dynamic CIO team and a truly engaged organizational enterprise, working together, sleeves rolled up collectively throughout.

Final Thought

Has your organization defined its required information roles? Begin by creating an organizational chart of current roles. Later in this book, compare the functional roles of managing information discussed in Chapter 9 and highlighted in Figure 9.2. Regardless of ongoing changes, revenue needs to be managed. Chapter 3 discusses ongoing patient financial services (PFS) considerations.

CIO Perspective

This chapter powerfully and succinctly reflects the current role and challenges of the modern CIO. In her cogent analysis, Ms. Busch alludes to the demands of the evolving healthcare business and technology, projecting that the more innovative and forward-thinking CIOs are better equipped to manage change and ultimately thrive in their professional roles.

—**Lac Van Tran**
Senior Vice President, Chief Information Officer, Associate Dean,
Rush University Medical Center, Chicago, Illinois

Endnotes

1. Connolly, B., How the CIO Came to Be: The History of Chief Information Officers, January 2013, http://www.cio.com.au/article/451627/how_cio_came_history_chief_information_officers/ (accessed August 2014).
2. Ibid.
3. Ibid.
4. Ibid.

5. Leviss, J., Kremsdorf, R., and Mohaideen, M., The CMIO—A New Leader for Health Systems, 2006, http://www.ncbi.nlm.nih.gov/pmc/articles/PMC1561791/ (accessed August 2014).

6. Murphy, J., The Nursing Informatics Workforce, http://www.medscape.com/viewarticle/746226_3 (accessed August 17, 2014).

7. Department of Health and Human Services, Chief Technology Office Feedback Forum, http://hhscto.uservoice.com/ (accessed August 2014).

8. Centers for Medicare and Medicaid Services (CMS), Our Mission, http://innovation.cms.gov/about/Our-Mission/index.html (accessed August 2014).

9. Chief Data Officer, 2014, http://en.wikipedia.org/wiki/Chief_data_officer (accessed August 2014).

10. CMS, Our Mission.

11. Eastwood, B., Top Challenges Facing Healthcare CIOs, August 2012, http://www.cio.com/article/2368501/healthcare/top-challenges-facing-healthcare-cios.html (accessed August 2014).

12. Gregg, H., A CISO's Biggest Challenge, June 2014, http://www.beckershospitalreview.com/health-care-information-technology/a-ciso-s-biggest-challenge.html (accessed August 2014).

13. HealthIT.gov, Health Information Exchange, June 2014, http://www.healthit.gov/HIE (accessed August 2014).

14. Murphy, K., What Are the Top Barriers to Health Information Exchange? January 2013, http://ehrintelligence.com/2013/01/22/what-are-the-top-barriers-to-health-information-exchange/ (accessed August 2014).

15. Ibid.

16. Ibid.

17. Ibid.

18. Ibid.

19. Ibid.

20. Verel, D., Are We on the Cusp of Compatibility for Health Information Exchanges? July 2014, http://medcitynews.com/2014/07/health-exchange-compatibility-cusp/ (accessed August 2014).

21. Ibid.

22. Ibid.

23. Eastwood, Top Challenges Facing Healthcare CIOs.

24. Accountable Care Organization, 2014, http://en.wikipedia.org/wiki/Accountable_care_organization (accessed August 2014).

25. Wyman, O., Accountable Care Organizations Now Serve up to 17% of Americans, April 2014, http://www.oliverwyman.com/who-we-are/press-releases/2014/accountable-care-organizations-now-serve-up-to-17—of-americans.html (accessed August 2014).

26. Verel, Are We on the Cusp?

27. Wyman, Accountable Care Organizations Now Serve up to 17% of Americans.

28. Economist Intelligence Unit, Under Pressure: The Changing Role of the Healthcare CIO, http://www.economistinsights.com/sites/default/files/presentations/Under_pressure_Slides.pdf (accessed August 2014).

29. Ibid.

30. Economist Intelligence Unit, Under Pressure: The Changing Role of the Healthcare CIO, April 2012, http://www.slideshare.net/Management-Thinking/under-pressure-the-changing-role-of-the-healthcare-cio (accessed August 2014).

31. Ibid.

Chapter 3

The Role of Patient Financial Services

It is amazing that people who think we cannot afford to pay for doctors, hospitals, and medication somehow think that we can afford to pay for doctors, hospitals, medication and a government bureaucracy to administer it.

—**Thomas Sowell**
American economist

The operational concept that defines patient financial services (PFS) is simple in theory. PFS is focused on managing patient accounts for healthcare services rendered or anticipated. PFS internal infrastructure requires the generation and management of six critical data points. To accurately generate a bill requires eligibility, proper registration, charges, diagnosis codes, procedure codes, and someone to pay the bill.

In addition, PFS is dependent on external partners who have the ability to receive and process these same six critical data points. Any future conceptualization of patient financial services will require the healthcare industry to fundamentally shift away from its current segmented operation. Today's focus is the management of patient services: the payer and the provider responding to their respective contractual agreements prior to servicing the patient. A patient-centric healthcare system requires the patient to be the primary driver of financial management, followed by providers and the payers.

PFS is also directly involved in revenue cycle support, works with other departments that document patient care services, and is dependent on the information they receive from other supporting organizational elements. Therefore, it is imperative that PFS has a revenue cycle strategy that facilitates specific processes to ensure data integrity. Today, the management of patient financial services is heavily focused on transactions between payers and providers. Other areas for PFS's direct or indirect involvement may include activities that support price transparency (such as the ability to evaluate and assess the actual cost of delivering a particular service so that that service can be appropriately priced), revenue strategies that support a variety of patient payment options and methodologies, and mechanisms that can help external organizations evaluate the value of care delivered (which requires weighing the cost of receiving care with the quality of care delivered). The rapidly changing technological environment should be viewed as an opportunity to strengthen the substance and breadth of data in order to enhance patient financial support services that generate revenue through the door.

A Bit of History

Financial management has an extensive global history. In 400 BC, Socrates philosophized about the respectable calling of management in Xenophon's *Oeconomicus* (Household Management), setting a foundation for PFS functional attributes that exist today. Financial management is both an art and a science—and ultimately a social responsibility. Contributing to the art, science, and social responsibility of financial management requires an understanding and appreciation of Socrates's work. Socrates set the ethical stage for integrating social responsibility with the pursuit of profit by fulfilling a human want.

Efficiency of workflow is important to be effective in financial management. Plato (350 BC) contributes to this notion in his writings. In Plato's works, he discusses efficiency and the attributes that are achieved through division of functions and specialization. Even today, financial management can be traced back to the acts of bartering and trading, which date back to the origin of man.[1] Trading between cultures (contracts) was documented in the Mediterranean region between 25 and 30,000 BC.[2] Planning and control systems were identified in the Chinese culture dating back to 1100 BC.[3] Hammurabi, the Babylonian king from 1792 to 1750 BC, developed a minimum wage system.[4] Record keeping and planning development systems were implemented and used in the Sumerian cultures in 4000 BC.[5] Therefore, the attributes of financial management as an art, science, and social responsibility have set the stage for the development of efficiency, planning, internal controls, systems, wages, and fiduciary responsibility throughout human history.

The attributes of financial management have evolved throughout history and continue to evolve in response to market developments. The core concepts of managing, planning, negotiating, collecting, and recording are inescapable; they have formed the basis for all successful historical financial transacting and will impact all future financial management systems. For example, U.S. history tells us that after the discovery of antibiotics and the development of modern surgery in the late 1800s and early 1900s, hospitals were viewed as places for treatment versus places in which patients were sent to die.

Between the cessation of the Civil War and 1925, the number of hospitals in the United States grew from approximately 170 to 7,000, creating an additional 825,000 hospital beds.[6] During that time, hospital administrators (current-day hospital chief executive officers [CEOs]) were referred to as superintendents and received their formal education and financial training for hospital administration from a book published by Michael Davis, *Hospital Administration, a Career: The Need of Trained Executives for a Billion Dollar Business, and How They May Be Trained*.

Davis approached the American College of Hospital Administrators (now the American College of Healthcare Executives) and proposed that formal financial training should be provided to the Committee on the Costs of Medical Care (the practice standards organization of the day) in October 1932 by stating, "Hospitals and clinics are not only medical institutions, they are social and business enterprises."[7] And so began our focus on the business enterprise of healthcare.

William G. Follmer, consulting accountant for Rochester Hospital Council, wrote a letter in August 1945 to the members of the Organizing Committee of the American Association of Hospital Accountants (AAHA) discussing the unique attributes of hospital accounting. Follmer emphasized the need for a specialized organization within the healthcare provider system that focused on the unique attributes and importance of finance in this industry.

It is interesting to recognize that the AAHA organization was predated by a small group of hospital superintendents that started the American Hospital Association (AHA) in 1898 and the American College of Healthcare Executives in 1933. The AAHA later changed its name to the Healthcare Financial Management Association (HFMA) in 1982.[8] In 1949, the HFMA established its first educational conference, with the objectives focused on education, communication, and the provision of didactic services, and set the stage for follow-on medical conferences. The HFMA identified a number of key functional areas necessary for members to improve workflows within their individual organizations, including accounting statements, internal control methods and procedures, work simplification, graphic presentations of budget reports, depreciation, appraisals, insurance, cost analysis, inventory control, credit and collections, mechanical accounting, and disbursements for payroll and accounts payable.

HFMA's reputation as an educational resource for ongoing practice standards has been well known since its inception. In addition, HFMA has established market standards known as MAP Keys as practice guidelines to measure effective revenue cycle management.

Hybrid Roles of Patient Financial Services

The name change from AAHA to HFMA in 1982 facilitated HFMA to broaden the developing roles in hospital finance beyond the chief financial officer (CFO). Hospitals subsequently created traditional accounting departments to manage ongoing operations; however, the management of patient accounts (patient financial services) continued to increase in complexity, breadth, and scope. The scope and roles within the business office and patient accounts evolved over time to support burgeoning patient financial services. These changing roles continued to be directly proportional to the complexity of healthcare reimbursement that was itself developing into a behemoth.

As an example, in 1929, Baylor Hospital in Texas initiated an agreement with a local teachers' union to provide hospital care to the union's members for a set monthly premium. This type of agreement created a need to handle patient accounts from a managed care perspective—meaning that the hospital was guaranteeing coverage to teachers for hospital care, for a predetermined number of days, and at a preset premium. Other organizations quickly followed suit, creating the need to manage ongoing privately negotiated agreements, including the management of legislated (mandated employee injury coverage) benefit plan arrangements. This quickly became a PFS function. The 1965 passage of Medicare and Medicaid also required PFS to increase the sophistication of resources utilized to effectively manage patient accounts from the dual perspective of both private and government-sponsored reimbursement systems. Each health plan had rules and guideline provisions for its beneficiaries. The plan provisions varied, thus requiring management controls.

As medical health system accounting and business offices have evolved, the role of patient registration has increased in importance—primarily due to the complexity of healthcare plans. If the patient is not registered correctly, the downstream financial effects relevant to this individual will be experienced throughout his or her entire healthcare experience. The impact is often financial for the patient; unapproved services will not be reimbursed. The adoption of varied and sophisticated registration functions varies significantly throughout the U.S. healthcare market. A recent experience with my son's emergency room visit afforded me the opportunity to reflect on the use of the provider's patient registration (system) technology.

My son's experience began with an acute clinical condition: an uncontrolled 8-hour nosebleed. We checked into the emergency room at 8:00 p.m. "Technology" greeted us at the door when the registrant scanned my son's ID and quickly found his insurance information from a prior visit. Registration was completed in less than 3 minutes, and we were assigned to ER bed 7.

Within 5 minutes, the doctor was in the room calling up my son's information on a portable screen. The attending physician documented my son's condition (assessment) online and initiated directives for treatment. Nursing staff promptly responded with supplies, and my son was adequately treated, followed by a patient financial services representative entering the room with an iPad. We electronically signed a consent form, benefits were verified, and the representative identified a $400 co-pay and requested that it be paid by check or credit card before checking out.

The use of technology to effectively manage patient care has entered the patient financial services arena. The above example demonstrates how billing and collection processes have been integrated into a patient's treatment experience via the use of technology compatible with an iPad, enabling the gathering of a patient's consent for treatment and options for collection of patient financial responsibility.

The Affordable Care Act (ACA), ongoing Centers for Medicare and Medicaid Services (CMS) mandates, and private plan arrangements expand the need for comprehensive skill sets that comply with private and public healthcare benefit programs. PFS and other departmental functions have expanded into inpatient versus outpatient reporting and are further subdivided by patient access, billing, collection, and clerical support. In addition, healthcare systems within their PFS departments have gone the extra mile by hiring patient advocates to comprehensively support patient needs at every juncture in the process. Furthermore, the need for price transparency in communications with patients is critical to the success for any healthcare provider wishing to remain solvent.

Author's Note: The market struggles in placing the patient as the primary driver of healthcare expense management. Is your organization prepared to facilitate the patient as the primary payer?

Patient Financial Services Today

Today PFS is heavily focused on managing the dollars triggered by the provision of healthcare services within a specific healthcare delivery system. In the context of the emerging role of the chief information officer (CIO), this chapter focuses on the data needs (information) required by PFS, which include the ability to measure productivity and resource utilization. Specific focus is placed on practice standards for critical data metrics in the following key areas: patient access, claim adjudication, revenue integrity, and management. Furthermore, facility (brick-and-mortar) and professional (physician) billing have different sets of dynamics that need to be addressed. The management of services provided and billed by healthcare facilities (hospital and health system) is delineated at all levels of core competency, from the actual management of services provided and billed by professional (physician) staff, and further separated by their measurement of diverse performance metrics. Our initial focus will be hospital and health system metrics, followed by a review of the metrics associated with the billing of professional services.

HFMA's MAP Keys in Revenue Cycle Management

HFMA's MAP Keys greatly assists in the regulation of revenue cycles within the healthcare industry. MAP Keys is a tool that has been readily adopted by health service providers across the country, with the simple approach of allowing users to track the progress of their facility compared to the national landscape of providers. MAP Keys provides both hospital- and physician-based practices with a set of unbiased, industry-wide standards used to manage revenue cycle performance and allow users to identify problems that directly impact bottom-line issues. When problem areas are identified, appropriate adjustments to policies and procedures can be made to more effectively increase revenue.

HFMA's MAP Keys for hospital and health systems can be broken down into four smaller sections, the first of which is patient access. Patient access is implemented to measure and improve a patient's access to healthcare services. This includes developing ways to expedite a patient's check-in process and providing assistance with financial and clinical processes upon arrival. Patient access encompasses the following subtopics: preregistration rate, insurance verification rate, service authorization rate, point-of-service (POS) cash collections, and conversion rate of uninsured patient to payer source. This section highlights scheduling and registration issues, the verification of patient insurance, financial approvals, a patient's eligibility for specific screenings, the delivery of services, and documenting service charges as well as encouraging up-front collections to increase the likelihood of reimbursement for services provided.

The second critical focus for HFMA's MAP Keys is supporting hospital and health system revenue integrity. Revenue integrity is that portion of MAP Key data that ensures compliance for services provided by hospital and health systems. This particular component of MAP Keys is responsible for confirming that all information is accurate, complete, documented correctly, and charged appropriately, and that all medical claims submitted meet set requirements. These set requirements identify charge capture, diagnosis coding, and unbilled claims, including documentation.

Claim adjudication is the third designation of HFMA's MAP Keys for hospital and health systems. Claim adjudication focuses on accuracy and the amount of time required for a claim to be sent to a third-party payer (patient's insurance provider) and for that third-party payer to reimburse the hospital a predetermined amount for those services rendered. In this section, the following subtopics are also addressed: days in final billed not submitted to payer (FBNS), universal billing form (UB-04/837I) clean claim rate, denial rate—zero pay, denial rate—partial pay, denials overturned by appeal, denial write-offs as a percent of net revenue, and aged accounts receivable (A/R) as a percent of billed A/R by payer group. A conversation of these larger topical subgroups, such as claim submissions, third-party follow-ups, and payment processing, needs to be addressed in order to understand the entire picture.

The fourth and final designation within HFMA's MAP Keys for hospital and health systems is management. Management includes the capability to gauge and keep track of overall performance. Doing so can help the organization goals and objectives and identify problem solutions before they escalate. Subtopical areas relating to the management of hospital and health systems are as follows:

Net days in A/R: Average numbers of days it takes to collect payment. Numbers much higher than 40–50 days indicate collection problems. Numbers that are much lower than 40–50 days indicate overly strict credit policies that might prevent higher sales revenue.[9] *Formula:* Average accounts payable × 365/Sales revenue.[10]

Aged A/R as a percentage of billed A/R: Aged accounts receivable is the process of determining which customers are paying on time and which are not and how far they are behind the payment date.[11] This analysis assists in estimating bad debts and establishing credit guidelines. The aged receivable number is then taken by a percentage of bills, especially bills of exchange, which are due to be paid by a company's debtors.[12]

Cash collections as a percent of adjusted net patient service revenue: Cash collections is the ability to keep track of payments and receipts of cash and securities.[13] The cash collection number is then taken as a percentage of patient revenues postadjustment.

Bad debt, charity care, and charity as a percent of uncompensated care: Bad debt for the purpose of uncompensated care is the unpaid dollar amount for services rendered from a patient or third-party payer for which the provider expected payment, excluding Medicare bad debt, combined with charity care (health services for which hospital policies determine the patient is unable to pay). Charity care results from a provider's policy to provide health-care services free of charge (or where only partial payment is expected, not to include contractual allowances for otherwise insured patients) to individuals who meet certain financial criteria. For the purpose of uncompensated care, charity care is measured on the basis of revenue forgone, at full established rates. Charity care does not include contractual write-offs and is taken as a percentage of uncompensated care (defined as charity care and bad debt).[14]

Uninsured discount and total uncompensated care: Uninsured discount,[15] under the current proposed definition, is for individuals who have no health insurance (or other source of third-party coverage) for the services furnished during the year, taken as a percentage of uncompensated care.

Cost to collect: The expenses incurred in realizing a due or promised payment.[16]

Cost to collect by functional area: The expenses incurred in realizing a due or promised payment broken down by each functional area.

Case mix index (CMI): A hospital's CMI represents the average diagnosis-related group (DRG) relative weight for that hospital. It is calculated by summing the DRG weights for all Medicare discharges and dividing by the number of discharges.[17]

Implementing the subtopic content listed above is crucial to an organization achieving effective management and cash liquidity.

Physician Practice Management and the Use of HFMA's MAP Keys in Revenue Cycle Management

Similar to HFMA's MAP Keys for hospital and health systems, its MAP Keys for physician practice management can be divided into four components, starting with patient access. In terms of physician practice management, patient access is geared toward providing satisfactory care, assisting patients in the registration process, and coordinating all other financial and clinical preparations necessary prior to patient arrival. The patient access component is also broken into several subtopics:

Percent of patient schedule occupied: This measures available capacity in a patient's schedule. *Formula:* Number of patient hours occupied/Number of patient hours available.

POS collection rate: This identifies opportunity for increased POS collections. *Formula:* Total POS collections/Total patient cash collected—all self-pay.

Scheduling process: A process to test and delineate the workflows associated with appointments and the timing and coordination of healthcare services.

Registration process: A process to test and delineate workflows associated with registering patients, including validating insurance benefits, determining a patient's eligibility for specific screenings, and delivering those services.

Proper claim submission: A process to test and delineate the workflows associated with the PFS services involved with generating, processing, and submitting claims, in addition to the workflows associated with processing payments and collecting co-pays collected at the time of service.

The next section in HFMA's MAP Keys for physician practice management is revenue integrity. In the world of healthcare, service providers know how important it is to manage their revenue integrity. Measuring revenue integrity allows service providers to ensure that all clinical and financial information is completed correctly and recorded appropriately (in the right place), and medical claims meet requirements. The more rapidly physicians are able to accomplish these tasks, the faster they are reimbursed for services. The only subtopic within revenue integrity is

Total charge lag days: This gauges charge capture workflow effectiveness and pinpoints any delay in cash flow. Monitoring total charge lag days can help accelerate cash flow.

The third section in HFMA's MAP Keys for physician practice management is claim adjudication. Claim adjudication deals with a patient's payment responsibility after his or her insurance benefits have been applied to the medical claim. Within claim adjudication, there are two subtopics:

Professional services denial percentage: Professional services denial percentage follows denials and determines the impact they will have on cash flow.

Aged A/R by payer group as a percentage of outstanding total A/R: This subtopic deals with accounts receivable, accounts outstanding, and collectability by various payer groups (types of insurance coverage). This manages the timeliness of claims sent out to patients and third-party payers.

The fourth and final component of the HFMA's physician practice management is management. This focuses on the ability to gauge and track revenue cycles. It allows the provider to create and track the progress of goals and identify problem areas before they result in issues affecting overall cash flow. There are nine subtopics that fall under the category of management:

Aged A/R as a percentage of outstanding A/R: This calculation indicates payment delays or the revenue cycle's ability to liquidate accounts receivables. *Formula:* 0–30, >30, >60, >90, >120 days/total outstanding A/R.

Primary physician practice operating margin ratio: This calculation determines the state of financial health and sustainability of current practice operations for primary practice operations. *Formula:* Net income from primary practice operations/Primary practice operating revenue.

Specialty physician practice operating margin ratio: This calculation determines the state of financial health and sustainability of current practice operations for specialty operations. *Formula:* Net income from specialty operations/Specialty operating revenue.

Net income or loss per primary full-time employee (FTE) physician: This calculation determines the financial health on a physician FTE level. It can be used for tracking and trending the profitability of the entity based on a physician level, and it supports the need for strategy development to minimize losses. *Formula:* Net income from operations/Number of FTE physicians.

Net income or loss per specialty FTE physician: This calculation determines the financial health on a physician FTE level. It can be used for tracking and trending the profitability of the entity based on a physician level, and it supports the need for strategy development to minimize losses. *Formula:* Net income from operations/Number of FTE physicians.

Total primary physician compensation as a percentage of net revenue: This calculation predicts the reasonableness of primary physician compensation relative to revenue (direct contribution of a physician [DCOH]). *Formula:* Total primary physician compensation/Total net primary patient service revenue.

Total specialty physician compensation as a percentage of net revenue: This calculation predicts the reasonableness of specialty physician compensation relative to revenue (DCOH). *Formula:* Total specialty physician compensation/Net specialty patient service revenue.

Practice net days in A/R: Used as a potential proxy for DCOH (cash inventory). Determines the effectiveness of patient care collections and can be used for budgeting and cash flow projections. *Formula:* Net patient service A/R/Average daily net patient service revenue.

Practice cash collection percentage: Provides an opportunity to increase cash flow and forecasts accuracy of expected revenues. *Formula:* Actual patient service cash collections/Net patient service revenue.

Key Market Barriers to Overcome

In preparing for this particular chapter, retired patient financial professionals with 30+ years of experience were interviewed. The trend in title and role was driven by the level of responsibility the individual achieved within his or her respective organization. The following is an illustrative perspective of observations noted within PFS services:

At my local community hospital, I started as the director of patient accounts and had responsibility for outpatient registration, admitting, and patient accounts. By the end of my tenure I assumed additional responsibility for preadmission, medical records, transcription, charging, and other smaller related departments. My first title was director of patient financial services. It was then changed to director of patient information management services. Revenue cycle management [RCM] came into use after I had left. While employed as an electronic health systems vendor and a revenue cycle consultant, RCM covered only patient access and patient accounts. Medical records may have been under the CFO, but it did not report to the PFS area. Back in the day, the position of patient account manager usually transitioned to director. However, some facilities would have both positions concurrently. The director of patient financial services often took on the responsibility of patient access as well. I find that with most open, posted positions, they are still using the director title for the basic functions, and the revenue cycle management positions may include call centers or other cycle-related areas. I worked for three hospitals, and the goal at each one was to increase the bottom line, reduce costs and bad debt, while simultaneously maintaining customer satisfaction. From what I have read, those goals are still the same. However, these goals have been enhanced to include a long list of current needs. I arranged to subcontract the collection department at my local community hospital 6 months after I started, and it remained that way until a local hospital chain took over. Outsourcing has become very commonplace within the medical community. Centralization of related departments was instituted at the same time, and we did that as well. I am not totally in touch with current practices, but recently did some research on PFS and the related world. I found it very interesting that hospitals are still fighting the same battles we fought 25 or 30 years ago … it is all cyclical. The paper and information overflow is still there, regardless of technological advances, and the paper seems to come from all sectors. I am hooked once more … researching this is interesting and disappointing at the same time.

The reoccurring theme of fighting the same battle was pervasive in the interviews conducted with seasoned PFS professionals and further compounded by the unintended consequences of the Affordable Care Act and other legislated markets. One of these unintended consequences is the number of healthcare plan options for patients. The number of new players in the industry, in addition to existing players that are expanding their scope, has increased significantly.

As an example, in Illinois, 31 health maintenance organization (HMO) Medicaid options are available within the exchanges. If a provider does not have a contractual relationship with each and every HMO, a provider will not have an effective ability to correspond with, verify, and or get paid from these plans. The PFS requirements for effective registration and eligibility have expanded and become more complex. Furthermore, even under contract, new players in the market may not have the infrastructure to manage relationships with providers or ensure the effective management of their insured among the providers they select. As one specific example, independent of ACA, the switch to the International Classification of Diseases, 10th revision (ICD-10) will have detrimental short-term effects.

Author's Note: Many providers are opting out of accepting patients who have purchased plans on the exchanges, creating a narrow network phenomenon. The net effect is that patients are unaware of the out-of-network status of services received by their provider at the time of service.

The specific issue providers will face here is the code expansion under ICD-10; all procedure codes documented and mapped to diagnosis codes listed under ICD-9 will be further subdivided into current and emerging procedure codes to an expanded diagnosis listing under ICD-10. The operational issues require mapping and associated database programming within an organization. This is followed by updating the orderable services, supplies, and documentation requirements inside the provider's EHR system. Professional caregivers will also need to change their mindsets regarding the documentation of patient care. All caregivers will require training to enable them to accurately document the specific care provided and select the proper diagnosis codes. Once providers get up to date within their own system, their external partners will need to come to parity or suffer revenue integrity themselves. If a provider transmits accurate ICD-10 codes to a payer, that payer's system must contain the same (exact) code files in order to receive and process that claim.

This begs the question, what needs to change? Ultimately, the patient financial services sector is driven by the accuracy of the front-end patient (registration) data collection process, which directly correlates to the accuracy of the final output (the bill that represents services rendered). This all leads directly back to data—garbage in, garbage out.

The PFS functions are dependent on data that is generated by many diverse users in the overall organization. Therefore, in addition to the CIO, added emphasis is now placed on the need for a data strategy that falls under the emerging role and responsibility of a chief data officer (CDO). A study published in the *Economist* regarding industries' management of big data noted that more than 500 global executives who have managed diverse companies or corporations are still trying to learn how to manage big data.[18]

Furthermore, companies that do exercise effective management of their data outperform those that do not. This could not be truer within the healthcare industry. Current technology initiatives, coupled with the requirements for patient engagement and population health presented by the Centers for Medicare and Medicaid Services and the Affordable Care Act, require a data management strategy. An organization's ability to develop, execute, and maintain a data management strategy will ultimately define winners and losers.

Author's Note: How will PFS manage the increase in collection work from patients who are utilizing an increasing number of out-of-network services?

Role of Data and Revenue Integrity Management

As these hybrid roles develop, organizations struggle to make decisions regarding the following questions:

- Who is responsible for data integrity and revenue cycle–type activities?
- How will these requirements be bridged within these two functions and throughout the organization?
- Is data integrity an IT or a finance function?

Information drives solutions—consider the following within your organization:

- Who is responsible for data integrity?
- Are data integrity functions aligned with IT support capabilities?
- Who will mitigate risk at multiple levels (patient engagement, clinical operations, regulatory, business, individual, and staff) by ensuring continued data integrity and access for priority business functions (production, transaction processing, etc.)?
- Who will ensure regulatory compliance and ongoing initiatives, such as meaningful use, population health management, and patient engagement?
- Who will align business processes and information systems?
- Who will define and roll out the roadmap to implement, enhance, and sustain business continuity capability and supporting IT requirements (CIO and CDO)?
- Who assumes the critical tasks and responsibility associated with risk assessment and gap mitigation planning and implementation concerning IT integration?

It would appear that these questions are best served within the various chief information roles discussed in Chapters 1 and 2. They can and will overlap.

The chief information officer (CIO) typically directs the information and data integrity of an organization and provides assurance that information technology functions are aligned to the mission and enterprise objectives.

The chief medical information officer (CMIO) is carving a niche in the implementation of clinical information systems being utilized by physicians.[19] An illustrative market shift is the advent of computerized physician order entry (CPOE), where physicians electronically submit patient care instructions to other medical professionals and staff, which requires the physicians themselves to have or develop functional technical knowledge.

The chief nursing information officer (CNIO) typically focuses on "heavy clinical involvement in all aspects of HIT implementation and subsequent workflow optimization and clinical transformation."[20] The CNIO is the senior informatics nurse guiding the implementation and optimization of HIT systems for an organization. The word *nurse* in the acronym does not necessarily mean nursing is the only discipline for which the CNIO is responsible, but rather that the position is typically filled by an individual who has experience and education in informatics.

The chief information security officer (CISO) focuses on the ability to accumulate, exchange, and manage data without compromising the information through the unauthorized access, theft, or sabotage of that data.

The chief technology officer (CTO) and his or her role in healthcare are described by the Department of Health and Human Services: "The CTO oversees the opportunities to leverage underutilized assets—initially identified as data and our human capital."

The chief data officer (CDO) focuses on the organization's data strategy, data governance, including collaboration with internal and external partners, data space, and value impact of data. This role bridges the gap in accountability and effectuating data needs throughout the organization.

A chief revenue officer (CRO) is responsible for all activities that generate revenue. In most companies, the CRO is tasked with primary or shared responsibility for operations, sales, corporate development, and marketing, pricing, and revenue management, since these functions extend across multiple teams in most companies.

Without question, healthcare is in a transitional state. Today's market is going through accelerated changes, which leads to questions concerning the management of internal and external resources. Which circumstances limit the utilization of in-house resources and potentially invite cosourcing, and when must the enterprise outsource? Survival typically exemplifies the latter. Consider these self-assessment issues:

- Are your employees fundamentally engaged in the process of change?
- Are you a public or private entity? Public sector entities have a fiduciary responsibility to taxpayers to produce self-assessments or performance surveys (report cards) and be audited. Private sector corporations have fiduciary accountability and must sustain profitability or fold.
- Do your employees have the technical subject matter expertise, competencies, and experience to rapidly implement complex time-sensitive bottom-line projects or tasks?
  - You may already be looking internally for resolution to issues or problems at hand.
- Will an outsource partner rapidly assess issues or problems and provide a positive resolution and a return on investment?
- Will the outsource partner provide solutions to identify and negate adverse financial situations?
- Will supporting outsource assets be effective in engaging internal partners?
- What are the costs of bringing in outside resources? What are the risks?
  - Is your internal organization's experience helping or limiting the successful outcome on any particular initiative?
  - Is your organization's perspective helping or hurting initiatives?

- Does your organization have the scalability to execute this project?
  - Do you have immediate resource capacity to accomplish this initiative, or will you require additional resources?
  - Is this project best internalized or outsourced considering available resources, time, and best use of capital?
- Will the need for support be infrequent or recurring?
  - Can we achieve a sufficient result on our own? Can we get "close enough"?
  - Is the project aligned to other critical tasks?
  - How tied to a source of competitive advantage is this initiative?
  - Is it efficient to use internal resources or outside experts? (Note that this question isn't asking which costs more; the focus is on the risk-adjusted return on investment.)
- Are there other factors at play, such as retaining employees on the payroll rather than discharging them?
- Can we hire the "consultant" directly?
- Can we realistically recruit and train our own resources?
- How much money are we losing while ramping up?
  - Can we hire all the skill sets needed to achieve project goals? Can we provide full-time work in order to take full advantage of the long list of skill sets offered by vendors?
  - What will we do with permanent staff (ramped up) when workflow slows?
  - What will we do if we have a surge in workflow? (Consultants are paid an hourly rate; cost goes down when workload goes down. When we have a crunch, can we quickly secure additional capable and managed manpower?)

Author's Note: Issues versus Problems

Issues: Issues typically require a solution. People are working to quickly determine the best course of action.

Problem: A problem is a person or persons standing in the way of a solution.

Some free advice: When someone comes to you and indicates he or she has an issue, ask, "What is it?" When that same person comes to you and says he or she has a problem, ask, "Who is it?"

On a parallel track to managing critical business functions is the notion of employee engagement, where employees take ownership of a task and assume a sense of accountability for results. This begs the question, how do we create an accountable, engaged organization?

The following is a discussion on the topic of accountability, which introduces two new roles: senior information risk owner (SIRO) and senior responsible owner (SRO). These two new roles or management identifiers provide assurance that digital continuity remains an integral part of change management, information management, data management, and the information assurance processes.

In essence, an organization that requires a SIRO may want to first assign an SRO to assure digital continuity for the organization. The SRO process of managing digital continuity may consider the following principal guidelines:

- Plan for action.
- Define digital continuity requirements.
- Assess and address risks to digital continuity.
- Maintain digital continuity.

In any successful contemporary organization, the absence of, or limited (partial) access to, critical information will have a significant impact on its day-to-day efficiencies, effectiveness, and profitability. If information crucial to maintaining business continuity is lost or key data that ensures a transparent accountable record of governance is missing, the organization could incur significant reputational damage, government intervention (oversight), and severe financial costs.

If the organization can effectively manage and maintain digital continuity, then confidence will be established that the information required to operate transparently, maintain the public's confidence, and protect the organization's reputation and revenue integrity and profitability is trustworthy. The organization can account for its decisions, document its actions, and meet bottom-line requirements.

If risks that create change are managed properly, the organization will be able to maintain digital continuity information, create organizational efficiencies as a business, and enable wider organizational agendas. The process of managing digital continuity involves identifying the organization's information assets, understanding the technical environment, and ensuring proper alignment to support organizational needs.

Managing digital continuity ultimately provides an organization with information that identifies which technology best supports the utilization of essential information and what doesn't. Organizations use this information to streamline their technical environment to increase data efficiency within processes that are deployed by various end users. These efforts can bring numerous financial, quality, and efficiency service benefits to the organization. Managing digital continuity will help streamline the overall use of people, processes, and technology.

Final Thought

The PFS's ability (function) to evolve is directly proportional to the level of data sophistication employed by a spectrum of internal and external partners. Your contractual arrangements with external partners should include provisions for being current on the ability or requirement to receive updated claim data. Your organizational data strategy should identify the integration and creation of workflows that place the patient as the primary focus; adopting these statements as operational standards will define your organization's ability to utilize available technology to your fullest advantage. Revenue is an ongoing agenda item in the C-suite. Chapter 4 discusses other paradigm shifts that are occurring within the C-suite.

CRO Perspective

Our ability to collect every dollar owed to a provider has become much more difficult and complex. PFS operations are required now more than ever to utilize multiple systems and third-party vendors to maximize collections. With this expansion comes the need to not only utilize data, but to put it in a readable and useful format. PFS and IT leadership will need to work hand in hand in order to capitalize on the information/data being gathered, and then utilize that information to drive processes.

—Duane Lisowski
Chief Revenue Officer, Hospital Physician Partners, Hollywood, Florida

References

1. Watson, P., *Ideas: A History of Thought and Invention, from Fire to Freud* (New York: HarperCollins, 2005).
2. Abulafia, D., Rackham, P.O., and Suano, M., *The Mediterranean in History,* 1st ed. (Los Angeles: J. Paul Getty Trust Publications, 2011).
3. Bateman, T., and Snell, S., *Management: Leading and Collaborating in the Competitive World,* 10th ed. (Columbus, OH: McGraw Hill Higher Education, 2012).
4. Andrews, E., 8 Things You May Not Know about Hammurabi's Code, 2013, http://www.history.com/news/history-lists/8-things-you-may-not-know-about-hammurabis-code (accessed December 2014).
5. Guisepi, R., The History of Ancient Sumeria, 1980, http://history-world.org/sumeria.htm (accessed December 2014).
6. Rosner, D., Doing Well or Doing Good: The Ambivalent Focus of Hospital Administration, in *The American General Hospital: Communities and Social Contexts,* ed. D. Long and J. Golden (New York: Cornell University Press, 1989).
7. Davis, M., *Hospital Administration, a Career: The Need of Trained Executives for a Billion Dollar Business, and How They May Be Trained* (New York: 1929).
8. Sheldon, R., *From Acorn to Oak* (Healthcare Financial Management Association, Westchester, IL, 1991).
9. Cash Flow, http://www.businessdictionary.com/definition/cash-flow.html (accessed December 2014).
10. Days Accounts Receivable (Days A/R), http://www.businessdictionary.com/definition/days-accounts-receivable-Days-A-R.html#ixzz3DgNdoYss (accessed December 2014).
11. Bills Receivable, http://www.investorwords.com/8999/bills_receivable.html#ixzz3DgPCdi1F (accessed December 2014).
12. Accounts Receivable Aging, http://www.businessdictionary.com/definition/accounts-receivable-aging.html#ixzz3DgOiRhG8 (accessed December 2014).
13. Cash Collections, http://www.businessdictionary.com/definition/cash-collections.html#ixzz3DgPuueXT (accessed December 2014).
14. Details for Title: CMS 2552-96, http://www.cms.gov/Medicare/CMS-Forms/CMS-Forms/CMS-Forms-Items/CMS019505.html (accessed December 2014).
15. Medicaid Program; Disproportionate Share Hospital Payments—Uninsured Definition, *Federal Register* 77: 2012.
16. Cost of Collection, http://www.businessdictionary.com/definition/cost-of-collection.html#ixzz3DgVbu9ji (accessed December 2014).
17. Details for Title: FY 2012 Final Rule Data File, 2012, http://www.cms.gov/Medicare/Medicare-Fee-for-Service-Payment/AcuteInpatientPPS/FY-2012-IPPS-Final-Rule-Home-Page-Items/CMS1250507.html (accessed December 2014).
18. Big Data: Harnessing a Game-Changing Asset, 2011, http://www.sas.com/reg/gen/corp/1583148 (accessed December 2014).
19. Leviss, J., The CMIO—A New Leader for Health Systems, National Institutes of Health, 2006, http://www.ncbi.nlm.nih.gov/pmc/articles/PMC1561791/ (accessed December 2014)
20. Murphy, J., The Nursing Informatics Workforce: Who Are They and What Do They Do? 2011, http://www.medscape.com/viewarticle/746226_3 (accessed August 2014).

Chapter 4

The Paradigm Shift in the C-Suite

Those organizations that have a collaborative technology infrastructure in place will be able to harness the neuronic power of all their people as if the organization had one super brain.

—Ade McCormack
Beyond Work-Life Balance, Auridian

The C-suite identifies where most corporations' strategic decisions are made, the heart and soul of the enterprise. The term *C-suite* gets its name due to the fact that most top senior executives' titles tend to start with the letter C, as in chief executive officer, chief operating officer, chief information officer, and they are referred to as C-level executives.[1]

C-suite personnel establish policy and attempt to set the tone from the top down. This chapter provides an overview of market activities that occur from a variety of perspectives and the impact on upper-level (C-suite) management. One example of perspective is a shift from the position of patient first to one of providers maneuvering to a marketing of services. This chapter will also consider patient engagement and retention, internal and external partners' development and utilization of data, a data strategy, and a starting framework or consideration for a public media strategy (communicating with internal and external partners).

A Bit of History

C-suite or *C-level* is an adjective used to describe high-ranking executive titles within an organization. Officers with C-level positions typically yield the most power and are very influential. Successful C-level executives demonstrate business expertise, lead by example, and cultivate a team-oriented atmosphere, rather than function strictly as high-level technical advisors. However, it is not uncommon to find all of the attributes listed above, including core competencies, in the IT technical arena, especially when high demands for data occur.

The C-suite executives can include, but are not limited to, chief executive officer (CEO), chief information officer (CIO), chief financial officer (CFO), chief marketing officer (CMO), chief compliance office (CCO), and chief operating officer (COO).

In healthcare, the function of the CIO can include chief medical information officer (CMIO), chief nursing information officer (CNIO), chief technology officer (CTO), chief data officer (CDO), and chief information security officer (CISO), as discussed in previous chapters. Complex health industry data models that support strategic planning initiatives require today's C-level executive to understand what many niche IT specialists considered their sole domain just a few years back. As a result, the executive needs at the top have expanded in breadth and depth and created new entry points and expanded core competencies in the executive office.

The path to the C-suite is changing. Highlighted in an article published by the *Harvard Business Review*, "The New Path to the C-Suite,"[2] once people reach the C-suite, technical and functional expertise matters less than leadership skills and a strong grasp of business fundamentals. The CEO is at the helm of the organization and directs, decides, leads, manages, and executes the mission of the business. This individual, the chief in charge, is navigating the ship and responsible for the welfare of the passengers and crew and avoiding danger at all costs.

The CIO, discussed in Chapter 3, is the information architect. The CFO focuses on the financial health of the organization. The chief human resource officer (CHRO) is the manager of the organization's personnel and responsible for workplace health and welfare. The chief marketing officer provides the message, creates interest, and develops the purchasing or selling of goods and services.

The chief operating officer's role varies across the board and is greatly impacted by specific industry needs. The COO is chiefly responsible for managing the implementation and execution of the overall mission objectives that involve strategy development, operational planning, mission execution, and staffing.

The COO ensures that the "commander's intent" is sustained and remains intact throughout the mission. C-level executives must support the chief executive officer to ensure the overall mission goals are achieved and performance exceeds the standard. The requirement for the acquisition of intelligent data necessary to effectively compete and thrive in the complex healthcare arena has created the need for executive-level strategic data planning and management roles. In addition to all of the various operational business layers a CEO must oversee, he or she must also oversee the generation of intelligent data. There has never before been a time when a dependency on this has been so critical. It is vital that corporate managers effectively use evolving technology, but it is equally important that they have an understanding of how external partners use the same technology to support those same operations. Consider information chiefs akin to adolescent teenagers—"It's all about me, right now!" Due to the changing dynamics of social media within professional and personal lives, the dynamics of social media should be on the radar of every C-suite member. This type of communication should be incorporated into an organization's data strategy.

Linda Tucci, a CIO headhunter for SearchCIO.com, wrote a great story about C-suite accountability when describing her 12-year-old son's use of social networking (Instagram) to do homework.[3,4]

When the teacher made homework assignments, her son sent texts to four other kids in his class to ask what needed to be done to complete the work, and all ended up collaborating. In addition, friends from other schools saw the postings and asked for the same help or provided information. They appear to have a completely different notion of privacy and a significantly different view on competition.

Shifting Roles at the C-Suite

According to the *Cambridge Dictionary*,[5] The C-suite group has been defined as "the most important managers in a company … those whose titles begin with the letter 'C', for 'chief'," with businessdictionary.com referring to them as "corporate officers and directors."[6]

The CFOs, COOs, CIOs, and their counterparts who make up the C-suite are increasingly being viewed on par with the traditionally labeled CEO in charge. This indicates a potential shift from the single-leader mode at the head of the corporate line and block to a team of leaders working together to guide the company in an increasingly technological and globalized business environment.

A *Harvard Business Review* article explained that C-suite executives are no longer those with the greatest degree of technical knowledge, but rather those who can best fuse the leadership and business skill sets with the "overall big picture" understanding of their field.

The chief security officer (CSO) or chief information security officer (CISO) may also find himself or herself at the C-table. As security shifts from information management to risk management, CSOs find themselves looking at a bigger picture and designing programs that balance acceptable risks versus threats.

To say this is the era of the data breach would be a gross understatement—what hasn't been breached? Networks and intranet-connected devices of healthcare organizations—ranging from hospitals to insurance carriers to pharmaceutical companies to basic business operation vendors—are being compromised at an alarming rate. Data breaches at a major brick-and-mortar retail store such as Target and an online retailer such as eBay could be precursors of what's in store for healthcare providers.

The CSO has one of the toughest tasks—protecting patient data while ensuring clinicians have access to the necessary data to provide adequate care. In a labor market stifled by economic factors, the need for qualified CSOs and CISOs has skyrocketed. That being said, it can be a thankless endeavor considering when security breaches occur, the CSO is often maligned and held responsible in a lose–lose situation. No matter what the CSO does, if someone wants to break in, he or she will. One CIO interviewed is always asked by the board, "Have we done everything to stop breaches?" He always pauses. According to a recent survey by Threat Track Security, "No Respect: Chief Information Security Officers Misunderstood and Underappreciated by Their C-Level Peers,"[7] 74% of the 200 executives responding said they thought CISOs should not be part of an organization's leadership team. Forty-four percent of respondents indicated that the primary role of the CSO or CISO is to be held accountable for any organization data breaches—another way of saying "chief scapegoat officer."

In addition to adapting to the globalization of the market, C-suite executives must also meet the skill set requirements to effectively communicate the dynamics of team building. The C-suite increasingly works as a team to make decisions for the company, with each officer using his or her individual knowledge to weigh in on company decisions, rather than simply reporting on his or her individual progress.[8]

Shawn Banerji, managing director at Russell Reynolds Associates in New York and a CIO headhunter, has a similar view, explaining that he has seen companies assembling "much more robust teams," similar to a "leadership ecosystem." He told SearchCIO.com, "It is a far more collaborative approach to conceiving and executing ideas and less of the top-down dictatorial leader. People who have that top-down type of DNA are not moving into these top jobs."

Banerji indicates that this shift is a result of the complex responsibilities that C-suite executives have to decide. Banerji further indicated, "These C-Suite jobs are so complex and these decisions have such significant implications that to expect any one individual to take on the personal accountability to get it right is not reasonable and it's bad business. It puts the business at risk."[9]

The reinvention of the C-suite is coming at the same time that the healthcare industry itself is undergoing a huge shift from a volume-based model to a value-based one. The implementation of the Affordable Care Act (ACA) and other Centers for Medicare and Medicaid Services (CMS) initiatives is forcing hospitals to place focus less on treating patients after they become ill and more on preventing the conditions that require hospitalization.

Dr. Kenneth L. Davis, CEO and president of the Mount Sinai Health System in New York City, explains the shift this way: "The hospital of today is a stand-alone facility where services are provided mostly within its walls, and quality of care is too often measured by number of inpatient beds…. The hospital of tomorrow needs to be a large, integrated system providing extensive outpatient care beyond its primary facility, dedicated to keeping community members healthy."[10]

Under CMS initiatives, hospitals will be given Medicare reimbursement (or subsidies) based on how well a patient recovers, rather than on how much treatment a patient receives. The current fee-for-service model rewards hospitals for overtesting and overtreating patients because hospitals are paid based on the individual services delivered; thus, they receive additional fees for treating complications and readmissions and have little financial incentive to reduce readmissions and complications.

"The last thing a surgeon or oncologist should be paid for are complications. Right now, if you have more of them you do better," said Dr. James Mohler, associate director and senior vice president for translational research at Roswell Park Cancer Institute and chairman of the institute's urology department. "What you're really talking about is paying for outcomes. Because that's what healthcare is about. You want to deliver the right care, and do it really well, so that the net cost to the country and to a patient will be less."[11]

By moving away from this fee-for-service model, hospitals have more incentive to keep patients healthy and out of the hospital. Therefore, complications and readmissions will begin to drain hospital resources rather than provide them. In addition, the federal government can withhold Medicare payments if hospitals experience too many patients readmitted within a 30-day period. To avoid unnecessary readmissions, hospitals will be required to spend more time on postdischarge planning and ensuring that patients have follow-up appointments with their primary physicians to identify likely complications before they occur.[12]

Hospitals see the increase in insurance coverage as a positive for patients. Dr. Stephanie Mayfield Gibson, Kentucky's commissioner of public health, said the Appalachian region hasn't "seen a change like that since LBJ brought Medicaid into existence. That's huge. For people to have access to care, that is the right thing, the compassionate thing. And we expect to see the (health) statistics changing there."[13] Mortenson Construction conducted a survey of 190 healthcare facilities' leaders, architects, and administrators and found that four out of five of those surveyed felt that focusing on health outcomes is the right way to go.[14]

Hospitals are supposed to receive financial assistance by the insurance mandate and the expansion of Medicaid. As more people obtain health insurance, the expectation is that they will begin seeing their doctor more regularly, as opposed to just those times when illness occurs. The uninsured often go to the emergency room for treatment because by law emergency rooms cannot turn them away for lack of insurance. This influx into ERs is a huge drain on hospital resources because they are forced to absorb the costs of acute treatment for conditions that could have been managed easily through regular care. However, the higher deductibles associated with the benefit plan offerings and the resulting narrow networks that are being created (providers opting out of more benefit plan offerings) may have unintended adverse effects on how patients utilize their healthcare dollars. Providers are opting out of certain plans because they are unable to provide the services within the fee schedule payments offered under certain plans. Payment reductions and quality metrics are being applied prior to the market achieving the alleged economies of scale derived from an increased number of insured individuals.

Kerry McKean Kelly of the New Jersey Hospital Association comments, "The problem is those cuts have begun before we've had the chance to see the benefits of seeing more insured patients, in the end, we hope it all balances out, and it's the perfect balance."[15]

Even worse for hospitals, the Affordable Care Act ushered in $155 billion worth of Medicare reimbursement cuts and other payments throughout the next decade to offset reform costs.[16] This means that even as hospitals adjust to a new payment methodology, they will receive smaller reimbursements for the care provided. At the same time, the Affordable Care Act eliminates the notion of patients not receiving coverage due to preexisting conditions and that customers, at minimum, will have access to some type of coverage through the exchanges.

Hospitals face another financial hurdle: electronic medical records. The 2009 American Recovery and Reinvestment Act mandates that hospitals must implement electronic records. For many hospitals, the biggest hurdle to accomplish an electronic medical record (EMR) system isn't digitizing, electronic storage, or training personnel, but actually paying for the EMR system, which costs, at a minimum, between $800,000 and $1.5 million in a perfect world.[17]

Many of the 2000+ small-town and rural hospitals in the United States are experiencing great difficulty implementing these changes. Brock Slabach, with the National Rural Health Association, explains that the average loss in profit margin for a rural hospital is 8% a year,[18] with no options but to comply as dictated by federal mandate. Ultimately, the switch to EMRs is good for the patient because doctors would have both the patient's medical history and input from specialists at their fingertips. Dr. Billy Oley, who works at the small Red Lodge, Montana, hospital, explained that he can get timely expert opinions from doctors at larger nearby hospitals on an almost daily basis now that he can transmit his patients' information electronically.[19]

As hospitals are increasingly forced to balance patient care, government regulations, and staying financially afloat, the leadership of the C-suite becomes more and more important. Rural hospitals trying to afford EMR systems are left to choose between figuring out ways to scrape together nearly $1 million on their own or joining a larger hospital system. Joining a large hospital system might bridge the financial gap, but it might also eliminate the freedom of rural hospitals to control their own patient care decisions in the process.[20] Hospitals losing money to Medicare cuts need executives who can effectively generate revenue and cut costs in new and creative ways and turn cost optimization into an ongoing priority. Teamwork skills, business savvy, and technical knowledge are musts for executives who will be guiding hospitals through today's ever-changing healthcare landscape.

The hospital of tomorrow needs to be a large, integrated system providing extensive outpatient care beyond its primary facility, dedicated to keeping community members healthy.

C-Suite Today

The C-suite today has to be fluid, innovative, and collaborative. The following is a list of attributes facing C-suite leaders:

Set the tone: Today's C-suite—or business architecture team—must come together and develop the blueprint to effectively and efficiently drive the strategy. Dell's CIO "Andi" Karaboutis states, "Stop asking the business what it wants and start futuring," defining futuring by quoting another entrepreneur with the Midas touch, Henry Ford. "If I had asked people what they wanted, they would have said faster horses." Andi wants her team to imagine the future. Benchmarking is looking at what everyone else is doing. Futuring is asking the question "What if?" and putting new ideas out to incubate. Not only must the C-suite members collaborate, but also they must conduct plenty of futuring.

Manage your people: Les Meyer, author of "People Strategists Reveal Key C-Suite Secrets to Bend the Trend," reports on the critical mission to tame runaway employee healthcare costs, as current methods no longer work. The next generation of solutions must be found in the notion of value realization. He states, "The bleeding edge of this thinking can be found in the C-Suite emergence of 'disruptive innovation' (DI), a business term used to describe how a more nimble or entrepreneurial approach to creating value and sustaining a competitive advantage can disrupt certain markets."

Disruptive innovation (DI) is about profound change in the C-suite. It is the bedrock of strategic business process improvement (SBPI). It's innovation that transforms an existing market or creates a new market through simplicity, convenience, accessibility, or affordability. Maintaining the status quo is not disruptive. It is a change in approach to one that better addresses critical business issues in the C-suite and the demands to create and sustain customer value. A balanced view of the business requires continuous predictive data analytics for insight.

C-suite leaders must simultaneously realize greater employee trust, talent engagement, and customer value realization, as well as prevent spiraling healthcare costs and "bend the trend." According to Kathleen Yeager, "SBPI and DI spotlight creative execution and encourage organizations to focus on critical talent management … the new value-centric HR professional who has a DI mindset would be an ideal role model and business leader in the C-Suite to promote the meaningful use of HR systematic performance improvement processes and best practices."

C-suite competency discussions, recommendations, and value realization barriers can't be tackled or resolved without metrics. What gets measured gets improved. People strategists have created next-generation SBPI C-suite level benefits and reporting dashboards and scorecards. Value realization materializes when action is taken on SBPI measurement insights. People strategists in the C-suite realize that keeping people healthy is a critical business strategy and serious economic imperative. Business is driven by value and value creation. No value, no sustainability. People are the biggest source of a sustainable competitive advantage. A C-suite active engagement survey was performed by C-suite executives. Some highlights included the most important needs revealed by the CEOs:

1. Evidence-based, high-value workforce well-being standards of practice
2. Proven high-touch, employee engagement (health behaviors) returns on investments that are integrated with high-value well-being results

3. Keen insights into comprehensive health promotion and neighborhood health assurance business models

4. Know-how to replicate "experience curve" of efficiency gains and bend-the-trend investment output effort

5. Expertise of informed physician executive leaders as frontline people strategists whose integrated role enables them to be more effective and focused

Additionally,

▪ Too few C-suite executives were aware that employee healthcare costs have both a direct and an indirect impact on profits, or that the workplace environment affects workforce healthcare costs.

▪ Only 38% of executives correctly stated how much their company spent on healthcare. Most of those with wrong answers underestimated their spending, and more than half of them believed the figure was more than 50% below the actual tab.

▪ Many executives did not know their company's disability incidence rate or the C-suite's knowledge of the health of their workforce.

The C-suite active engagement survey revealed that a profound disconnect exists between awareness and understanding of traditional C-suite critical business issues and financial key performance indicators. People strategists who embrace an HR application of DI may help drive success and reserve a permanent place in the C-suite.

Drive security initiatives: High-profile breaches abound. At the root of many serious breaches are advanced persistent threats (APTs) that can install advanced malware and collect data over an extended period of time. Protecting against APTs was the top security initiative for 2014, as cited in a recent survey by IDG Research Services. The next top two security issues were encryption and data loss prevention and next-generation firewalls (NGFWs).[21]

According to "Security Concerns in the C-Suite and How Next-Generation Firewalls Can Help,"[22] addressing APTs and data breaches is a high-C-level concern.

The Balancing Act

In addition to the attributes mentioned above, a key factor for C-suite success will be in the management's ability to take their organization to the next level and transform it into an intelligent data–driven entity.

Regardless of opinions, commentaries, or political posturing regarding the current legislation (e.g., ACA), the patients and their health needs will remain unchanged. For example, those providers focusing on emerging technologies or implementing components of the ACA will still have patients requiring healthcare services. Patients will need to be registered, assessed, treated, and sent along to the next provider managing the individuals.

However, it is the context in which those services are provided that will require a delicate balancing act during the transition period. Expect to see significant growing pains among all market players and business models for providers and payers to change. Some organizations may not survive. The questions of survival parallel the organization's ability to anticipate change and transition the organization to new ground rules established by government legislation, market standards, and the patient.

The C-suite should incorporate into their strategy an ongoing market concern—that the patient has yet to be front and center in the conversation. Further, from a revenue management perspective, the focus still remains on what providers need to do to get claims processed and paid by the payer. Future benchmarks on health and wellness should be measured by the ability to achieve patient self-determined health and welfare milestones.

Key Market Barriers to Overcome

The C-suite has ongoing market conditions that may impact the organization's overall strategic direction. For example, how do we adapt quickly enough to effectively address the current healthcare issues? The level of data mobility and access control necessary to safely interact with the electronic management of healthcare makes security a primary concern. The challenge is not so much managing the current state of affairs, but managing new terms and determining what they mean.

Imagine managing the architecture of a healthcare system like you would manage your own home. You own a state-of-the-art entertainment center, including satellite, movies, audio, and surround-sound and Internet access. For whatever reason, you decide to change providers (satellite to cable) and all the system controls change, requiring you to learn how to navigate new territory, similar to learning a new language.

Hospitals now have to learn a new language called population health. What does the population health mandate look like? What are the goals and objectives? As you can see, managing a new language is the first barrier to overcome, followed closely by the ability and rate of adaption to that new language. New statement-of-work requests are often confusing and lack a clear picture of the requirements that healthcare management personnel are accustomed to dealing with, let alone understand.

Rapid change also requires new and different skill sets. These new skill sets will be necessary to overcome the next barrier: access to human capital. The ability to lead in an ever-changing healthcare environment is critical. Institutions must not shortcut those costs associated with the development and training of staff. In this environment of change, we need a human capital strategy. We need to have the right person for the right job. A Chicago area CIO advises, "Recruit talented people and do not spare any costs for development of people assets." What is your human capital strategy? In essence, how do we maximize our existing talent and identify the right people for the right job?

A CIO's critical skill set must include the ability to understand the healthcare business and the interrelationships of all its business components, in addition to having an analytic mindset.[23] A firsthand knowledge of people, process, and technology must be a component of the skill set.

Effective survival strategies include the ability to conduct a thorough self-assessment of the organization's core competencies. Self-assessments are followed by recommendations for organizational changes necessary to survive the current dynamics within healthcare.

For example, in academic facilities (environments), the core competency includes treating patients with complex care needs because that is their focus. Academic facilities receive patients from referrals, so they invest in building a referral base. Academic facilities develop strong primary care relationships to protect their referral methodology as their model for patient access. However, with the changing dynamics in healthcare currently underway, the focus is on a patient-centric environment and patient selection. Therefore, reliance on referrals (the traditional model) may no longer work. Competition and cost-effectiveness, with the goal of doing a better job than your competitors, place the patient at the front of the line.

The focus in changing the model of care by affiliations pushes complex care packages outside of organization's walls, providing access and relaying information directly to the patient. The traditional medical center model is to develop a strong referral network with physician providers able to manage niche clinical problems. The provider must now incorporate some type of social media strategy to get to the patient first, before treatment is needed. The system's message is now being sent directly to the patient versus through provider affiliation networks. Organizations are using technology to achieve this transition. Models to provide care without walls will see a great deal of innovation. Models will include expanded use of telehealth, telemedicine, and home monitoring systems. All of these issues should be incorporated into the organization's overall strategy.

Role of Data and Revenue Integrity Management

Ongoing business model changes in healthcare and the messages sent to the patient will have an interesting impact on healthcare marketing. How will we communicate to our patients? In the example of the academic healthcare facility, the core competency is understood to be the treatment and management of complex healthcare services. The referral base is communicating to other healthcare professionals, "Hey, we can manage your patients' needs."

In the midst of changing healthcare models, providers are introduced to a new language that they will need to be responsive to in order to thrive and survive. One emerging reference term in this new language that providers need to become intimately familiar with is *patient-centric*. A patient-centric model is the movement of the patient as a recipient of care toward becoming the driver of his or her own healthcare needs. How will providers operationalize this new patient-centric model? How does an organization accustomed to receiving referrals from other professionals adapt to patients selecting their physicians "cafeteria style"? Many times a patient's health has deteriorated to such a point that he or she is not in any condition to be the astute shopper of healthcare services. What if his or her choice is strictly driven by cost, or his or her selection is inhibited by the barriers of understanding a complex language used by healthcare providers?

With this understanding, the strategy for an academic organization in transition is to make patients aware of their services before the patient has an acute need. This strategy also demands a change for all healthcare entities. Providers accustomed to reacting to symptoms presented by the patient will now need to move into a preventive versus reactive mode. Education outreach programs will be an opportunity to prepare patients prior to the onset of symptoms.

In fact, proactive organizations are taking it one step farther by incorporating health prevention strategies. If you want to change your future wellness outcome, then contact your provider for various health and wellness strategies. Consider developing a patient healthcare management portfolio to organize all of your health information and, if needed, hire a patient advocate to manage your health. This is no different from organizing all of your personal finances and, if required, hiring a financial advisor to manage your investments.

Final Thought

Does your organization have a social media strategy? If yes, how is it integrated into your data management strategy? How will your business model change, and how will it impact the organization's marketing strategy? Finally, have you developed a strategy to help patients develop a healthcare portfolio and partner with you in keeping them well? Accurate and complete data will impact the quality of strategic direction set at the C-suite level. Chapter 5 reviews a data and information strategy assessment tool.

CEO Perspective

This chapter provides some great insights as to the changing dynamic in leadership teams at hospitals and health systems. The C-suite is expanding within new segmented roles, and the need for information subject matter experts by information type continues to evolve. Intelligent information is an evolving commodity.

—**Scott Becker**

Chief Executive Officer, Publisher of Becker's Hospital Review, Chicago, Illinois

References

1. C-Suite, Investopedia, 2009, http://www.investopedia.com/terms/c/c-suite.asp (accessed December 2014).
2. Groysberg, B., Kelly, K., and MacDonald, B., The New Path to the C-Suite, *Harvard Business Review*, March 2011, https://hbr.org/2011/03/the-new-path-to-the-c-suite (accessed August 2014).
3. Tucci, L., http://www.techtarget.com/contributor/Linda-Tucci (accessed September 2014).
4. Tucci, L., C-Suite Looking for Team Members, Not Captains of Industry, 2013, http://searchcio.techtarget.com/opinion/C-suite-looking-for-team-members-not-captains-of-industry (accessed September 2014).
5. C-Suite, http://dictionary.cambridge.org/us/dictionary/business-english/c-suite (accessed September 2015).
6. C-Suite, http://www.businessdictionary.com/definition/c-suite.html (accessed December 2014).
7. Threat Track Security, No Respect: Chief Information Security Officers Misunderstood and Underappreciated by Their C-Level Peers, http://media.scmagazine.com/documents/89/threattrack_study_on_cisos_22034.pdf (accessed August 2014).
8. Groysberg et al., The New Path to the C-Suite.
9. Tucci, C-Suite Looking for Team Members.
10. Lenzner, R., The Hospital of Tomorrow: Redefining Hospitals under the Affordable Care Act, *Forbes*, May 2014, http://www.forbes.com/sites/robertlenzner/2014/05/21/the-hospital-of-tomorrow-redefining-hospitals-under-the-affordable-care-act/ (accessed August 2014).
11. Hospitals Affordable Care Act Means Right Sizing Healthcare, 2014, http://medcitynews.com/2014/01/hospitals-affordable-care-act-means-right-sizing-healthcare/ (accessed August 2014).
12. O'Brien, K., 5 Ways Obamacare Affects Hospitals, Doctors and More, 2013, http://www.nj.com/news/index.ssf/2013/09/5_ways_obamacare_affects_hospitals_doctors_and_more.html (accessed September 2014).
13. Ungar, L., and Hampson, R., Doctors Worry about Obamacare's Impact on Hospitals, 2014, http://www.courier-journal.com/longform/news/investigations/2014/04/26/doctors-worry-obamacares-impact-hospitals/8152137/ (accessed September 2014).
14. Moore, J., Affordable Care Act Will Change the Way Hospitals Are Built, Used, *Star Tribune Business*, 2014, http://www.startribune.com/business/247893521.html (accessed September 2014).
15. O'Brien, 5 Ways Obamacare Affects Hospitals, Doctors and More.
16. Why Was the American Hospital Association (AHA) So Interested in the Creation of the Affordable Care Act? 2012, http://www.medicarenewsgroup.com/news/medicare-faqs/individual-faq?faqId=a7693994-8416-4824-ab6f-ab93ab3e7246 (accessed September 2014).
17. Keenan, C., Electronic Medical Records: The Costly and Time-Consuming Process for Small, Rural Hospitals, 2014, http://thegazette.com/subject/news/electronic-medical-records-the-costly-and-time-consuming-process-for-small-rural-hospitals-20140601 (accessed September 2014).
18. Whitney, E., Rural Hospitals Face Tough Choices on Computerized Records, 2014, http://kaiserhealthnews.org/news/rural-hospitals-face-tough-choices-on-computerized-records/ (accessed September 2014).

19. Ibid.
20. Ibid.
21. Security Concerns in the C-Suite and How Next-Generation Firewalls Can Help, http://www.fortinet.com/sites/default/files/whitepapers/CSO-NGFW-WP.pdf (accessed August 2014).
22. Ibid.
23. Interview with Lac Van Tran, CIO, Rush University Health System, Chicago.

Chapter 5

Data and Information Strategy Assessment Tool

It is a capital mistake to theorize before one has data.

—Sherlock Holmes
A Study in Scarlett *(Arthur Conan Doyle)*

Organizations must develop a process to identify the resources required to manage data, formulate an information strategy, and execute the mission with the right person at the helm, gaining the initiative and maintaining the momentum. The individual most likely to spearhead this mission is the chief information officer (CIO).

The CIO's chief deputy or chief data officer (CDO) has emerged as another critical C-suite member to have his or her fingerprints all over the big data management process. The promise of our nation's health data file system (patient files), and the treasure trove of potential clinical intelligence borne from its analysis, is stifled by the fact that this information is locked away in obsolete, layered, fragmented databases stored in data silos.

A data silo is simply a provider's (hospital, doctor's office, clinic, lab, etc.) patient files that remain on site without ever being pushed forward or collected into a medium that can be queried or accessed by another provider. Patient information, or our nation's clinical intelligence (health data files), begins at hard-copy record or separate electronic check-in and most often terminates in the office file cabinet or purged computer file. A file cabinet can take the form of some 20-year-old proprietary and now obsolete database fed by a patchwork "data-capture template" or barely legible handwritten or fragmented dictated physician observations, prognoses, and directives stored in manila folders (electronic files) that are buried in cardboard (disc) storage boxes.

In today's healthcare industry, technological integration has been difficult to achieve without a sound data strategy. Leading-edge providers seek to maximize the potential health data intelligence that they derive from IT and associated data mining systems on both a clinical and a business front.

Unfortunately, the reality of the situation is that much of available IT spending is currently geared toward moving and storing data. While expending significant efforts on electronic storage and management of data as a necessary step toward creating and analyzing big data, CIOs face increasing pressure on concurrent data demands. Increasing at a faster rate are the budget dollars for data analysts to respond to internal data call requests throughout the organization. Budget dollars and resources shift toward data mapping and mining when providers or health industry participants recognize the tremendous value that knowledge provides. The value of this knowledge is on the radar screen because providers' survival and ability to thrive will be dependent on the quality of information they have to make business and clinical decisions. Quantum shifts in this direction would demonstrate a tremendous move toward a long-term investment, saving providers time and money and essential to contributing to better healthcare outcomes.

A Bit of History

Several Centers for Medicare and Medicaid Services (CMS) initiatives are noted in Table 1.1, including the Affordable Care Act of 2010 (ACA), the American Recovery and Reinvestment Act of 2009 (ARRA), and the HITECH Act of 2009. These legislative initiatives (and ongoing updates) launched the healthcare industry's health IT (HIT) efforts into high gear and propelled them uncontrollably down the highway in a rainstorm without windshield wipers, a roadmap, GPS, or more importantly, any sense of simple dead reckoning.

A direct consequence of these legislated initiatives is market indecision; however, incentives to push providers to adopt and utilize electronic health records (EHRs) may have gained some ground. The meaningful use enacted through the HITECH Act with incentive payment provision stipulated in the American Recovery and Investment Act has spurned significant investment in EHR, with hospitals adopting varying levels of functional interoperability.

The key to survival under this new legislation is to develop an integrated collection of data-driven healthcare technology tools and services. Although many hospitals have exceeded expectations in terms of information system capabilities, many more are struggling to identify and implement systems that significantly impact the provision of care at reduced cost. That being said, hospitals that are making progress in implementing these changes will continue to drive the overall healthcare system to better levels of data analytics that result in productive business intelligence to refine business practices and quality metrics to enhance clinical intelligence development. The following quotes provide an interesting perspective on the topic of electronic health records.

> More than half of eligible professionals and 80 percent of eligible hospitals have adopted these systems, which are critical to modernizing our healthcare system.[1]
>
> **—Kathleen Sebelius**
> *Secretary of Health and Human Services*

> Once you close a paper file it's dead. You're not able to move it or learn from it.[2]
>
> **—Dr. Farzad Mostashari**

> Continued technological advances in how medical information is shared will be key to helping healthcare providers and patients make more informed decisions.[3]
>
> **—President Barack Obama**

Current State from the CIO Perspective

CIOs are finding themselves working harder to meet the demands of their own organization's internal users. In a series of interviews conducted with current CIO healthcare executives, we began by examining the question "What is one of the biggest challenges facing CIOs today?"

In these discussions, several pervasive themes emerged, the first being the constantly changing environment regarding IT. CIOs are often faced with defining IT's role within an organization in comparison to what they feel it should be. In fact, many CIOs in the healthcare industry stated that the CIO function and IT department are still largely misunderstood by many C-suite executives, which in large part may be due to a lack of overall operational knowledge on the subject.

One CIO stated, "Yes, the CEO just asked me to figure out how to manage meaningful use criteria!"

Another CIO commented, "We've become the dumping ground and final resting place of all requests."

Yet another CIO commented, "Everyone comes to you with their expectations, and the expectation of course is you do what I want, when I want, how I want, and how you pay for it, staff it out, is your problem, not mine." Thus, "I think that we are all struggling with this a little bit in terms of what is the expectation that the organization really has for IT, and what they are willing to fund and support in order to fulfill that expectation."

Most likely, any IT department could double its resources and still fall short of being able to meet all its organization's demands because IT departments exist to service an endless list of requests.

One CIO's critical objective is triaging the endless list of requests that filter into the department to determine which resources are best suited to solving the problem. However, the limiting or deferral of a request does not negate the value or need for the person making the request. Therefore, IT departments are often faced with a lot of pressure. Their perceived value is often associated with their ability to meet the demands of their users in an effective and timely manner. Organizations that do perform self-assessment surveys regarding IT support within their organization may find user feedback focused on service. For example,

- "You didn't call me back."
- "You didn't call me back fast enough."
- "You didn't follow up appropriately."
- "You didn't give me the resource as I requested."

Many IT departments are simply overwhelmed and do not have the capacity to meet their own user needs.[4] Compounding this with new initiatives handed down from the C-suite team, one could only begin to imagine that the CIO perspective tends to be reactive versus proactive.

Within the context of managing data, a historical analogy can be found to put the CIO role into perspective. Provider IT departments traditionally assumed the role and responsibility of working with databases. The role was typically referred to as a database administrator, charged with managing the company database. However, the explosive growth of information resources and complex databases required a resource team to manage these systems.

Today, those traditional roles have been carved up and distributed to groups of IT business analysts who generate reports. At a minimum, contemporary business analysts have experience working with Crystal, SQL Server Reporting Services, or other reporting systems. Today's data analytic personnel need to have a working knowledge of clinical data and associated workflow patterns, in addition to the analytic skills required to manipulate and mine data from dissimilar database systems.

It appears that over time, the basic title of database administrator has virtually disappeared and reemerged as a highly technical position. The mantra often heard from IT people is "We are managing the data from a technical position," which is coordinating the storage and the interfaces versus controlling the data in and of itself.

In one interview, a CIO reported, "It is my job to give them the data they asked for and not tell them what to ask for." All data users have a need for sophisticated analytics; however, the skill sets of data scientists may be lacking within IT departments and associated business unit end users. This could be addressed with the formal adoption of a CDO and competent data science personnel made available to the organization.

Recent trends indicate that health enterprise companies are hiring business unit analysts for their respective areas because business units desperately need critical information and may not have the data scientist role to facilitate the development of business and clinical intelligence. IT is often placed in a position to react to corporate intelligence needs (analysis) while simultaneously installing software, running applications, and ensuring overall system integrity.

Companies must anticipate that the role of a business intelligence analyst will emerge in various forms and require the tools and equipment to conduct accurate and timely information analytics. The question for your organization is, will these data scientist (intelligence analyst) roles emerge within your corporate domain and, if so, where?

Based on a competent job task analysis (JTA), job functions can range from basic data analytic personnel to formal data scientist requirements. Data analytics typically fall under the CIO's domain or are deeply embedded in each separate business unit, especially if an organization does not have a designated CDO. That aside, a data scientist would typically organize and implement the normalization of information and extraction of measures and capture meaningful use criteria as established by CMS for the enterprise database.

One of the CIOs interviewed during the preparation of this book commented that "many healthcare systems are limiting themselves by using legacy IT infrastructures developed in the 1970s and 1980s. These data structures fall dramatically short for meeting the demands of present-day data use and management requirements." The old mantra of "if it is anything electronic, it must belong to IT" is still prevalent and often returns the burden of accountability back into the lap of IT. This accountability shift occurs frequently regardless of IT's analytic subject matter expertise to comprehend data content or intelligence value.

The need to understand data content has inspired many new roles, such as the chief medical information officer (CMIO) and the chief nursing information officer (CNIO). The use of CMIOs and CNIOs promotes clinical end-user participation in the codevelopment of departmental technology initiatives by having a clinician involved with the process. The adoption of a new technology is much more palatable in terms of end-user effectiveness and its integration when the end user is involved in the development.

Technology infrastructures need to match the data content required by the subject matter experts (intelligence analysts), who must understand and think like the end-user community, including the C-suite staff. Organizations that require a massive overhaul of data analytics and new technology platforms may want to consider the role of a CDO (a data scientist) to achieve this future data-driven state.

Our CIO interviews confirmed that security is a constant concern. One university-based system CIO noted:

Every day you just wonder is something going to happen? We spend a lot of time and money on it [security]…. We think that we're secure and we hire people that try to break in to see if our firewalls are secure…. We make sure that we have done all of our due diligence, but you just constantly live with this threat of stealing. Every time we add another data point or a data interface or add another contact, we wonder whether we are opening ourselves up to a breach situation. There are just so many places and so many ways that it can happen; it's just something that lingers over you all the time. I get the question all the time from our board and from our leadership: 'Can you guarantee us that a [breach] won't happen?' How do you explain to people that we live in a world where there are no guarantees and breaches pose a constant threat? So that's something that just 'is' … it takes up an enormous amount of our time, and worry, and it's unfortunate, but that is the world we live in.

This was a typical "top of mind" CIO comment and a constant reminder that potential security breaches were a headline theme in the C-suite.[5] Cyber security is a specialized niche and requires core competency in the tactics, techniques, and procedures that information thieves use in this "dark art" community of invaders.

In medical jargon, cyber security is similar to a diabetic in that the patient's condition is chronic, requiring constant monitoring and intervention, and the patient must study, look for, and avoid complications to halt progression of disease.

In this case, IT must either prevent or halt malicious or mischievous activity that appears to be a favorite sport of some of our more ethically challenged individuals. Beyond the nightmares and liability issues that CIOs must manage on a daily basis looms the heavy burden of managing the entire corporate technology platform.

Effective utilization of applied technology's full bandwidth requires a constant dedication to training. Dedication to training requires that individuals devote a portion of their time to keeping pace with industry trends and future applications. The difference in technology applications really comes down to being on the offense or defense: proactive education places the individual on the offensive side of the line, and the offense typically scores. This is part of the balancing act that CIOs face when budgeting time and money for ongoing education. "Do I provide the opportunity, time, and budget to sustain basic capabilities or position my people to perform above the standard?"

Right now you have to look very closely to identify standards and metrics for information systems and data management. Organizations have recognized the need and have begun to increase investments in a variety of training programs to reach their users, including online courses and "learn as you go." Educational programs such as these will benefit all by way of providing access to training programs at the users' convenience.

The question for the CIO is how to identify and measure the end-user educational requirements that meet their functional utilization. A glaring example is a registration nurse who only utilizes 20% of the hospital's registration system capability because that's what his or her mentor used and that's what that individual taught. Metrics must evolve to a system of creating and measuring the success of programs that permit end users to gain knowledge of and confidently command 100% of any vital system's full functionality. A major frustration and constant complaint emanating from healthcare corporations is that many applied technologies that were identified, purchased, and implemented are grossly underutilized due to a simple lack of "line and staff" (end-user) training.

Metrics to measure performance, goals, and objectives are critical to user adoption. They are also critical to the use of technology, in addition to developing data analytics that provide both clinical and business intelligence. Carefully defined metrics will facilitate the effective management of expectations.

For example, the HITECH Act implemented meaningful use criteria in the management of patient care. The use of defined clinical indicator metrics will better facilitate the measurement of quality patient care.

Other metrics will afford the opportunity to measure objectives that impact things such as patient safety. Within the healthcare market, the level of interoperability that exists between an organization's internal and external partners will increase as partners enhance their familiarity and use of similar technology.

From a patient satisfaction and safety perspective, overall accountability within departmental or clinic workflow is also segmented. The notion of hospital clinic business units being responsible for their respective clinical and business functions is not feasible when personnel responsible for data generation or capture either are unfamiliar with or lack specific training in technology tools that record, track, and transfer vital data points regarding a patient's care. This segmented culture is extremely pervasive within a clinical setting.

For example, a cardiologist may solely focus on a patient's cardiac condition and subsequently send that same patient back to a pulmonologist to tackle respiratory issues without a smidgeon of crosswalk consultation concerning the patient as a whole. This segmented mindset must change or the patient will end up crisscrossing the country consulting six specialists, all treating the symptom but ignoring the cause.

On a recent bicycle trip, one of our team members fell and hit her head on the gravel road. There were 12 cyclists in the group, including a cardiologist, pediatric neonatal intensive care nurse, and adult intensive care nurse. The two nurses began assisting the injured cyclist and asked the cardiologist for advice and assistance, after which the cardiologist responded, "I am just a cardiologist. I don't do trauma or head injuries." Last time I looked, the heart was still connected to the brain! The notion of "I take care of patient issues relevant to my own area of expertise, under my conditions and setting, and then turn them over to somebody else and hope it all works out" is over. The general notion of coordinating patient care can at times appear to be insurmountable. However, as a concept, it must be addressed or the patient loses in the end.

In my lifetime, I have yet to meet an individual who has not had some type of encounter with the healthcare system. For professionals well versed in healthcare, a tour on the patient's side of the equation can be a humbling reminder of what needs to be accomplished. A personal encounter with the healthcare system afforded me many frontline patient care experiences concerning my mother, who recently became a patient in an acute care facility for a period lasting 4 months.

My father, a retired general practitioner, and all of us siblings stood vigil in shifts, never leaving mom alone for fear that something would be overlooked, misconstrued, ignored, or mistaken. How we managed to accomplish this task of "standing post" without ever leaving her alone was a feat in and of itself. Our mother had one scheduled (intended) surgery that led to another four unintended surgeries. During this ordeal, our family members had to continually remind each new nursing shift about the history surrounding our mother's medical condition, including specific adverse reactions to treatment regimen and food products she was allergic to. What is the etiology (the cause or causes of a disease or abnormal condition) of what our mom experienced? It went well beyond any semblance of organized physician or staff interoperability; it required a true coordination of care. However, in this example, true coordination occurred because family members were vigilant of all the data points required to take care of this patient. The data points were not connected within the provider's system and process. They were independently coordinated by the family providing the day-to-day data points required to manage her care. They were not coming from a nursing care plan or progression of notes from one clinical staff to another, which begs the question, what would have happened if the family was not present to connect all the dots?

One very important set of metrics to include in your organization's data schema is to ask the following: Are we connecting all the dots? Are all data points accessible by the decision maker? Does the patient have access to these data points in order to properly consent to treatment and ultimately become the decision maker for his or her own health and well-being?

A nonprofit healthcare system CIO I interviewed recalled his own experience:

> This past year, I went through the end-of-life process with my mother, so I was able to experience many things at my own facility. My takeaway was the caregivers were great, the care was great, but the process itself is lacking. It was a real challenge navigating her through all these pieces, and I know the system, and I know the people, so I was able to navigate her. But how does one manage when they don't know the system? And so, I think that's where we as an industry still have a ways to go. And I think that other industries have solved it better than we have to date. I am optimistic because I think that people are thinking more along those routes, but I still think that the process flow and all the information that goes with it still holds us back. In healthcare, we also have people set in their ways about their job requirements. You know, we still have people who don't understand that part of their job is documentation; part of their job is entering information into the system. You can't pick and choose what you want to do, as all of it fits into the whole process of taking care of the patient.

Imagine healthcare professionals becoming frustrated with the systems that they work in, and then consider those patients who have absolutely no knowledge of the healthcare industry's inner workings. If a patient was to take an active interest in his or her care regimen, where would he or she begin, and whom would he or she rely on for information?

My interview with this nonprofit health system CIO continued with the following: "The other thing I find frustrating about healthcare providers is that quite often the professional staff will refer the medical issue back to the patient and ask the patient what they want to do."

He relayed a personal conversation he had with one physician. The patient and a family member go to the professional to ask for his expert advice. Even when the family member repeatedly asks the practitioner what he would suggest as a treatment, the healthcare professional continued with the response, "Well, you're the patient, what would you like to do?"

Patients are looking for the best path forward and reach out to medical providers for answers; if the patient were the provider, he or she would be in a much better position to answer his or her own question. If the provider wants the patient to diagnose the condition and suggest treatment, then great, send the bill to the doctor for your services rendered.

Another nonprofit healthcare system CIO posed the question to a doctor in the following manner. "If this was your mother, what would you do?" The doctor paused and responded what he would do if it were in fact his mother. By personalizing the healthcare question and forcing the provider to visualize his own mother as the patient, this nonprofit healthcare system CIO was able to get his question answered.

CIOs are voicing a shared concern in not having sufficient resources to effectively respond to the ever-increasing need for data that supports a wide range of operability requirements. A challenge of equal proportion is the acceptance and adoption of new technologies by internal partners and professional staff. Eventually, healthcare organizations must overcome these challenges in order to survive and effectively serve their patient consumer. The ACA, in addition to an increasing number of health information exchanges (HIEs), has facilitated the creation of an infrastructure to provide approved offerings of various healthcare plan options for patients. The relative impact of patient choice under the ACA will ultimately impact how health professionals will respond. Physicians, hospitals, insurance corporations, or health industry enterprises (patients, providers, and payers) of any persuasion that fall short or fail to leverage the necessary technology to satisfy patient needs for information access will simply die on the vine. Other providers will simply choose to remain independent and not be participating providers; this will result in an increased number of barely participating network providers.

Consumers ultimately respond to value-based purchasing. Health industry performance models require the aggregation of clinical intelligent data; however, information shortcomings will result in a parallel scenario developing from a business intelligence perspective. Anticipated healthcare market shifts will eliminate participants who choose not to engage these changes, and those who survive must accurately predict market trends.

Accurate forecasting is crucial in order to effectively prepare for a future that might very well present limited capital and operational resources. Misdirected resources, lack of focus, or moving the entire health market in the wrong direction could very well result in the demise of the healthcare system as we know it today. Technology initiatives are inherently disruptive to an organization; missing the mark on preparing and executing requirements will separate those who will survive from those who fail. This rings true regardless of what industry a CIO operates in.

Therefore, an organization's ability to be proactive versus reactive to market trends is critical. To ease the growing pains of change, a CIO must be on top of strategies that address and support emerging trends. An effective strategy to adapt and plan for these trends will be directly proportional to the amount of pain the organization will be able to endure. That being said, the following sections present illustrative tools that can be utilized by any chief in charge, including, but not limited to, CIO, CDO, CMIO, and CNIO. The models include disciplines from internal audit, compliance, risk management, and forensic support–type approaches.

Author's Note: Does your organization have a data strategy? If yes, how will that data strategy be operationalized? Finally, once it is operationalized, what controls and resources are in place to keep the strategy sustainable?

Key Principles: Healthcare Data and Information Strategies

From a provider's perspective, raw data in and of itself is almost useless unless it can inform or improve decisions or other business processes. In other words, data represents the ingredients that form the end product, which in this case is knowledge or intelligence. This chapter highlights the two main branches of intelligence that are available to providers who successfully implement the appropriate information technology solutions.

Business intelligence (BI) refers to all intelligence that is relevant to the business functions of the entity. Whether it concerns cost management, resource allocation, the billing process, or staffing, any successful health IT systems must allow providers to act on all available relevant data to efficiently streamline operations. As the healthcare community shifts from a volume-based system to an efficiency-based system, providers will need to ensure that their business operations are structured to minimize wasteful spending.

As with any other business, understanding the relevant information related to performance is crucial in determining best practices. When all is said and done, businesses that identify and implement effective data and information strategies will be in a position to fully analyze business performance metrics from a data-driven standpoint and eliminate guesswork related to operations, management, and limited resource allocation.

Clinical intelligence (CI) focuses on the subject of health. Healthcare tends to be clinically driven and primarily focused on saving lives and making decisions that affect the well-being of patients. A major component of decision making in the healthcare continuum is the philosophy that any decision made is as good as the available information.

When it pertains to doctors deciding on patient care regimens, the goal of a successful data or information system is to maximize the interconnectivity of all patient data. Information should be viewed as a tool for doctors and staff, with IT providing the information, analytic, and decision tree tools required to properly treat patients. Clinical intelligence, when properly harnessed by effective IT systems, places doctors in a better position to affect successful patient outcomes. CI can also support population health management strategies where analytics are required to identify gaps and provide clinical decision support.

Another perspective might involve an individual patient with x-rays and test results from several different providers. An effective database and intelligent information system will blend all the significant clinical data in a fashion that allows clinicians to maximize their performance in caring for patients by creating a data-driven process. The ultimate benefit of accurate CI is a better patient care experience and patients benefiting from improvements in their overall health. The following items should be considered, with defined metrics, when implementing any data and information strategy:

- Information and data must be readily available to relevant end users within the organization.
- Information and data must be protected from unauthorized access.
- Information and data collected by the entity is effectively captured, stored, mined, and analyzed to maximize utility.
- Information and data must be a principal component of all decision making.
- Information and data must be utilized to conduct vulnerability analysis and measure risk on both the clinical and the business side of operations.
- Developers of information and data systems must work with all system end users throughout the development process to ensure that the end product efficiently and effectively supports workflow.
- If applicable, provider information and data systems must properly align with the objectives and requirements of the health information exchange (HIE) and accountable care organizations (ACO).
- Information and data strategies must be fluid and responsive to emerging market trends.
- Information and data strategies must consider compliance and changing legislation.
- Information and data must be patient-centric.

A health data and information strategy requires the appropriate leadership, skill sets, and structure to be successful. In this rapidly changing environment, it is not unusual for traditional departments to feel at a disadvantage when it comes to having the "right person for the right job." The previously discussed role of a chief data officer would appear to be timely.

Author's Note: Raw data in and of itself is almost useless unless it can inform or improve decisions or other business processes.

CDO Cubic Approach

Chapter 2 introduced the history and emerging role of the chief data officer. Chapter 12 will further define the role of the CDO. This chapter will review a cubic framework to fully assess, identify, and develop the requirements for the role of a CDO within the organization. The following is a recap of the cubic framework strategic approach. The cubic framework outlined in a *MIS Quarterly Executive* article by Lee et al.[6] can also be used to identify the role and need for a CDO in an organization. These steps are

1. Assess current status of your organization's data-related business practices (based on the three dimensions of the CDO cube).
2. Determine the CDO role profile needed for your organization (based on the eight roles described), and whether an executive-level CDO is required to fulfill these needs.
3. Strategize the likely path for the CDO based on a projection of organizational future needs.

This model provides guidance for establishing the infrastructure, process, and leadership necessary to begin developing a data strategic plan for an organization. Details of this model are reviewed in Chapter 12. The following section focuses on the data and information strategies required to achieve the objectives set forth. This section also identifies an organization's strategic data plan through the use of one component within the behavioral continuum model, framework, and analytic roadmap tool.[7]

This component is identified as the interactive, iterative, and reiterating behavioral continuum model, framework, and analytic roadmap used to identify, collect, authenticate, process, transform, and unify fragmented data (IIRB model, framework, and analytic roadmap). The continuum aspect relevant to any data and information strategy is the process of first identifying critical data points, followed by integrating any fragmented data. Healthcare is heavily inundated with deeply fragmented, underutilized, and undercapitalized data—all orbiting derivative intelligence.

Therefore, a mechanism to identify critical data points is set forth within IIRB model, framework, and analytic roadmap.[8]

IIRB Model, Framework, and Analytic Roadmap[9]

Once a data strategy is identified and developed, it must be tested to determine whether it meets organizational goals and objectives. The fundamental behavioral principles that must be understood when determining data points fall into the following categories:

Player component: A person, place, or thing that takes part; a participant, provider, or entity.

Benchmark component: The identified player's standard, point of reference, or measurement for each identified player, as well as within and among each component within the behavioral continuum.

Functional information component: All relational knowledge derived by persons, communication systems, circumstances, research, processes, technology, and behaviors realized by each identified player, as well as within and among each component within the behavioral continuum.

Rule-based component: All related principles, regulations, governing conducts, actions, procedures, arrangements, contracts, legislature, dominions, and controls generated by each identified player, as well as within and among each component within the behavioral continuum.

Transparency, opaqueness, and obstruction component: The identification of the quality of being transparent, opaque, or obstructed (barriers, impediments, obstacles, and stoppage) by each player, as well as within and among each component within the behavioral continuum.

Consequence component: The identification of issues, upshots, sequels, damages, acts, instances, effects, results, outcomes, conclusion importance, significance, rank, position, monetary value, or state of being of each player and within and among each component within the behavioral continuum.

Detailed workflows and data roadmaps should be delineated to include all people, process, and technology components. Within each of these continuums (healthcare specifically) the following components should be highlighted:

- Data capture that identifies and defines all workflow
- Mechanism of data and its movement
- Data workflows mapped
- Drivers of data components
- Activity of daily functions (ADF) associated with workflow
- Business intelligence data flows
- Clinical intelligence data flows
- Revenue cycle data flows
- Operational data flows
- Service delivery data flows
- Product delivery data flows

Adapt or die has been repeatedly identified as a Darwin-like prognosis for players in the healthcare industry. Accurately forecasting trends and being prepared to support your organization's need to adapt and thrive as new trends develop will be critical for an organization's survival as we go forward. The following list of models and data profilers may be used to measure an organization's ability to adapt to emerging trends. The components of a data and information strategy (DIS) assessment tool should include

DIS assessment: The act of evaluation, valuation, and assessment as applied to the organization's current data roadmap in comparison to its defined strategic plan.

DIS prevention: The process to identify postimplementation a data strategic plan and the effectual hindrance or the act of preventing adoption to a new business model.

DIS detection: The discovery of, the act of, or the process of extracting information from the data sets that is not consistent with the organization's data strategy or data policy.

DIS mitigation: The lessening of the force, intensity, adverse circumstances, conditions, or event consequences of data deficiencies that have been detected within the defined data strategic plan.

A function of the CDO would involve the management, handling, directing, controlling, and tracking of the data and strategic plan for the organization's information. The IIRB model, framework, and analytic roadmap will be further expanded as a data intelligence strategy framework.

Data Intelligence Strategy Using the Healthcare Continuum

The principal concepts of the healthcare continuum (HCC) can be applied to any provider business attempting to maximize utility gained from successful data and information systems. In essence, the continuum audit and investigative model focuses on the following layers:

- The players (P-HCC)
- Benchmark data (S-HCC)
- Information systems—location, format, and housing of data (I-HCC)
- Risk—identification of roadblocks (T-HCC)
- Ability to measure damages and impact (C-HCC)
- Rules—private, public, and statutory (R-HCC)[10]

Within each segment and contemporaneous to each continuum level of the behavior pipelines are

- Primary healthcare continuum (P-HCC): Identify market players.
- Accounts receivable pipeline (ARP): Identify the monetary impact.
- Operational flow assessment (OFA): Identify the relevant business functions.
- Product market activity (PMA): Identify the relevant product.
- Service market activity (SMA): Identify the relevant service.
- Consumer market activity (CMA): Identify the appropriate type of patient.[11]

The healthcare continuum model (six in total) serves as a framework to fully address the questions that any CIO or CDO must consider when implementing a successful data and information strategy for his or her provider entity. The model is structured to provide a comprehensive listing of critical components and includes all relevant sources of information, as well as all parties and processes that rely on information collected by the entity.

The following six figures integrate the continuum model with the patient as the starting point. The six components of the healthcare continuum (HCC) model are broken down by the key behavioral components and illustrative operational considerations.

P-HCC Definition[12]

The first level of analysis is based on the primary healthcare continuum (P-HCC). P-HCC analysis, illustrated in Figure 5.1, identifies the parties that provide direct or indirect healthcare services, how they work together, and the information shared.

S-HCC Definition[13]

The second level of analysis is based on the secondary healthcare continuum (S-HCC). S-HCC (Figure 5.2) analysis identifies each entity that uses information generated from the P-HCC for data intelligence. The DIS strategy must include authoritative benchmarks and metrics to be applied. For example, the meaningful use criterion is defined under the rule-based continuum. However,

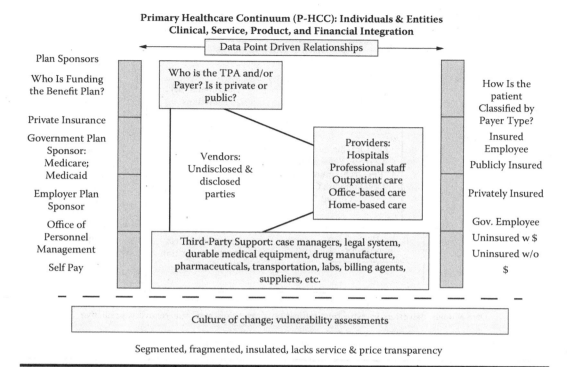

**Primary Healthcare Continuum (P-HCC): Individuals & Entities
Clinical, Service, Product, and Financial Integration**

Data Point Driven Relationships

Plan Sponsors

Who Is Funding
the Benefit Plan?

Private Insurance

Government Plan
Sponsor:
Medicare;
Medicaid

Employer Plan
Sponsor

Office of
Personnel
Management

Self Pay

Who is the TPA and/or
Payer? Is it private or
public?

Vendors:
Undisclosed &
disclosed
parties

Providers:
Hospitals
Professional staff
Outpatient care
Office-based care
Home-based care

Third-Party Support: case managers, legal system,
durable medical equipment, drug manufacture,
pharmaceuticals, transportation, labs, billing agents,
suppliers, etc.

How Is the
patient
Classified by
Payer Type?

Insured
Employee

Publicly Insured

Privately Insured

Gov. Employee

Uninsured w $

Uninsured w/o
$

Culture of change; vulnerability assessments

Segmented, fragmented, insulated, lacks service & price transparency

Figure 5.1   Primary healthcare continuum. (Adapted from Busch, R. *Healthcare Fraud: Auditing and Detection Guide*, New York: John Wiley & Sons, 2012.[10])

the secondary continuum describes the mechanics of how to implement legislated rules or rules contracted between two parties.

I-HCC Definition[14]

The third level of analysis is based on the information healthcare continuum (I-HCC). I-HCC (Figure 5.3) analysis identifies the operational issues within the entities of the P-HCC, and the users and uses of the S-HCC. Figure 5.3 illustrates elements that are important to identify within a provider's current operating practices and procedures, and how they interact with other parties within the healthcare marketplace. It is also necessary to identify electronic interoperability drivers, such as compatible Internet, intranet, and extranet systems, and electronic interoperability impediments, such as incompatible or detached electronic and paper systems. At each layer, the people, processes, and technology workflows must be identified within each business unit, including internal and external partner groups. A comprehensive DIS will delineate all workflows and respective applied technologies.

C-HCC Definition[15]

The fourth level of analysis is based on the consequences healthcare continuum (C-HCC). C-HCC (Figure 5.4) analysis identifies and measures risk of all associated behaviors and activities to ensure that all required processes are present in the healthcare marketplace. A DIS should include all active risk assessments and risk mitigation strategies.

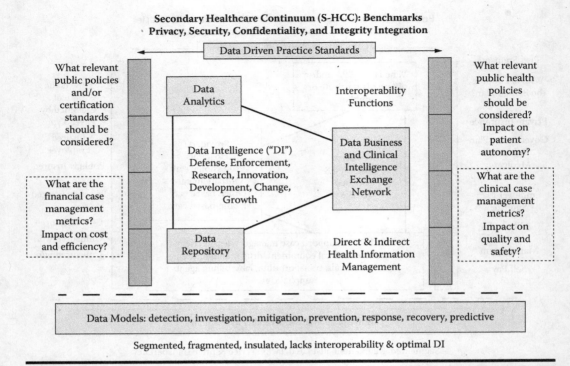

Figure 5.2 Secondary healthcare continuum. (Adapted from Busch, R. *Healthcare Fraud: Auditing and Detection Guide*, New York: John Wiley & Sons, 2012.[10])

T-HCC Definition[16]

The fifth continuum integrates risk. This analysis is based on the transparency continuum (T-HCC). T-HCC (Figure 5.5) analysis identifies transparency issues that may exist for any number of reasons and affect numerous market player processes. Transparency issues can pertain to both business and personal disclosures and are motivated by social assumptions, laws and legislation, and limitations of access due to technology, contracts, and other intentional and unintentional constraints. An example of a roadblock is security. The purpose of the transparency continuum is to recognize any roadblocks that would impact the operational objectives. Therefore, the inclusion of a mitigation strategy to address roadblocks and settle on opportunities to evaluate should be incorporated in order to be vigilant, or an ongoing threat remains.

R-HCC Definition[17]

The sixth and final continuum incorporates an understanding of rules by each continuum that all market players are subject to. Figure 5.6 illustrates components of the rule-based continuum. This is further layered by the subject matter of each pipeline (P-HCC, ARP, OFA, PMA, SMA, and CMA) within each segment. In essence, the process is structured to avoid missing information, identify gaps, and generate incontrovertible facts. The rules consider the monetary and business drivers that may or may not be contractually driven. The DIS must incorporate and update any new requirements that are contracted or legislated.

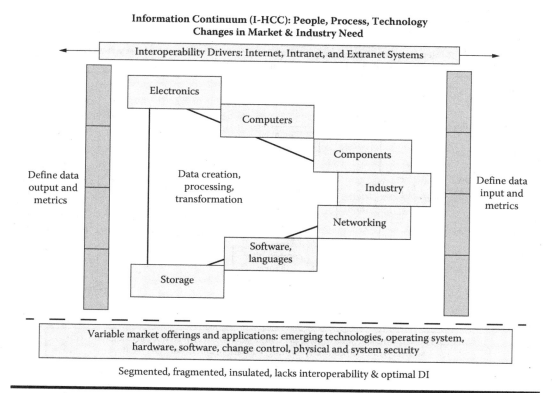

Information Continuum (I-HCC): People, Process, Technology Changes in Market & Industry Need

Figure 5.3 Information healthcare continuum. (Adapted from Busch, R. *Healthcare Fraud: Auditing and Detection Guide*, New York: John Wiley & Sons, 2012.[10])

Overall, several data and information strategy tools have been provided. How to obtain clinical and business intelligence is a running theme in all healthcare settings. Once again, Chapter 2 introduced the history and emerging role of the chief data officer to build a data strategy for the organization. At some point, an organization will want to determine whether its data needs require a specific executive role to manage the data requirements for the overall organization. This chapter presented the cubic framework outlined in the *MIS Quarterly Executive* article by Lee et al. to further evaluate a formal CDO position. With respect to the actual analytics, this chapter also provided an interactive, iterative, and reiterating behavioral continuum model, framework, and analytic roadmap to identify, collect, authenticate, process, transform, and unify fragmented data referenced in short as the IIRB model, framework, and analytic roadmap. This can be an effective tool in managing high-volume data points that are heavily fragmented, underutilized, and undercapitalized in order to gain extremely high-value operational intelligence. This model was further extrapolated into the provider market under a framework referenced as a healthcare continuum model for the development and management of a strategic data plan.

Final Thought

Do you understand the new trends or older reoccurring trends emerging in your market? How are you adjusting your strategy in order to adapt to these market events? How is the CIO reacting

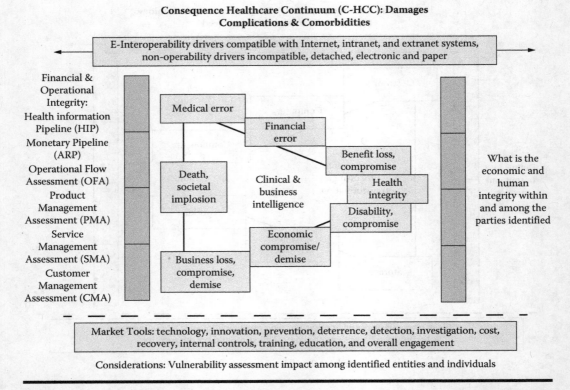

Consequence Healthcare Continuum (C-HCC): Damages Complications & Comorbidities

E-Interoperability drivers compatible with Internet, intranet, and extranet systems, non-operability drivers incompatible, detached, electronic and paper

Financial & Operational Integrity:
Health information Pipeline (HIP)
Monetary Pipeline (ARP)
Operational Flow Assessment (OFA)
Product Management Assessment (PMA)
Service Management Assessment (SMA)
Customer Management Assessment (CMA)

Medical error

Financial error

Benefit loss, compromise

Death, societal implosion

Clinical & business intelligence

Health integrity

Disability, compromise

Economic compromise/ demise

Business loss, compromise, demise

What is the economic and human integrity within and among the parties identified

Market Tools: technology, innovation, prevention, deterrence, detection, investigation, cost, recovery, internal controls, training, education, and overall engagement

Considerations: Vulnerability assessment impact among identified entities and individuals

Figure 5.4 Consequence healthcare continuum. (Adapted from Busch, R. *Healthcare Fraud: Auditing and Detection Guide*, New York: John Wiley & Sons, 2012.[10])

to an aggressive and dynamic IT market and developing response strategies? Finally, are the data needs reaching a level of intensity that a formal CDO needs to emerge and run on a parallel track to the CIO? In order to effectuate and execute new strategies, gap analysis management is critical in moving your operations from their current to desired future defined state. Chapter 6 discusses key gap management considerations.

CCO Perspective

Ms. Busch does well to point out the challenges and pitfalls of data integration in the evolving healthcare climate. Covered entities under HITECH demonstrate massive variability in capacity, operability, and connectivity from within their organizations as well as between entities in communication for individual patient treatment, payment, and the emerging myriad services provided to healthcare organizations as the use of outsourced expertise increases. The resultant risks and vulnerabilities of escalating analytical use and data flow directly impact healthcare compliance programs in the management of quality standards, assuring medical necessity, protecting health information and the accuracy of billing/reimbursement activities—with regulatory implications for failure existing on both federal and state levels. In this and in

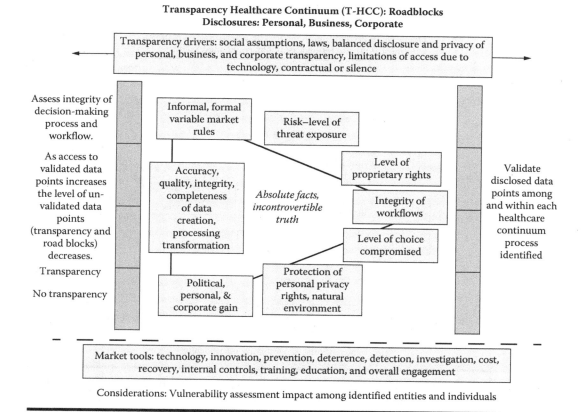

Figure 5.5 Transparency healthcare continuum. (Adapted from Busch, R. *Healthcare Fraud: Auditing and Detection Guide*, New York: John Wiley & Sons, 2012.[10])

many regards, effective CIO/CDO relationships are absolutely essential to compliance officers. Understanding and addressing opportunities within the various healthcare-related continuums, as effectively outlined in the "Data Intelligence Strategy" section of Chapter 5, generate superior return on investment for business development as well as for safeguarding practices.

—Andre Boucher
Compliance Officer, Tenet Healthcare, Coral Springs, Florida

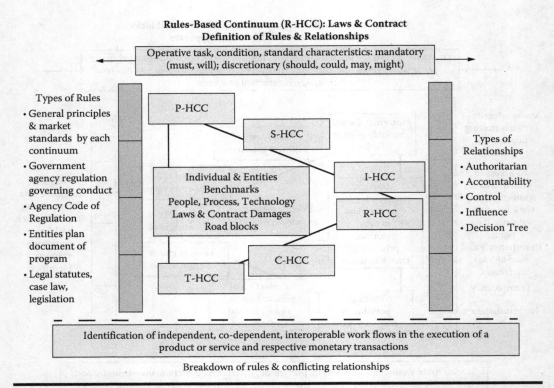

Figure 5.6 Rule-based healthcare continuum. (Adapted from Busch, R. *Healthcare Fraud: Auditing and Detection Guide*, New York: John Wiley & Sons, 2012.[10])

References

1. Doctors and Hospitals' Use of Health IT More Than Doubles Since 2012, http://www.hhs.gov/news/press/2013pres/05/20130522a.html (accessed August 2014).

2. Better Data = Better Health: Farzad Mostashari Q&A, http://www.rwjf.org/en/about-rwjf/newsroom/newsroom-content/2012/10/better-data—-better-health—a-conversation-with-farzad-mostasha.html (accessed August 2014).

3. Ackerman, K., What the Presidential Election Could Mean for Health IT, October 2012, http://www.ihealthbeat.org/insight/2012/what-the-presidential-election-could-mean-for-health-it?view=print (accessed August 2014).

4. Sondergaard, P., Many CIOs Are Unprepared for the Next Era in Enterprise IT, *Forbes*, February 11, 2014, http://www.forbes.com/sites/gartnergroup/2014/02/11/many-cios-are-unprepared-for-the-next-era-in-enterprise-it/.

5. Von Hoffman, C., Cybersecurity Expert: US Critical Infrastructure Threat Is Real—but 'the Sky Isn't Falling,' 2012, http://www.cio.com/article/2371081/security0/cybersecurity-expert—us-critical-infrastructure-threat-is-real—-but—the-sky-isn-t-falli.html (accessed September 2015).

6. Lee, Y., Madnick, S., Wang, F., Wang, R., and Zhang, H., A Cubic Framework for the Chief Data Officer (CDO): Succeeding in a World of Big Data, http://www.mitcdoiq.org/wp-content/uploads/2014/01/Lee-et-al.-A-Cubic-Framework-for-the-CDO-MISQE-Forthcoming-2014-copy.pdf (accessed August 2014).

7. Busch, R., Interactive and Iterative Behavioral Model, System, and Method for Detecting Fraud, Waste, and Abuse (Iterative and/or Reiterating Behavioral Continuum Model, Framework, and Analytic Roadmap to Identify, Collect, Authenticate, Process, Transform and/or Unify Fragmented Data [IIRB Model, Framework, and Analytic Roadmap]), 62026556, patent pending, July 18, 2014.
8. Ibid.
9. Ibid.
10. Busch, R., *Healthcare Fraud: Auditing and Detection Guide*, 2nd ed. (New York: John Wiley & Sons, 2012).
11. Ibid.
12. Ibid.
13. Busch, R., *Healthcare Fraud: Auditing and Detection Guide*, 1st ed. (Chichester: John & Sons Wiley, 2007).
14. Busch, *Healthcare Fraud*, 2nd ed.
15. Busch, *Healthcare Fraud*, 2nd ed.
16. Ibid.
17. Ibid.

Chapter 6

Gap Analysis Management

Illusion is an anodyne, bred by the gap between wish and reality.

—**Herman Wouk**
Pulitzer Prize–winning American author

This chapter reviews the process of preparing a gap analysis and identifying a "tool" checklist for providers to begin the journey. Given the requirement to conduct a gap analysis, mission success is dependent on already having or acquiring the basic skill sets to identify and articulate your current state, future state, and all gaps within the margins. This is key to surviving the treacherous twists and turns encountered when navigating through a comprehensive gap analysis, which in many cases may determine the fate of the organization. Those who create the illusion of normalcy, as a form of anesthetic to avoid the pain and suffering of discovering their true economic state or disregarding simple change within their environment, will not survive.

A Bit of History

The definition of a formal business gap analysis states, "A technique that businesses use to determine what steps need to be taken to move from their current state to a desired future state."[1] This technique is also referred to as a need-gap analysis, needs analysis, or needs assessment. A gap analysis consists of (1) identifying characteristic factors (such as attributes, competencies, or performance levels) of the present situation (*what is*), (2) identifying factors that are necessary to achieve future objectives (*what should be*), and (3) highlighting existing gaps that need to be filled to achieve that future state.

The gap analysis process forces companies to reflect on what they are at present and what they strive to be in the future. A scientifically based gap analysis approach will include a problem or scope definition, the relevant data to review, and a hypothesis formulation. In the context of a scientifically driven gap analysis, the hypothesis will be a derivative of a needs assessment or driven by the data output of a prior gap analysis. Regardless, the process and its resulting product must be documented in a manner that will allow the results to be repeated and confirmed by a third party. Again, the basic tenet of a gap analysis is determining where you are verses where you should be.

The shortfall in a gap analysis is the identified gap between current and desired future state. Once gaps are identified, the question then becomes how to bridge the difference that stands between the present and future states.

Author's Note: This biggest challenge to creating a gap analysis is defining your future state.

Hybrid Roles of Gap Analysis Management

The literature is inundated with the topic of gap analysis. As mentioned before, it is the process of comparing actual performance, possible performance, or ideal performance to a desired future state, and the analysis module will identify any deficits or gaps. Once the deficits are identified, a plan is created to achieve that desired state. The steps in Table 6.1 provide a general framework to conduct a gap analysis (GA). Each step is incremental and will impact the successful execution of all subsequent steps.

The minimum skill sets involved in conducting a gap analysis vary by industry but are typically guided by the leadership component of the company's business division. Analysis of the current state must involve individuals who possess a comprehensive specific business unit expertise, in addition to overall organization knowledge. In addition to step 2 mentioned above, step 3 skill sets require the ability to effectively communicate with internal and external business partners.

The knowledge, skills, and ability necessary to accurately collect the relevant data and conduct an accurate operational flow assessment considering the numerous personnel obstacles, undocumented internal processes, and obsolete technology hurdles are critical to the successful completion of steps 4–8. These steps demand the right personnel resources with the right analytical and

Table 6.1   Gap Analysis General Framework: Overall Process

Step 1: Establish a defined expectation or topic for consideration.
Step 2: Define the process to document and articulate the current state relative to a defined expectation.
Step 3: Define and articulate the future state; typically follows the completion of a needs assessment.
Step 4: Conduct a current and future state analysis and compare the two.
Step 5: Define and articulate the variances from the current and future states.
Step 6: Review original expectations and establish the need for any modifications to achieve the defined future state.
Step 7: Develop an implementation plan on how to achieve the future state with or without modifications of the defined expectation.
Step 8: Define the appropriate metrics to measure, test, and validate findings and provide assurance that the plan can mitigate the identified gaps have succeeded and then test the implementation of remedies.

internal audit and investigation subject matter expertise to complete this mission and ultimately withstand the demanding management scrutiny.

Although it is not unusual to identify a "corporate" team of individuals that collectively possess the necessary combined skill sets required to tackle this difficult mission, at least one team member must recognize the mission parameters and possess the leadership skills to report and defend the original mission intent.

Author's Note: Assuming competent personnel and clear mission intent, be cautious of what you ask for if you are not comfortable with managing root cause issues. The ability to map and create business flow and reflect that in work product documentation is also very important. Documenting the analysis provides an opportunity to vet and validate all investigative or report findings. It's what is referred to as the quality review board (QRB) process. QRB is a process by which a team of subject matter experts or senior-level management review the documentation for factual accuracy, appropriate analytical systems used to support findings, order of dialogue syntax, and proper grammar, and ensure the material remains focused on the issue at hand. An interim report is produced by an audit, investigation, or review of field elements. An interim report (in its entirety) is reviewed by all team members for reasonability checks (mistakes, backup analysis proofs, inaccuracies, clarity, grammar, spelling, and tone) and "marked up," after which it is redrafted for another review by the same team of auditors, investigators, or authors. The draft is presented to a team lead writer for the final draft, and a final review is conducted by the same team members. This interim draft goes to the QRB panel for a full review and challenges. This report must stand up to public and board scrutiny because the information contained within it impacts funding, fines, safety, and reputation. *Analysis and reporting are subject to an unbridled, no-holds-barred peer review that seeks to invalidate findings with prejudice.* If the gap involves procuring data intelligence as an objective, the process would be enhanced by the use of a data scientist to facilitate objectives that involve analytics.

Gap Analysis Management Today

The healthcare industry is transitional at best, and the market players need a formal gap department to move from one new trend to the next. Regardless of this rapidly changing health marketplace, many providers have conducted some type of gap triage and are reacting.

Providers are beginning to identify specific roles and hire or internally reassign personnel to address intermittent gaps in their operations on a daily basis. Revenue cycle management is the art of ensuring that all operations associated with the generation and receipt of revenue are present and operate with a high degree of integrity. This typically involves the integration of professional medical auditors who bring impartiality, efficiencies, and comprehensive skill sets to work with their industry counterparts in order to ensure the accurate and timely resolution of insurance claim issues.

Author's Note: As the patient portion of a claim increases, revenue cycle efforts may be refocused on private pay revenues.

In addition, revenue integrity management provides another mechanism to address not so visible disruption of mission-critical issues buried within the organization. Many of the newly recognized roles have been developed to respond to recently legislated requirements, and some organizations have already deployed mature revenue integrity teams that are dispersed throughout the organization, ready to address issues as they arrive.

Within this rapidly changing environment, another emerging need has surfaced for medical data auditors (discussed in Chapter 8) that support both providers and other healthcare continuum organizations. Medical data is expressed in a language that requires personnel with special knowledge, skills, and abilities to effectively comprehend and analyze it in context.

Balancing Act

The balancing act in conducting a gap analysis is to have a thorough understanding of your industry niche and of your respective organization's internal and external partners. Table 6.2 is an application of the behavioral continuum audit model for conducting a gap analysis.

Chapter 5 introduced the interactive, iterative, and reiterating behavioral continuum model, framework, and analytic roadmap used to identify, collect, authenticate, process, transform, and unify fragmented data (IIRB model, framework, and analytic roadmap). The IIRB model, framework, and analytic roadmap were introduced and applied in the context of developing a data and information strategy (DIS) assessment tool. However, the application of this framework was specifically adapted to conduct gap assessments, which have similar behaviors; however, the context of the application may be adjusted.

Leadership for these respective business units (provider departments) or C-suite involves managing, handling, directing, controlling, and tracking the gap work process and monitoring all future state objectives. The IIRB model, framework, and analytic roadmap will be further expanded in this chapter as a gap analysis tool and framework strategy.

Table 6.2 IIRB Model, Framework, and Analytic Roadmap Core Models

Gap assessment: The act of evaluating, valuating, and assessing deficit variances as applied to the organization's current state in comparison to the desired state.
Gap prevention: The process of identifying a future state postimplementation as defined in the gap's desired state and the controls to minimize the effectual hindrance or the act of preventing the adoption of the future state as defined by the organization.
Gap detection: The discovery of, the act of, or the process of extracting information from the identified gaps that is not consistent with the organization's desired future state.
Gap mitigation: The lessening of the force, intensity, adverse circumstances, conditions, or event consequences of identified gaps that have been detected within the defined future state.

IIRB Model, Framework, and Analytic Roadmap

Once a gap assessment scope has been defined and developed, it must be tested to see whether it meets the organization's goals and objectives. This may require a formal needs assessment to validate the future state requirements. When the future needs assessment has been validated, the gap analysis can move forward immediately following the identification of current state data points. The driving behavioral principles in understanding data points fall into the categories shown in Table 6.3.

Please note that behavioral components can be applied in a variety of data analytic tasks. For example, in Chapter 5, the model was applied to conduct a DIS assessment. In this chapter, the model will be modified to conduct a straightforward gap analysis. In subsequent chapters, it will be applied in other "provider review" activities. These behavioral components are applicable as a basis to provide confidence in the relevant data captured when conducting any types of analyses, audits, or other reviews of data.

A review of the first step listed earlier, "establish a defined expectation or topic for consideration," will illustrate the application of this data collection model. For example, an organization might choose as its future state the adoption of meaningful use criteria. This defined future state can be used to initiate a gap analysis and progress to step 2, "define the process to document and articulate the current state relative to a defined expectation," which requires extensive mapping. Detailed workflows and a data roadmap must be delineated to include all people, process, and technology components involved in current and future state activities. In healthcare continuums, the components in Table 6.4 must be highlighted.

Table 6.3 IIRB Model, Framework, and Analytic Roadmap Core Continuums

Player component: A person, place, or thing that takes part; a participant, provider, or entity.
Benchmark component: An identified player's standards, point of reference, or measurement for each identified player, as well as within and among each component within the behavioral continuum.
Functional information component: All relational knowledge derived by persons, communication systems, circumstances, research, processes, technology, and behaviors realized by each identified player, as well as within and among each component within the behavioral continuum.
Rule-based component: All related principles, regulations, governing conducts, actions, procedures, arrangements, contracts, legislature, dominions, and controls generated by each identified player, as well as within and among each component within the behavioral continuum.
Transparency, opaqueness, and obstruction component: The identification of the quality of being transparent, opaque, or obstructed (barriers, impediments, obstacles, or stoppages by each player), as well as within and among each component within the behavioral continuum.
Consequence component: The identification of issues, upshots, sequels, damages, acts, instances, effects, results, outcomes, conclusion importance, significance, rank, position, monetary value, or state of being of each player and within and among each component within the behavioral continuum.

Source: Busch, R., patent pending, 2014.

Table 6.4   IIRB Illustrative Revenue Cycle Data Call

Step 1: Define the data elements supporting the workflows identified.
Step 2: Define the mechanism of data and its movement.
Step 3: Map data workflows.
Step 4: Identify drivers of data components.
Step 5: Identify activities of daily functions (ADFs) associated with the workflow.
Step 6: Define the business intelligence data flows.
Step 7: Define the clinical intelligence data flows.
Step 8: Define the revenue cycle data flows.
Step 9: Define the operational data flows.
Step 10: Define the service delivery data flows.
Step 11: Define the product delivery data flows.
Step 12: Define the metrics collected, measured, and analyzed.

A workflow analysis similar to that described for step 2 can be repeated to operationalize the future state. Step 3 states, "Define and articulate the future state; typically follows the completion of a needs assessment." The above steps hypothesize what the future state should look like. Once these workflows are defined and documented, the gap analysis team can proceed to step 4, "conduct a current and future state analysis and compare the two." Anticipate this to be a very time-consuming task. It is recommended that analysts visually display the current state as a workflow diagram. The visual display of workflow diagrams provides a pictorial image to be used to validate the process articulated by the users.

This is followed by literally walking through the physical current state while documenting the components. This review step must be repeated several times to validate completeness, followed by the development of desired state mapping. Once the gaps are mitigated, the process should be repeated. Another common but extremely valuable exercise is a provider's initiative to adopt meaningful use criteria. Gaps in documentation requirements to achieve meaningful use criteria are noted. This is followed by initiating provisions to implement a process to address and correct the deficits identified in the gaps.

To illustrate the testing component of this process, a provider may have implemented the desired workflows to achieve the objectives of the meaningful use criteria. A postgap repeat analysis may include testing the system to see whether any additional gaps exist in the use and implementation of tools utilized to achieve meaningful use objectives.

If a postreassessment gap is justified, then step 5, "define and articulate the variances from the current and future states," would articulate what components (i.e., people, processes, and technology) should be reviewed. The postreassessment gap could be an old issue or something entirely new; however, any deficiencies must be revalidated against the original expectation. In this illustration, the gap involves the adoption and/or correction of meaningful use criteria.

This validation process is identified in step 6, "review original expectations and establish the need for any modifications to achieve the defined future state." In this continued illustration of meaningful use, a physician's documentation is a factor in the success or failure of meeting objectives. For example, Dr. A is not completing the second requirement of meaningful use.

Step 7, "develop an implementation plan on how to achieve the future state with or without modifications of the defined expectation," may include provider education and validation of access to the system to enter documentation by Dr. A. Finally, in step 8, the process would further progress with "define the appropriate metrics to measure, test, and validate findings and provide assurance that the plan can mitigate the identified gaps have succeeded and then test the implementation of remedies."

In the case of our Dr. A, this may include the review of education materials or random audits of future patient medical records to validate that Dr. A is now consistently including the second criterion for meaningful use in his documentation. Gap areas should run parallel to any forecasting or strategic plans established by the organization's leadership. Support for gap initiatives should originate from the organization's medical audit support function or any type of business analytic support role.

Regardless of the role (individual or team), initiating and managing the gap, accountability, and ownership for the project should be defined. The IIRB model, framework, and analytic roadmap model will be further expanded in this chapter as a gap strategy framework.

Author's Note: The chief data officer (CDO) role may involve functions before, during, and after a gap analysis event to evaluate any impact to the organization's overall data strategy, policies and standards, data integration, data architecture, governance, metadata, data quality, analytics, and delivery of data.

Gap Analysis Strategy Using the Healthcare Continuum

The concepts of the healthcare continuum (HCC) can be applied to any business provider attempting to achieve a desired future state or evaluate why a future state has not been achieved. The

Table 6.5 IIRB Model, Framework, and Analytic Roadmap Core HHC

Step 1: The players (P-HCC): List all known entities and professional roles involved.
Step 2: Benchmark data (S-HCC): List practice standards by each noun identified.
Step 3: Information systems (I-HCC): Location, format, and housing of data: Identify and create business flowcharts of all people, processes, and technology.
Step 4: Risk—identification of roadblocks (T-HCC): Identify any potential adverse outcomes and impediments.
Step 5: Ability to measure damages and impact (C-HCC): Measure any financial adverse outcome.
Step 6: Rules—private–public statutory (R-HCC): Understand the applicable laws associated with the review.

Table 6.6   IIRB Model, Framework, and Analytic Roadmap Core Data Pipelines

Step 1: Primary healthcare continuum (P-HCC): Identify the market players.
Step 2: Accounts receivable pipeline (ARP): Identify the monetary impact.
Step 3: Operational flow assessment (OFA): Identify the relevant business functions.
Step 4: Product market activity (PMA): Identify the relevant product.
Step 5: Service market activity (SMA): Identify the relevant service.
Step 6: Consumer market activity (CMA): Identify the appropriate type of patient.

behavioral components are described in Table 6.5. Within each segment and contemporaneous to each continuum level of the behavior pipelines are the steps shown in Table 6.6.

The following section integrates the continuum model with the patient as a starting point. The six components of the healthcare continuum model (HCC) are broken down by the six key behavioral components, with operational considerations illustrated.

The healthcare continuum model (six items in total) serves as a framework to fully understand and address questions that a competent data scientist or business analyst should consider when executing a successful gap analysis for his or her provider. The model is structured to provide a comprehensive listing of critical components and to include all relevant sources of information, as well as all parties and processes that rely on information collected by the entity. The following is an explanation of each level of the model, in the order in which it should occur.

Primary healthcare continuum (P-HCC): Identify all relevant entities and professionals associated with the gap review. P-HCC analysis identifies the parties that provide direct or indirect healthcare services, how they cooperate, and the shared information among internal and external partners. This is a critical step because it continues to build with respect to the collection of data points as the continuum audit model is applied. This step will ensure that the analyst has taken into consideration all relevant data points.

Secondary healthcare continuum (S-HCC): Identify and document all authoritative practice standards by each professional and entity identified. S-HCC analysis will identify each entity that utilizes information generated from the P-HCC for the comparison of current to future state objectives. The gap analysis strategy must include authoritative benchmarks and metrics to be applied. For example, meaningful use criteria (CMS criteria) are defined within this model under the rule-based continuum; however, the secondary continuum is about the mechanics of how to implement the rules legislated or rules contracted between two parties. Again, the analyst conducting the review must reflect on the future state defined by the gap objective and identify any inconsistencies with the practice standards.

Information healthcare continuum (I-HCC): Identify all workflow considerations by people, processes, and technology used. I-HCC analysis will identify the operational issues within P-HCC entities and the users and uses of the S-HCC. It is also necessary to identify electronic interoperability drivers, such as compatible Internet, intranet, and extranet systems, and electronic interoperability impediments, such as incompatible or detached electronic and paper systems. At each layer, analysts must identify all people, process, and technology workflows within each business unit, among all internal and external partners. A comprehensive gap analysis strategy will delineate all workflows and their applied technologies, respectively.

Consequences healthcare continuum (C-HCC): Identify adverse monetary, compliance, and risk exposure. C-HCC analysis identifies and measures risks of all associated behaviors and activities to ensure that all required processes are present in the healthcare marketplace. A gap analysis should include active risk assessments and risk mitigation strategies.

Transparency healthcare continuum (T-HCC): Identify roadblocks and create a plan to mitigate. The fifth continuum integrates risk. T-HCC analysis will identify transparency issues that may exist for any number of reasons and affect a market player's processes. Transparency issues can pertain to both business and personal disclosures and are typically driven by social assumptions, legislation, and access limitations due to technology shortfalls, contracts, and other intentional and unintentional constraints. An example of a roadblock or barrier to achievement of a future state would be a provider failing to adopt a new technology. This can be seen with the adoption of meaningful use. A doctor may state, "I don't have time to train on the new system and take care of my patients at the same time." Or the physician may state that any changes to the workflow impact the amount of time spent with patients. The recognition of roadblocks and barriers is very important in a gap analysis because it will drive the processes to validate the desired future state or the strategies to mitigate barriers.

Rule-based healthcare continuum (R-HCC): What does the law or contract state you have to do? Rules are defined as any legislated or contractually driven requirement of an entity or among entities. This is further layered by the many subject matter pipelines (P-HCC, accounts receivable pipeline [ARP], operational flow assessment [OFA], product market activity [PMA], service market activity [SMA], and consumer market activity [CMA]) within each segment. This process is structured to avoid missing information, identify gaps, and generate incontrovertible facts. These rules govern the monetary and business drivers that may or may not be contractually driven. The gap analysis strategy must incorporate and update any new requirements that are contracted or legislated that impact a desired future state.

Table 6.7 is an illustrative template developed for a provider setting out to evaluate department gaps involving clinical settings. Each task documents who has ownership, the date it was assigned, the date it was completed, and the date the findings were submitted, along with any documentation support. It is important to include the dates that tasks are assigned and completed and by whom.

The steps in this model are discussed in this chapter within the provider facility example. This example is tracked in MS Excel. The subsequent Excel sheets are utilized to document the data collected and the audit support for each item reviewed for the identified gap.

Key Market Barriers to Overcome

This biggest challenge to creating a gap analysis is defining your future state. If you fail to definitively identify the direction your organization wants to move, then it becomes extremely difficult to evaluate what needs to be changed and, equally important, what should not change. If the organization or business unit fails to define its future state, consider conducting a thorough needs assessment first. Once the future state is defined, initiate a gap analysis. Remember, step 1 of the gap analysis requires that the future desired state is articulated to a level of sufficiency that the resulting gap analysis is productive.

Table 6.7 Illustrative Provider Audit Gap Template

No.	Task I
I.	***Pregap Audit Preparation***
	1. Establish a defined expectation for consideration.
	2. Schedule business unit kickoff meeting to discuss upcoming audit.
	3. Define the process to articulate and document the current state relative to the defined expectation.
	4. Define and articulate the future state, typically after the completion of a needs assessment.
	5. Compile notes or minutes from scope validation kickoff meeting.
	6. Determine roles and responsibilities of all gap audit, operations, and business analytic staff to be involved.
	7. Schedule initial meeting with management of user client department.
	8. Compile notes or minutes from meeting with management of client department.
	9. Create auditor binders and documentation.
	10. Generate, review, and confirm data call requirements, including user interviews.
No.	**Tasks II and III**
II.	***Obtain Copy of Statement of Work (SOW) or Audit Charter Requirement (ACR)/ Audit Scope***
	1. Review SOW/ACR—desired state.
	2. Create documentation file of SOW/ACR.
	3. Define metrics of SOW/ACR.
III.	***Create a Project Management Profile to Monitor SOW/ACR***
	1. Conduct the analysis of and comparison of the current and future states.
	2. Review gap deliverables.
	3. Define and articulate the variances from the current and future states.
	4. Review the original expectation and whether any modifications are to occur to the defined future state.
	5. Develop an implementation plan on how to achieve that future state with or without modifications of the defined expectation.
	6. Define appropriate metrics to measure and provide assurance that the plan will mitigate the gaps identified, and test the implementation of those gaps.

(Continued)

Table 6.7 (Continued)   Illustrative Provider Audit Gap Template

	7. Confirm deliverables with user client.
	8. Prepare report findings.
No.	**Tasks IV and V**
IV.	***Create User Client Contact Sheet by GAP Area***
	1. Identify all internal and external resources working on the gap review.
	2. Contact information of all auditors within organization, business owner, and leadership.
	3. Create an organizational chart (IIRB model framework, Chapter 5).
V.	***Identify Clinical or Department Area***
	1. Identify all contacts.
	2. Identify all systems.
	3. Sample of charge description master (CDM).
	4. Sample of all hard-copy paper.
	5. Sample layout of personal healthcare information (PHI).
	6. Collect any known issues.
	7. Current Procedural Terminology (CPT) and Healthcare Common Procedure Coding System (HCPCS) sample sources; applicable revenue models.
	8. Data call on any information impacting clinical or business functions.
	9. Compile any documents on managed care contractual considerations.
	10. Compile any mandated compliance requirements.
No.	**Tasks VI and VII**
VI.	***Walk through Clinical or Department Area***
	1. Follow the patient clinical area and business processes.
	2. Follow the proper PHI.
	3. Obtain or create a copy of floor plan for clinical or department area.
	4. List clinical supplies.
	5. List medication or supply inventory.
	6. Request procedure process (policy and procedure protocols if available).
	7. Compile department specific policy and procedures.
	8. Compile departmental notes, history, and staffing profiles.

(Continued)

Table 6.7 (Continued)   Illustrative Provider Audit Gap Template

VII.	*Create Workflow and Data Mapping (Visio) Diagrams with Confirmation People, Process, and Technology (PPT)*
	1. Create first draft of Visio diagram.
	2. Have user client validate first draft of Visio diagram.
	3. Create second draft of Visio diagram.
	4. Have user client validate second draft of Visio diagram.
	5. Create third draft of Visio diagram.
	6. Have user client validate of third draft of Visio diagram.
	7. Obtain weekly update of Visio diagram.
	8. Obtain weekly update of Visio diagram.
	9. Obtain weekly update of Visio diagram.
	10. Obtain weekly update of Visio diagram.
No.	**Tasks VIII–XI**
VIII.	*Collect Sample Management Reports on Defined Metrics*
	1. Review report.
	2. Denials.
	3. Discharge—no final bill (DSNF).
	4. Exception report.
	5. Other applicable metrics; Healthcare Financial Management Association (HFMA) metrics (Chapter 3).
IX.	*Document Rules Being Applied*
	1. List each rule, compliance, and contractual requirement.
X.	*Create Audit Worksheet—Data Elements for Review*
	1. Identify the entities, people, and parties involved (players).
	2. Identify the standards (benchmarks—what is normal), policy issues, etc. (secondary).
	3. Identify the sample, process, and technology issues (information); observations include CDM issues and clinical documentation.
	4. Consequences—conduct a risk assessment of vulnerabilities.
	5. Rules—list relevant legislated compliance requirements or contractual obligations.
	6. List transparency issues, unforeseen (roadblocks).

(Continued)

Table 6.7 (Continued)   Illustrative Provider Audit Gap Template

	7. Other (charges, revenue, etc.).
XI.	*Test Audit Worksheet*
	1. Test audit worksheet in clinical areas.
	2. Update audit worksheet.
No.	**Tasks XII–XV**
XII.	*Create Audit Memo*
	1. Identify weekly reporting objectives.
	2. Identify monthly reporting objectives.
	3. Identify quarterly reporting objectives.
	4. Identify internal reporting objectives.
	5. Identify external reporting objectives.
XIII.	*Determine Data Warehouse*
	1. Submit audit findings as audit process—first draft.
	2. Submit audit findings as audit process.
	3. Submit to internal quality review process.
XIV.	*Document Roadblocks*
	1. People.
	2. Systems.
	3. Process.
XV.	*GAP Analysis Report*
	1. Determine which medical data audit (MDA) staff will write the report at the user client kickoff meeting.
	2. Report should be initiated within the first week the audit begins.
	3. Report should be updated weekly based on all auditors' findings

The second barrier to overcome is the inability to effectively articulate a detailed understanding of the current state. There are numerous examples of audit staff making the assumption that an identified policy or procedure presented during a review of a particular business unit is not even close to the actual steps being executed by staffers within that area. Remember, you get what you inspect (validate), not what you expect.

The gap audit template referenced in Table 6.1 illustrates the steps under documentation of workflows by creating a Visio diagram of the people, processes, and technology involved with the business unit. Please note that this process is repeated and validated several times throughout the gap analysis. The quality of your conclusion is only as accurate as your understanding of the current state. A significant amount of time should be given to this step in the overall process.

The next barrier to overcome is assurance that the gap team has access to the relevant data that will enable a comprehensive review.

Finally, the last barrier to overcome is securing qualified resources to conduct the gap analysis. If these conditions cannot be satisfied internally, the organization must obtain competent external partners to facilitate the review. This chapter provided a general audit gap overview approach, highlighted in Table 6.1, and a detailed IIRB model, framework, and analytic roadmap gap template in Table 6.2,[3] followed by application illustrations in Tables 6.4 through 6.6 to develop an effective gap strategy. Again, process, structure, and a scientifically based gap analysis methodology will dramatically increase the probability of success in achieving the stated objectives.

Final Thought

Has your organization defined its future state? Do you possess the internal resources to conduct a gap analysis, and if so, are they the right persons for the right job? Again, with ongoing change, the need to manage revenue streams for sustainability (getting the claim out the door) includes denial management (getting dollars in for claims that are denied). Denial management should remain an active component on the radar screen. Chapter 7 discusses denial management considerations.

CDO Perspective

Organizations aspiring to meet the challenges of the future head on would be prudent to consider the frameworks and processes outlined by Ms. Busch in evaluating the state of their healthcare data. As big data moves beyond "hype" to realized value for organizations, those responsible understand they face a daunting task. Because medical data is expressed in a language that requires special knowledge, skills, and abilities to effectively evaluate, comprehend, and analyze it in context, a rigorous and comprehensive evaluation framework is critical to producing information that can be trusted and acted on. Ms. Busch outlines the people, processes, assumptions/constraints, and technology competencies that should be considered in conducting effective gap analysis management. Kudos for developing a roadmap for this complex body of work.

—**Michelle Currie**
CDO, CETA Performance Services LLC, San Francisco, California

References

1. Gap Analysis, http://www.businessdictionary.com/definition/gap-analysis.html (accessed September 2014).
2. Busch, R., Interactive and Iterative Behavioral Model, System, and Method for Detecting Fraud, Waste, and Abuse (Iterative and/or Reiterating Behavioral Continuum Model, Framework, and Analytic Roadmap to Identify, Collect, Authenticate, Process, Transform and/or Unify Fragmented Data [IIRB Model, Framework, and Analytic Roadmap]), 62026556, patent pending, July 18, 2014.
3. Ibid.

Chapter 7

Denial Management Analysis

Denial ain't just a river in Egypt.

—Mark Twain
American author and humorist

This chapter provides an overview of contemporary denial management analytical tools that incorporate a checklist approach as their central theme. Healthcare denial management is, by and large, one of the most unwieldy and burdensome areas within patient financial services. Generally speaking, a denial occurs when a payer rejects a claim due to some difference in policies or procedures until further information is provided.

For individuals deeply immersed in the process, it could appear at times that denial management is simply an unconscious defense mechanism characterized by a refusal to acknowledge or process a claim for services rendered. Many providers claim that payers often deny a significant percentage of claims because the process of denial management, providing a justification, resubmitting, and managing this laborious process, is so cumbersome that it is easier to simply write it off. In fact, the process of collecting payment for claims is one of the major reasons why many healthcare professionals abandon independent practice.

Denial management is heavily reliant on data analytics that utilize established or, in some cases, proprietary metrics to identify and evaluate the conditions that result in a denial and then lay the groundwork to prevent future claims from being denied.

A Bit of History

The ability to turn no into yes and recover denied payment for services rendered is the "art" that defines any successful denial management program. Navigating the process of denial management is a daunting task for any hospital, physician, or provider. Consider the fact that a significant percentage of claims denied ("nos") in a provider's accounts receivable can tie up reimbursements for periods in excess of a year and potentially place a provider at financial risk. Mitigation efforts often prove to be excessively difficult, time-consuming, and an additional drain on the provider's resources.

Denials can account for 1%–3% of a provider's net revenue potential,[1] which is an enormous amount of money that cannot be ignored. Claims can be denied for any number of reasons, requiring providers to have the commensurate knowledge, skills, and abilities (KSAs) to rapidly correct the issue and incorporate specific mechanisms to prevent future denials. Although the process of mitigating denials may at times seem insurmountable, the results are well worth the effort if a systematic "checklist" approach is implemented. The conversion rate of pended or denied claims to a paid status typically ranges from 55% to 98% of resubmitted claims, depending on the level of KSAs of the denial management team.[2]

The denial process is made even more difficult for the reason that there is no clear-cut definition as to why the claim was actually denied. The burden is on the provider to discern the real cause of the denial in the absence of a reason code. Each payer system may provide somewhat different interpretations, or reason codes have been misapplied or lack clarity, resulting in a denial. In fact, it would not be uncommon for a payer to transmit a note to the provider indicating a reason for a rejection and simultaneously recommending a code that is inconsistent with the payer's reasoning. Each provider has a tendency to classify and resolve denials such as rejected claims, underpayments, and suspended claims differently.

Underpayments occur when payers fail to compensate providers with the full amount of the submitted claim. This may be due to any number of reasons, for example, difference in options or policies negotiated between the insurance company and the provider, charges submitted by an in-network provider versus an out-of-network provider, and nonconcurring codes. Regardless of cause, underpayments present a multitude of unique and difficult problems to overcome, and they often go unnoticed.

Lost revenue represents everything from unnoticed underpayments to incorrect payments to missing charges from claims.[3] Denials generally fall into two categories: hard and soft, which are then subdivided by classification. Hard denials require the provider to resubmit the entire claim, whereas soft denials generally require additional information or clarification to be reconsidered. Nevertheless, providers must possess the knowledge and tools to quickly and accurately navigate through the differing and very complex payer denial system to ensure they are compensated.

Hybrid Roles of Denial Management Analysis

Job postings seeking professionals to manage denial issues and payments appear to parallel the scope of the provider's practice. For example, a recent job posting for a denial management specialist identified the following minimum requirements: "High school diploma with extensive on-the-job training in a clinical setting. Applicants must hold certified professional coder (CPC) credentials." Tables 7.1 and 7.2 are illustrative examples of job postings.

It is not unusual to see new specialized roles with titles such as clinical appeals specialist that invoke clinical discussions with payers in order to satisfy issues pertaining to denied claims. Tables 7.3 through 7.5 illustrate the experience, education, training, and skills required for this role.

The other category in which denial management roles tend to fall is in the context of an analyst. We call this discipline denial management analysis. The position of denial management analyst tends to have responsibilities in managing contractual relationships. For example, a task may include the maximization of reimbursement by identifying contractual variances between actual and expected reimbursement from contracted payers. General responsibilities may also include supporting the execution of strategic initiatives, process redesign, root cause analysis, metric and report development, and special projects as they relate to denial management (Tables 7.6 and 7.7).

Table 7.1   Essential Duties and Responsibilities: Denial Management Specialist

Research and analyze denial data and coordinate denial recovery responsibilities.
Identify, analyze, and develop denial root cause corrective action plans and resolution strategies.
Develop reporting tools that effectively measure and monitor processes throughout the denial management process to support process improvement.
Prioritize work overturn activity to eliminate untimely filings.
Categorize claim denials and organize overturn activity.
Identify and pursue opportunities for improvements in denial performance; supervise and assist with chart audits.
Process work lists to facilitate prompt intervention of insurance denials; research, respond to, and document insurer and patient correspondence and inquiry notes regarding coding coverage, benefits, and reimbursement on patient accounts.
Research explanation of benefits (EOB) rejections for resolution and file appropriately.
Inform management of issues or changes in the billing system, insurance carriers, or networks.
Reconcile daily registrations with insurance updates.
Advise and assist financial coordinator.

Table 7.2   KSA Requirements: Denial Management Specialist

Demonstrate knowledge of applicable medical terminology.
Demonstrate knowledge of patient confidentiality and Health Insurance Portability and Accountability Act (HIPAA) regulations.
Demonstrate knowledge of CPT, HCPCS, and ICD-9 coding requirements.
Demonstrate knowledge of medical billing and collection practices.
Demonstrate understanding of Medicare and medical assistance regulations as they apply to job functions.
Demonstrate understanding of electronic health or medical records (EHRs or EMRs) or healthcare-related computer systems.

All of these job descriptions tend to function within the finance arena. The ability to effectively mitigate denial management issues requires a cross section of expertise that must include clinical subject matter expertise, how a specific business office functions (revenue cycle, hospital or provider financial and clinical operations, healthcare finance, and payer contracts), and an operational understanding of patient services databases (patient deliverables).

However, understanding the root cause of any denial activity requires basic clinical knowledge in order to effectively analyze why a denial occurred. Therefore, a denial management strategy requires the analyst to have access to a multitude of database resources and business intelligence and clinical intelligence information to efficiently and accurately recover the full monetary value of services rendered.

Table 7.3   Knowledge, Education, and Ability Requirements: Clinical Appeals Specialist

A bachelor's degree in nursing or equivalent degree in a related discipline and current state-issued RN license.
Specialized knowledge of InterQual Level of Care Criteria and Milliman & Robertson criteria, as well as knowledge of third-party payer regulations related to utilization and quality review.
Experience in the healthcare field, including a minimum of 5 years working as a clinical nurse in an acute care setting.
At least 2 years of experience in case management, discharge planning, or utilization review is preferred.
Demonstrate knowledge of regulatory and payer requirements for reimbursement and reasons for denials by auditors.

Table 7.4   Essential Duties and Responsibilities: Clinical Appeals Specialist

Review patient medical records and utilize clinical and regulatory knowledge as well as knowledge of payer requirements to determine why cases are denied and whether appeals are necessary.
Utilize preexisting criteria, clinical evidence, and other resources to develop sound and well-supported appeal arguments where warranted.
Prepare convincing appeal arguments, using preexisting criteria sets or clinical evidence from existing library of clinical references or regulatory arguments, for an administrative law judge hearing. Participate in hearings to provide required testimony.
Conduct clinical evidence research to support appeal arguments when existing resources are unavailable.
Prepare feedback to clients and participate in client meetings.
Discuss document-related and level-of-care decisions independently with clients.
Understand abstract information from handwritten patient medical records.
Ensure compliance with HIPAA regulations, to include confidentiality, as required.

Author's Note: The best tactic or defense against denials is simply avoiding the conditions that create them in the first place.

Denial Management Today

The best tactic or defense against denials is simply avoiding the conditions that create them in the first place. Research on the topic of denials confirms that more than 90% of payer denials are avoidable.[4] The largest common denominator of denied claims is administrative mistakes introduced by the provider. This section will provide an understanding of the types of errors and denial

Table 7.5   Skills and Ability Requirements: Clinical Appeals Specialist

Possess analytical skills—to synthesize complex or diverse information.
Have ability to effectively collect and research data.
Use intuition and experience to complement data.
Design workflows and procedures.
Identify and resolve issues in a timely manner.
Gather and analyze information skillfully.
Develop alternative solutions.

Table 7.6   Essential Duties and Responsibilities: Denial Management Analyst

Evaluate and ensure that claims incorrectly denied or underpaid by payers are identified, appealed, and reversed.
Work closely with appropriate groups, e.g., HIM/coding and medical team, to review and obtain medical documentation required to facilitate denial appeal process.
Proactively work with multidisciplinary teams to develop procedures and reduce the number of denials received through reporting of denials and education of denial trends.
Work with management on payer contract interpretation, updating and distributing correspondence to hospital staff.
Compile, analyze, and report on data related to underpayments, denials, revenue opportunities, and revenue leakage.
Categorize denials based on root cause findings and distribute reports and applicable metrics to management.
Serve as a resource for billing and reimbursement issues.
Continuously review applicable regulations; update and maintain current knowledge base.
Perform special audit requests for denials and assist in drafting appeal letters.

Table 7.7   KSA Requirements: Denial Management Analyst

Bachelor's degree with preference toward health information management (HIM), business, nursing, or finance
Additional certifications, such as certified medical reimbursement specialist (CMRS), preferred
Subject matter expertise in provider billing, collections, payer contracting, and managed care contracting
Ability to reconcile patient accounts
Revenue cycle support, analytical skills, gap analysis, and root cause analysis, in addition to skills listed in all other job descriptions (roll-up)

patterns that require some form of mitigation. Manual errors, incorrect coding, timing issues, and oversights can all be caused by both providers and payers. One cannot also rule out that a denial may result from the payer's adjudication system not having been updated with the payer's most recent business rules. With the heavy workload experienced by many provider offices, it is not always easy to devote time to research every denied claim, but the information gained from these investigations may help the provider avoid claims being denied for the same or similar reasons in the future, saving both time and money in the long run.[5] Also, a strong data analytic denial management program can trend payment, underpayment, and denial patterns made by a payer, thus creating a data-driven process for denial management.

Other than manual errors, claim denials or rejections generally fall into five categories: clinical denials, technical or administrative denials, service-level denials, line-level denials, and short-pay or underpayment denials. Clinical denials occur when reimbursement is rejected because the service provided was determined to be unnecessary based on the diagnosis code provided, or the diagnosis itself is unsupported (there may be disagreements with treatments regarding missed diagnosis). Technical or administrative errors involve claims that were not billed correctly, including process, procedure, and data errors. Simple errors such as mistakes with coding are included in this category. service-level denials are characterized by the entire claim being denied because of an inaccurate diagnosis. Line-level denials are those that comprise a partial denial, but not necessarily a rejection of the entire claim. Short-pay or underpayment denials involve incorrect payments posted by the payer. Claims can also experience rejection because they weren't processed within a required time frame.

The best way to resolve denial issues is to identify, train, and deploy a team of representatives from various departments within the organization to determine the issues and develop solutions. This team can start by addressing each individual issue that causes a claim to go unpaid and move on to the next issue.

Shore Health Systems presents a good example of this kind of denial management team assembled to tackle these issues. To improve the process of resubmitting denied claims, Shore Health Systems assembled a revenue defense team that incorporated people from patient accounting, case management, medical records, coding, contracting, compliance, and patient access. The objective of this group was to review each rejected claim and determine which department would be best suited to resolve the problem and resubmit the claim.

The team approach proved to be extremely efficient relative to the burdensome demands placed on one person to determine the direct source of a problem and identify someone in the right department to address the issue. With this system in place, Shore Health Systems achieved a 0.5% denial rate, which is a significant improvement over the average rate of the typical provider.[6]

Another example of how a hospital developed best practices for managing denials is Children's National Medical Center in Washington, D.C. "Children's National's methodology was to bring together all departments that played a role in claims submission whose actions impacted whether a claim was accepted or denied, and identified solutions to all potential issues prior to submittal. In this way, each department or stakeholder assumed some form of ownership of the claim submittal process and worked to resolve issues before they rebounded as problems."[7]

Remember, an issue is a *thing* that involves identifying a solution or determining an option. A problem is a *person* standing in the way of a solution to any issue.

While that may sound simple enough, this system requires the cooperation of many different people. It is important for a department to take responsibility for a denied claim so its staff can use their expertise to find and correct the reason for rejection.

One of the best concepts driving Children's National's strategy was to employ an audit coordinator, defined as a person who ensures each denied claim is directed to the correct department for resolution. In addition, this individual tracks the status of all rejected claims being adjudicated and ensures that they are resubmitted in a timely manner. To achieve the desired results from any cross-departmental team requires members to maintain knowledge, skills, and abilities through ongoing education to stay current with coding and procedural issues that promote proper billing practices.

Children's also established a revenue cycle workflow analysis, making it possible to map and track the progress of denied claims. Each claim is tracked and sorted by audit type, payer, department, dollar value, and probability of successful overturn. In addition, the hospital tracks the efforts of each auditor working on denials and ensures that all personnel working on assigned issues are achieving results and maintaining process accountability.[8]

Hospital protocols vary greatly on levels of access provided to resources that are necessary to manage payment denials. Regardless of resources or access to those resources, a system or process must be in place to resolve denied claims.

Furthermore, a system must exist to track the various causes of claim denials by type and the peculiarities of each, and root cause analysis must support a process to improve system mitigation elements and prevent future claims from being denied. To further augment a denial mitigation process, a provider may consider creating incentive programs that enhance team motivation to manage claims and ultimately "discover and recover the money." Rewarding employees for successfully appealing a denial may help speed up this difficult and daunting process, as well as create healthy competition within departments.

The average denied claim costs a provider $25–$30 by the time it has been resubmitted.[9] It would be prudent to consider cost-effective measures to minimize the cost of processing a denial, in addition to denial teams rectifying the operational deficiencies that would consistently apply these corrective measures. There are several different options for software that support denial resolution, such as Cloud Care, Optum, Denial Defender from Health Fusion, and OnBase Revenue Cycle Management solutions. Electronic billing systems rank high among the options because they limit the number of denials due to human error. While there are many billing systems available on the market to choose from, there are certain generic capabilities that should be integrated in order to efficiently resolve denial issues.

Important software elements to recognize should be charge entry analysis, which checks billing and diagnoses codes before they are submitted, and a sophisticated rules engine that tracks limits and forms the basis for a denial. A rules engine distributes real-time, up-to-date rule-based parameters to providers, ultimately enhancing the accuracy of submitting claims and promoting speedy reimbursement. Claim alerts are an important software application because they track claim submissions and status to ensure that every claim is accounted for until reimbursement data is entered. In-depth analytics follow claims in real time to ensure everything is paid in full and no errors occur. Finally, the system must demonstrate functionality and flexibility to accommodate and store new code or rule changes as required.

The world of healthcare is an ever-changing environment, and so is the complex process of dealing with denial management. There are many different ways to help solve claim denial issues; however, there is no easy, single solution that will fit for every provider. Once a multidepartment denial management team has been established and reliable billing software accepted and established, and employees have been trained how to use it, a system of trial and error is required to develop a best-practice process to resolve denials for the hospital, clinic, or physician. In many cases, the only things that will move the process forward are sheer perseverance and patience.

Balancing Act

The balancing act in developing a comprehensive denial management program begins with selecting the right people for the right job. Once an organization has the right personnel in place, it must provide those individuals with access to data that feeds claim development, access to the operational business units that generate or impact this information, and the knowledge required to mitigate claims for resubmittal. Table 7.8 documents the established components of a typical denial management program.

This chapter examines other considerations when building or enhancing the denial management functions. The following section covers application of the behavioral continuum audit model modified to address a denial management program.

In Chapters 5 and 6, the IIRB model, framework, and analytic roadmap to identify, collect, authenticate, process, transform, and unify fragmented data were introduced and applied in the context of developing a data and information strategy (DIS) assessment tool, followed by conducting a gap analysis. Here the steps are presented in the context of creating a denial management program (Table 7.9).

The application of this framework is targeted toward the development and ongoing administration of a denial management program. The behavior for the model is the same as in previous examples; only the context of the application will be adjusted.

Table 7.8 Denial Management Program Components

Component 1: Create a standardized definition for denial categories.
Component 2: Create a process to manage denial categories by custom payer.
Component 3: Create a decision hierarchy tree of denial categories.
Component 4: Create a process to centralize fragmented data points.
Component 5: Create a centralized denial database.
Component 6: Create key performance indicators.
Component 7: Create accountability matrices.
Component 8: Create an infrastructure to measure, monitor, and mitigate corrections.

Table 7.9 IIRB Model, Framework, and Analytic Roadmap Core Models

Denial assessment: The act of evaluating, valuating, and assessing denial activity as applied to the organization in its relationship to third parties.
Denial prevention: The process of identifying corrective action postimplementation or execution of a task that results in a denial, followed by implementing controls to minimize the effectual hindrance, or the act of preventing similar denials in the future.
Denial detection: The discovery, act, or process of extracting information from the identified denial that is not consistent with the organization's current business or clinical processes.
Denial mitigation: The lessening of the force, intensity, adverse circumstances, conditions, or event consequences of denials that have been detected inside the business or clinical functions that generate claims.

Author's Note: Relevant CDO capabilities may include evaluating the critical data points required for effective denial management. Are the defined data points included in the organization's data strategy? What is the impact on the organization's master data management, operational data, and required content analytics?

A function of C-suite leadership for that respective business unit within an organization would involve the management, handling, directing, controlling, and tracking of the denial work process and the assurance of achieving a fluid way to minimize resources required within patient financial services (PFS). In the following section, The IIRB model, framework, and analytic roadmap will be further expanded as a denial management analysis tool and strategy framework.

IIRB Model, Framework, and Analytic Roadmap

Once the denial management components identified in Table 7.8 are defined and developed, they must be tested to determine to what degree they meet the organizational accurate billing standard goals and objectives. At some point, a revenue cycle gap analysis must be conducted based on the percentage of claims currently in a denial status. The denial management gap analysis proceeds to identify the current state data points. To understand the dynamic of this process, consider that the driving behavioral principles in understanding the data points fall into the categories shown in Table 7.10.

Table 7.10   IIRB Model, Framework, and Analytic Roadmap Core Continuums

Player component: A person, place, or thing that takes part; a participant, provider, or entity.
Benchmark component: The standards, points of reference, or measurements for each identified player, as well as within and among each component within the behavioral continuum.
Functional information component: All relational knowledge derived by persons, communication systems, circumstances, research, processes, technology, and behaviors realized by each identified player, as well as within and among each component within the behavioral continuum.
Rule-based component: All related principles, regulations, governing conducts, actions, procedures, arrangements, contracts, legislature, dominions, and controls generated by each identified player, as well as within and among each component within the behavioral continuum.
Transparency, opaqueness, and obstruction component: Identifying a measure of quality of being transparent, opaque, or obstructed (barriers, impediments, obstacles, and stoppage) by each player, as well as within and among each component within the behavioral continuum.
Consequence component: The identification of issues, upshots, sequels, damages, acts, instances, effects, results, outcomes, conclusion importance, significance, rank, position, monetary value, or state of being of each player, as well as within and among each component within the behavioral continuum.

As previously mentioned, the IIRB model, framework, and analytic roadmap behavioral components can be applied in a variety of data analytic tasks. For example, in Chapter 5, the IIRB model was applied in conducting a DIS assessment, and in Chapter 6, the model was applied in conducting a gap analysis. In this chapter, it is modified for the development and maintenance of a denial management program. These behaviors are applicable as a basis to provide assurance in capturing all of the relevant data when conducting all types of analyses, audits, or other reviews of data.

The IIRB model application is illustrated in Table 7.8 by a provider implementing a Recovery Audit Contractor (RAC) audit and denial response program. In this application, insufficient documentation could be identified as one reason a denial is issued. Table 7.11 illustrates a sample process that is influenced by a regulatory requirement. This table demonstrates a progressive process that is divided into three phases: aggregation of the resources to respond; the steps in responding to the denial, including subsequent appeals; and the opportunities to leverage the data, followed by conducting analytics and evaluating the impact on the organization. In this example, component 1 is "RAC denial due to insufficient documentation" and is one type of denial category (see Table 7.8). Components 2–5 would be illustrated in Table 7.8 as a general framework. Component 7, "accountability," would occur during phase 1 of Table 7.8. Finally, the creation of an infrastructure to measure, monitor, and mitigate corrections is illustrated in all three phases, with emphasis on the last phase in Table 7.11.

Table 7.11 Illustrative Process Flow of RAC Denial Audit Response: IIRB Application

Phase 1
Committee should include five areas (compliance, clinical, reimbursement, coding, and provider of care); a physician role is typically required for appeals.
Documentation must be submitted to the third-party auditor for review and payment determination. All agencies should have an internal process established to monitor claims selected for an alternative dispute resolution (ADR) and to ensure the documentation is submitted within the required time frame. If the documentation development request for medical records is not received in a timely manner, the claim will be automatically denied.
Request an extension if an inordinate amount of requests are made for medical documentation.
Phase 2
All refund request letters are to be directed to the assigned RAC coordinator.
All requests should be logged indicating the due date for a response.
Requests should be separated by issue, i.e., bilateral procedures, missing admit orders, etc.
All letters should fall into one of three categories: • Coding issues • Billing issues • Clinical issues

(Continued)

Table 7.11 (Continued)   Illustrative Process Flow of RAC Denial Audit Response: IIRB Application

Weekly or biweekly meetings should be scheduled to discuss selected cases the committee would like to appeal and the findings to support the appeal.
Once the case has been reviewed and the committee decides to proceed with an appeal, a response is drafted.
A tracking spreadsheet should be set up with all appeal details. This sheet should include the following: • Date of letter from audit contractor (versus CGI) • Description of the issue • Amount of refund requested • Date refund issued • Date refund processed by Medicare • Due date of response • Appealed (yes or no) • Date appeal submitted • Result of appeal • If favorable, date money paid back to the client
Develop an organizational policy to monitor and address monies taken through the recoup process.
Develop a process to ensure applicable refunds.
Develop a process to retrieve recouped dollars within a specified time period (45 days) on cases that are in appeal.
Phase 3
Develop a data strategy plan to mitigate any issues associated with claims that are not appealed.
Develop a strategy to avoid future losses. (For example, Medicare requires all signed admit orders to include the word *admit* and be signed by doctors with admitting privileges; some hospitals allow nurses to sign orders, but CMS does not.)

The denial management program requires a defined process and an appropriate skill set with defined accountability and ownership of each denial category identified. The IIRB model, framework, and analytic roadmap can be further expanded as a denial management strategy framework.

Denial Management Strategy Using the Healthcare Continuum

The concepts of the healthcare continuum (HCC) can be applied to any provider business developing or enhancing its current denial management program. Table 7.12 shows a review of the behavioral components. Within each segment and simultaneous to each continuum level of the behavior are the data pipelines (Table 7.13).

Table 7.12 IIRB Model, Framework, and Analytic Roadmap Core HCC

Players (P-HCC) example: Defined by payer group
Benchmark data (S-HCC) example: Sufficient documentation
Information systems—Location, format, and housing of data; people process and technology (I-HCC) example: Use of electronic health record system and further defined by the user
Risk—Identification of roadblocks (T-HCC) example: Exposure to fines secondary to a RAC audit
Ability to measure damages and impact (C-HCC) example: Fines and penalties resulting from insufficient documentation
Rules—Private–public statutory (R-HCC) example: Medicare and Medicaid manual requirements on documentation

Table 7.13 IIRB Model, Framework, and Analytic Roadmap Core Data Pipelines

Primary healthcare continuum (P-HCC) example: RAC auditor, HIM staff, PFS
Accounts receivable pipeline (ARP) example: 200 claims denied
Operational flow assessment (OFA) example: Admitting documentation does not match medical record
Product market activity (PMA) example: Emergency room supplies
Service market activity (SMA) example: Emergency room exam
Consumer market activity (CMA) example: Medicare patients

The following section integrates the continuum model with the patient as the starting point. The six components of the HCC model are broken down by the six key behavioral components, with illustrative operational considerations.

The six-layered healthcare continuum model serves as a framework to fully address questions that any denial management support team should consider when executing a successful denial management program for their organization. The model is structured to provide a comprehensive listing of critical components and to include all relevant sources of information, as well as all parties and processes that rely on information collected by the entity.

P-HCC: Define All Relevant Parties and Roles Involved

The first level of analysis is based on the primary healthcare continuum (P-HCC). P-HCC analysis identifies the parties that provide direct or indirect healthcare services, how they work together, and the information shared. In the RAC example, the critical departments involved included patient financial services (PFS), health information management services (HIM), finance, compliance, and a revenue integrity team. Each area has core competencies that facilitate the review process and follow-up mitigation support. Mitigation support came from business unit analysts who reviewed and analyzed the data, and internal auditors who facilitated the development of internal controls to prevent future issues. In addition, IT facilitates access to data and the creation and support of a centralized denial database system.

S-HCC: Define Relevant Practice Standards by Each Player Identified

The second level of analysis is based on the secondary healthcare continuum (S-HCC). S-HCC analysis identifies each entity that uses information generated from the P-HCC for the comparison of a current state (position) to a future state objective. The denial management strategy should include authoritative benchmarks and metrics to be applied. For example, under the rule-based continuum, the Centers for Medicare and Medicaid Services (CMS) published their policy on sufficient documentation requirements for services rendered. The secondary continuum describes the mechanics of how to implement provider internal controls to ensure sufficient documentation (required benchmarks). Consider the rule instructions that need to be followed and benchmark guidance on how to follow those rules.

I-HCC: Define People, Process, and Technology Workflows

The third level of analysis is based on the information healthcare continuum (I-HCC). I-HCC analysis identifies the operational issues concerning the components of the P-HCC and the uses of the S-HCC. It is important to illustrate and document all the people, process, and technology support utilized by each market player. It is also necessary to identify the electronic interoperability drivers, such as electronic attributes that are compatible with Internet, intranet, and extranet systems. In addition, electronic interoperability impediments, such as incompatible or detached electronic and paper systems, must be identified. Identified at each layer are all the people, process, and technology workflows within each business unit, among internal partners, and finally, by external partners. A comprehensive gap analysis will delineate all workflows and respective technologies applied.

C-HCC: Define Risks of Fines or Penalties

The fourth level of analysis is based on the consequences healthcare continuum (C-HCC). C-HCC analysis identifies and measures risks of all associated behaviors and activities to ensure that all required processes are present in the healthcare marketplace. A gap analysis of current denial support infrastructure must be conducted to ascertain sufficient controls in order to respond to denial from public programs (RAC and Medicare), as well as privately contracted benefit health programs.

T-HCC: Define Any Roadblocks to Data

The fifth continuum integrates risk. This analysis is based on the transparency continuum (T-HCC). T-HCC analysis identifies transparency issues that could exist for any number of reasons and affect any number of market player processes. Transparency issues can relate to both business and personal disclosures and are driven by social assumptions, laws and legislation, and limitations of access due to technology, contracts, and other intentional and unintentional constraints. An example of a roadblock or a barrier is insufficient information for the basis of the denial. Therefore, the successful achievement of an effective denial management program would have sufficient controls to respond to denials on a timely basis and ensure that all the information that fully explains the denial is provided. The greatest frustration in responding to a denial occurs when the error is attributed to a payer system with outdated codes. The payer system may also be missing the links that provide mapping to the claim form, for example, a claim system in which the second and third modifier placements are not recognized. External causes of denials are one category in which providers could leverage the utilization of data analytics to identify these patterns.

R-HCC: Define the Laws to Which Program Is Subject

The sixth and final continuum incorporates an understanding of rules by continuum that each market player is subject to. Rules are defined as any legislated or contractually driven requirement of an entity or among entities. This is further layered by the subject matter of each pipeline (P-HCC, accounts receivable pipeline [ARP], operational flow assessment [OFA], product market activity [PMA], service market activity [SMA], and consumer market activity [CMA]) within each segment. In essence, the process is structured to avoid missing information, identify gaps, and generate incontrovertible facts. The rules govern the monetary and business drivers that may or may not be associated with contractual requirements. The denial management process must have a strategy that incorporates and updates any new requirements that are contracted or legislated.

Key Market Barriers to Overcome

Denial ain't a river in Egypt. Addressing denials from known issues is simple in comparison to attempting to resolve denials when the issue is not clear or not known. If your organization is experiencing a high number of write-offs without any data capture that identifies the cause, your organization's ability to improve will be compromised. The problems we face are often within our grasp and in full view. This chapter focused on current denial management analysis tools, terms, and conditions and an illustrative checklist for more than one type of denial. Unfortunately, the new challenges presented by the Affordable Care Act, specifically new insurance plans, present a great number of growing pains. One provider interviewed noted that Illinois had developed 31 Medicaid insurance plans since the ACA exchanges opened. However, her organization only had contracts with 10 of them. The unfortunate implication of being the provider means you have no control of who walks in the door for treatment. Therefore, all claims associated with those noncontracted insured will be denied as covered beneficiaries. Data analytics and the role of the data scientist are critical to minimizing denial pains, especially denials that result from insufficient clinical documentation. As stated earlier, denial management is in need of data analytics and respective metrics to evaluate the efforts associated with collections and the ability to collect and process data points.

Final Thought

Compare your metrics on the percentage of claims denied by payer within your region to national benchmarks. What is your success rate in overturning denials by payer category? If your organization is experiencing higher than normal denial rates, consider the implementation of a revenue integrity team. Chapter 8 introduces key considerations in revenue integrity management.

CIO Perspective

Critical access hospitals (CAHs), like all hospitals, face increasing narrow margins with shrinking reimbursement rates. CAHs have the added dilemma of operating with normally low cash days on hand. It is imperative we get claims "out the door" in the most efficient way possible with low denial rates. Having standardized processes in place, from registration to nursing and training providers, is monumental to controlling denials. International Classification of Diseases, 10th revision (ICD-10) will create the added burden of denials based upon a predictable slow adoption of the new rules. Data analytics is the best resource for tracking denied claims with attention on the highest claim values first. Having a team approach is best to not only fix the issues postdenial, but to retrain employees to new workflows for efficient payment with low denial rates. It is almost impossible to get to a no-denial state. I feel with an engaged revenue cycle team, constant training of staff, and attention to data analytics, we can dramatically reduce unwarranted denials.

—Tom A. Hornburg
Chief Information Officer,
Mason General Hospital and Family of Clinics, Shelton, Washington

References

1. Managing Denials, 2014, http://www.hfsystems.com/denials/ (accessed August 2014).
2. Clayton, C., Best Practices in Denial Management, 2010, http://www.hfma-nca.org/documents/2010%20 Spring%20Conference/Thursday-March%2025/Compliance%20 (accessed August 2014).
3. Ibid.
4. Managing Denials.
5. Clayton, Best Practices in Denial Management.
6. Fontaine, C., Are You Getting to the True Root Cause of Your Denials? http://www.hfma.org/content.aspx?id=7235 (accessed August 2014).
7. Leach, R., Daymont, M., Roby, J., Metro, L., and Walter, S., A Multidisciplinary Approach to Denials Prevention, 2012, http://www.hfma.org/Content.aspx?id=3286 (accessed August 2014).
8. Ibid.
9. Mckee, S., Denial Management: How to Improve the Process, http://www.poweryourpractice.com/revenue-cycle-management/denial-management-how-to-improve-the-process./ (accessed August 2014).

Chapter 8

Revenue Integrity Management

If you build it, they will come.

—Field of Dreams
American movie, 1989

This chapter provides an overview of revenue integrity management and the emerging role of the medical data auditor (MDA) in a provider environment. The MDA can support any of the chief information roles discussed throughout this book. Chapter 6 focused on the development of financial metrics within the healthcare industry and the dynamics of the Healthcare Financial Management Association (HFMA). This chapter provides a broader perspective on revenue management through the use of MDAs.

A Bit of History

Dictionary.com defines revenue as a noun in several different forms:

1. The income of a government from taxation, excise duties, customs, or other sources, appropriated to the payment of the public expenses
2. The government department charged with the collection of such income
3. The collective items or amounts of income of a person, a state, etc.
4. The return or yield from any kind of property, patent, service, etc.
5. Income; an amount of money regularly coming in; a particular item or source of income[1]

The word *revenue* dates back to the year 1375 and was originally associated with income received by the government in the form of taxation. The establishment of fiscal organization was identified in the Ottoman Empire during the time period of Mehmet II the Conqueror and Süleyman I the Magnificent (1359–1389) and directly associated with managing revenue and expenses as a defined practice.[2] That being said, taxation as a system is as old as human society. Ancient civilizations levied some form of taxation to support the empire or government, its military expenses, and other public services. "The earliest known tax records, dating back 6000 years BC, were discovered on clay tablets found in the ancient city-state of Lagash in modern day Iraq. The reigning king implemented a tax system called 'bala', meaning rotation."[3]

The word *integrity* has its roots as a noun and dates back to the Middle English period of the late 1400s; it is defined as "adherence to moral and ethical principles; soundness of moral character; honesty; the state of being whole, entire, or undiminished: to preserve the integrity of the empire; a sound, unimpaired, or perfect condition."[4]

The term *management*, also a noun, traces its roots back to 1590 and is defined as "the act or manner of managing; handling, direction, or control; skill in managing; executive ability; great management and tact; the person or persons controlling and directing the affairs of a business, institution, etc.; the store is under new management; executives collectively, considered as a class (distinguished from labor)."[5]

The definition of *revenue integrity management* in the context of a healthcare environment appears to be something of a work in progress. First, consider *revenue* to be an amount of money in the form of receivables regularly coming in for healthcare services. *Integrity* we'll define as the state of being whole, and *management* the act of maintaining revenue and integrity. So these three terms, *revenue*, *integrity*, and *management*, have come together to define or describe a powerful tool available to healthcare providers that focuses on revenue streams that must be maintained in their whole state and the act of achieving this state.

Hybrid Roles of Revenue Integrity Management

To fully appreciate revenue integrity management's constantly evolving core competencies, it is equally important to understand the issues that affect the specific industry segment you work in. Within healthcare, the current focus is on developing technologies that contribute to the use of electronic health records (EHRs). Note the timeline shown in Table 8.1.

Electronic Medical Health Record

The Health Information Management Systems Society (HIMSS) defines a medical health record EHR:

> The Electronic Health Record (EHR) is a longitudinal electronic record of patient health information generated by one or more encounters in any care delivery setting. Included in this information are patient demographics, progress notes, problems, medications, vital signs, past medical history, immunizations, laboratory data, and radiology reports. The EHR automates and streamlines the clinician's workflow. The EHR has the ability to generate a complete record of a clinical patient encounter, as well as supporting other care-related activities directly or indirectly via interface including evidence-based decision support, quality management, and outcomes reporting.[18,19]

How did this new focus on electronic health records affect the traditional patient financial services (PFS) roles discussed in Chapter 3? The chief financial officer (CFO) and PFS functions,

Table 8.1   History of EHRs[6] and Event Timeline

Date	Event
January 2004	President Bush's State of the Union address conveys the issues associated with medical records and says that CMS will launch an initiative to make electronic health records available to most Americans within the next 10 years. "By computerizing health records, we can avoid dangerous medical mistakes, reduce costs, and improve care."[7]
2004	Department of Health and Human Services (HHS) Secretary Tommy Thompson appoints David Brailer as the national health information technology coordinator to provide "leadership for the development and nationwide implementation of an interoperable HIT infrastructure,"[8] with the goal of establishing electronic health records for all Americans within 10 years.
2006	CMS defines its role as providing "support for development of Electronic Health Records."[9]
January 2009	President Obama, in a speech at George Mason University, says, "[EHRs] will cut waste, eliminate red tape, and reduce the need to repeat expensive medical tests … it just won't save billions of dollars and thousands of jobs—it will save lives by reducing the deadly but preventable medical errors that pervade our healthcare system."[10]
February 2009	President Obama, in his State of the Union address, continues the momentum by indicating, "our recovery plan will invest in electronic health records and new technology that will reduce errors, bring down costs, ensure privacy, and save lives."[11]
February 2009	The HITECH Act is signed into law on February 17, 2009. Beginning in fiscal year 2012, CMS will rank hospitals based on 30-day readmission rate for heart attack, heart failure, and pneumonia. Those in the bottom quartile nationally from the prior year will have a percent of total Medicare payments withheld, up to 1% in 2013, up to 2% in 2014, and up to 3% in 2015.
March 23, 2010	The Affordable Care Act is passed by Congress and signed into law by the president.
March 2010	President Obama signs the Patient Protection and Affordable Care Act. Provisions in the act strengthen the HITECH Act and mandate the implementation of meaningful use by 2014. As part of meaningful use, physicians and hospitals must prove that they have met 25 different functional objectives with their use of an EHR product in order to be considered meaningful users. Among others, these objectives include computerized physician order entry (CPOE), the use of clinical decision alerts, incorporation of lab results into the EHR as discrete data, e-prescribing, and electronic information distribution to patients. Penalties for not implementing EHR may very likely include cuts to Medicare payments.

(Continued)

Table 8.1 (Continued)   History of EHRs[6] and Event Timeline

Date	Event
October 2011	Final rules for ACOs. The final rules for ACOs strengthen the need for robust EHRs with more financial incentives that target rural doctors and hospitals, digital data collection of 33 performance measures, "double points" for EHR as a quality measure, and other random audits. Electronic records will be the table stakes for all providers that participate in an ACO, because "failure to report quality data measures accurately, completely and timely (or to correct such data in a timely manner) will most likely result in the ACO being terminated from the program or subjected to sanctions."[12]
2011	**EHR adoption and meaningful use:** **Stage 1** of the CMS EHR Incentive Program, meaningful use, began in 2011 and defined the baseline functionality that meets incentive thresholds for EHRs. CMS requirements focus on providers capturing patient data and then sharing that data with the patient or other healthcare professionals for the betterment of the patient.[13]
June 2012	The Supreme Court upholds the Affordable Care Act (ACA) by a vote of 5–4. Hospitals and providers recognized that ACA EMR resultant efficiencies would increasingly align their enterprise with like-minded, data-driven partners who could prove successful outcomes, such as readmission prevention. Corporate compliance programs force nursing homes to demonstrate continuous improvement that can be validated by data. The ACA provides incentives for providers that recognize, establish, and implement the EMR process with the ultimate goal of total health record system interconnectivity. More than ever before, market forces are driving the rapid transition to EMR in postacute care. **Supreme Court response introduction:** "In 2010, Congress enacted the Patient Protection and Affordable Care Act in order to increase the number of Americans covered by health insurance and decrease the cost of healthcare. One key provision is the individual mandate, which requires most Americans to maintain 'minimum essential' health insurance coverage. 26 U. S. C. §5000A. For individuals who are not exempt, and who do not receive health insurance through an employer or government program, the means of satisfying the requirement is to purchase insurance from a private company. Beginning in 2014, those who do not comply with the mandate must make a 'shared responsibility payment' to the Federal Government. §5000A(b)(1). The Act provides that this 'penalty' will be paid to the Internal Revenue Service with an individual's taxes, and 'shall be assessed and collected in the same manner' as tax penalties. §§5000A(c), (g)(1). Another key provision of the Act is the Medicaid expansion. The current Medicaid program offers federal funding to states to assist pregnant women, children, needy families, the blind, the elderly, and the disabled in obtaining medical care. 42 U. S. C. §1396d(a).

(Continued)

Table 8.1 (Continued) History of EHRs[6] and Event Timeline

Date	Event
	Supreme Court response introduction: (continued)
	The Affordable Care Act expands the scope of the Medicaid program and increases the number of individuals the states must cover. For example, the Act requires state programs to provide Medicaid coverage by 2014 to adults with incomes up to 133 percent of the federal poverty level, whereas many states now cover adults with children only if their income is considerably lower, and do not cover childless adults at all. §1396a(a)(10)(A)(i)(VIII). The Act increases federal funding to cover the states' cost in expanding Medicaid coverage. §1396d(y)(1). But if a State does not comply with the Act's new coverage requirements, it may lose not only the federal funding for those requirements, but all of its federal Medicaid funds. §1396c. Twenty-six states, private citizens, and the National Federation of Independent Business brought suit in Federal District Court, challenging the constitutionality of the individual mandate and the Medicaid expansion. The Court of Appeals for the Eleventh Circuit upheld the Medicaid expansion as a valid exercise of Congress's spending power, but concluded that Congress lacked authority to enact the individual mandate. Finding the mandate severable from the Act's other provisions, the Eleventh Circuit left the rest of the Act intact."[14]
2013	Section 618 of the Food and Drug Administration Safety and Innovation Act (FDASIA) of 2012 directed the Secretary of Health and Human Services, acting through the commissioner of the U.S. Food and Drug Administration (FDA) and in consultation with the Office of the National Coordinator for Health Information Technology (ONC) and the chairman of the Federal Communications Commission (FCC), to develop a report that contains a proposed strategy and recommendations on an appropriate, risk-based regulatory framework for health IT, including medical mobile applications that promote innovation, protect patient safety, and avoid regulatory duplication. The Health IT Policy Committee formed an FDASIA work group and issued recommendations to ONC, FDA, and FCC as of the September 4, 2013, HIT Policy Committee meeting.[15]
2014	**EHR adoption and meaningful use:** Stage 2 of the CMS EHR Incentive Program begins in 2014 and concentrates on the documentation of advanced clinical processes and incentivizes providers to enable patients to access and exchange their health information online.[16]
2014	CMS creates new chief data officer post.
2016	**EHR adoption and meaningful use:** Stage 3 of the CMS EHR Incentive Program is scheduled to begin in 2016. However, the rule has not been finalized because policy and standards committees have not finalized decisions that may further expand meaningful use objectives to improve healthcare outcomes.[17]

(which should be aligned) would continue to manage all revenue cycle support and billing integrity functions and would not be expected to change as a result of the implementation of an electronic health record program. PFS and CFOs still need to foster the development of business and clinical intelligence initiatives that drive cost improvements and promote more favorable patient health outcomes. The market started to prepare by responding to technology standards. As chief information officers (CIOs) began to introduce this rapidly changing technology into their respective healthcare operations, the reciprocal effect presented the need for content subject matter expertise and forced the development of the previously discussed roles of the chief medical information officer (CMIO) and chief nursing information officer (CNIO).

In fact, the development and use of electronic health records preceded President George W. Bush's drive to implement technology initiatives that mitigate medical errors and control costs. Electronic healthcare software vendors have been providing electronic solutions since the early 1960s; however, the political debate on the use of electronic healthcare records really took a turn, as outlined in Table 8.1. President Obama addressed the issues of data errors and rising costs in his statement: "Our recovery plan will invest in electronic health records and new technology that will reduce errors, bring down costs, ensure privacy, and save lives." However, a careful analysis of the president's statement in concert with a detailed examination of the Affordable Care Act (ACA) suggests otherwise. The ACA legislation states, among other things discovered after the act was passed, nontransparent items, including detailed economic requirements of the individual mandates.

> Congress enacted the Patient Protection and Affordable Care Act (ACA) in order to increase the number of Americans covered by health insurance and decrease the cost of healthcare. One key provision is the individual mandate, which requires most Americans to maintain "minimum essential" health insurance coverage

From a revenue cycle perspective, the ACA shifted the focus to midstream revenue management by incorporating insurance coverage provisions and market initiatives that were primarily focused on developing electronic health records to support better health outcomes. The focus on better health outcomes by the development of electronic records does continue. However, the focus is shifting toward developing tax revenues to provide insurance coverage to all individuals. The fundamental focus on emerging technology shifted to mechanisms (taxes) to assist in the reimbursement of healthcare services.

Author's Note: The market was already on track and focusing on the development of electronic health records to help mitigate medical errors and reduce overall healthcare costs. The ACA dramatically expanded the focus of electronic health record technology and compounded the issue by forcing coverage through new mandated insurance plans that contained thousands of unknown variables. The ACA has forced a new revenue model for insurance coverage that has directly or, in many cases, dramatically impacted PFS and changed the dynamic of the provider's and payer's revenue cycle. The consequences or impacts on healthcare reimbursement have yet to be realized because many critical ACA technology components have not been developed or implemented.

The immense challenges of managing the changes resulting from the passage of the ACA have escalated beyond the traditional core competencies available in the market today. The market has placed the cart before the horse throughout the healthcare delivery system. This may explain one CIO's commentary that "health IT has been the primary recipient of all the emerging needs placed upon an organization." Further, within the healthcare insurance industry the phrase "minimizing pay and chase" has been the mantra of controlling the unauthorized fraudulent payment for healthcare services. In this constantly evolving and "hasty" tempo to build and implement electronic health record strategies, a new mantra of "implement, then validate" has emerged, as opposed to "validate, then implement," in response to third-party-mandated deadlines. This urgency to "implement, then validate" a sound electronic health record system has been driven more through fear of being penalized as an organization than a responsible by-product of healthy industry competition to excel and succeed.

The flip side of the EHR coin is an organization's financial systems. While the CMIO, CNIO, and others are updating meaningful use within their own clinical systems, PFS is forced to concentrate resources on the new health plans established under the ACA exchanges. Hypothetically, an organization may be on par with respect to the electronic recording of clinical services provided to the patient; however, the associated financial data that documents those same healthcare services on the payer's end may be completely out of sync or nonexistent. Consider this question during the next C-suite meeting. Are we, the provider, technologically aligned (trading properly coded and current data) with all our payers, including all Medicaid programs, from a contractual standpoint that mandates parity of information concerning financial recording requirements? For instance, if a patient walks in with one of the many ACA-mandated insurance plan options, will the provider's system recognize it as a contracted plan (financial recordings)? Will the payer recognize the plan on receipt of the clinical service from the provider?

The United States is in the process of converting the International Classification of Diseases, 9th revision (ICD-9) to ICD-10 (10th revision). ICD-10 dictates the proper recording of a diagnosis on the financial submission of claims. One PFS interviewed reflected on studies in Canada with respect to the implementation of ICD-10. The conversion of ICD-9 to ICD-10 in Canada resulted in a 30% drop in revenue, which has not yet been recovered. The Canadian PFS manager commented that he anticipates a similar drop in revenue in the United States after converting from ICD-9 to ICD-10. This drop in revenue will likely result from lost, nontranslatable, or deleted billing data following the implementation of different mapping and procedure codes from one system to another.

Author's Note: *ICD codes (diagnosis codes) document why a patient was treated; procedure codes communicate what was done to treat the patient.* A claim documents what was done and why it was done, including all associated costs. Therefore, insurance claim data might be considered the Bible of all-inclusive business or clinical intelligence information relevant to any patient, hospital, or provider. If the whats and whys do not appear on the claim form, a treatment never happened. If it happened and it does not appear on the claim, the organization will have exposure to fines and penalties, in particular if the claim is not supported within the clinical record.

Many providers have responded to the management of new Centers for Medicare and Medicaid Services (CMS) and private payer initiatives with the development of a revenue integrity team or the hybrid medical data auditor (MDA). This discipline has evolved from the former role of the medical auditor that was principally focused on auditing medical records as they compare to the billing statement and reconciling services documented with services billed. That role requires the knowledge, skills, and abilities of a registered nurse or healthcare professional with the requisite clinical background to meet with the payer representative and validate the bill for accuracy. The MDA must incorporate internal audit, mapping, and technology skills, in addition to basic business analytic skills, in order to effectively execute the tasks required to complete the mission in a complex environment requiring overlapping skill sets and multiple core competencies, such as IT and finance.

A professional MDA must fundamentally understand the healthcare subject matter from a clinical perspective, possess internal auditing skills, understand healthcare finance reimbursement, and display strong-minded determination to locate misplaced or missing data wherever it may exist within the organization. To assist their medical audit and investigative teams, Medical Business Associates, Inc. of Westmont, Illinois, has developed and patented a master behavioral assessment tool (roadmap) that significantly enhances an auditor's ability to rapidly and accurately identify critical data points during the execution of complex revenue integrity operations.

Although Medical Business Associates developed this investigative tool primarily for use within the medical (healthcare) auditor community, the fundamental system "mapping or tracking" principles that identify the what, who, where, when, and critically important why can be utilized in any industry or organization. (Note: Understanding the why is critical and categorized as a behavioral problem.) The organization must, at all costs, identify, define, and understand the root cause. Why? Failing or falling short in the execution of this critical task is commensurate to having a computer virus that invades your operating system, and regardless of what you do to "patch and isolate" the problem, the virus behaves in a fashion that ultimately reinvades your system at every opportunity. It is important to recognize that the application of this model to healthcare-centric revenue integrity auditing incorporates the business practices of IT and revenue cycle engagements, which include

...medical data auditors (MDAs) who are skilled in assessing personnel knowledge, skills and abilities (limits) and motivation or lack thereof to succeed, organizational process, and understanding client specific applied technology whether it is established or tribal. MDAs apply their operational experience, multidiscipline subject matter expertise, technical medical auditing skills, compliance and revenue cycle management to assessments and corrective actions in order to facilitate organizational objectives. MDAs bridge the data needs and data efforts of IT, finance, and departmental disciplines throughout the organization. The need for experienced MDAs is in direct response to market changes that require a higher level understanding and management of extensive (complex) payer contracts, an increased number of work streams that are cross disciplined, ACOs, new population health management directives, and the ongoing changing landscape to use data more strategically within healthcare.[20]

The use of MDAs should be embedded between the CIO and CFO functions and considered, from a revenue perspective, to be their intelligence agency. In the future, the MDA's role may be best positioned or optimally controlled and directed under the management of the CDO. As the market minimizes the impact of "implement and validate" to "validate and implement," the role of the MDA will be utilized more effectively to support forecasting, as opposed to just a search and cleanup mode. As a result of increasing demands for revenue management and rapid revenue growth demands in healthcare, another C-suite member, the chief revenue officer (CRO), has emerged. The CRO's basic functions should include the following skill sets:

- Understanding the customer base (marketing)
- Ability to define and effectively manage the organization's products and services (inventory)
- Ability to set pricing for services
- Ability to sustain an effective sales strategy and forecasting models for product and services
- Ability to effectively manage distribution and provision of the services and products

In healthcare, some of the operational functions of pricing and distribution may be found in corporate sections or divisions that are led by individuals with titles such as director of revenue management or director of revenue cycle.

The director of revenue cycle position typically requires or includes an undergraduate degree in accounting, business management, or health information administration. Furthermore, this role will typically have assigned the responsibility to supervise and manage the daily operations of revenue cycle functions and develop the associated processes, policies, and procedures. The director of revenue cycle position is also responsible for maintaining compliance with regulations, standards, and directives from regulatory agencies and third-party payers. Table 8.2 lists examples of audit support roles that may work with the revenue cycle.

Table 8.2 Illustrative Healthcare Audit Roles and Descriptions

Medical reviewer: Performs audits on all medical records contained in a healthcare facility. Also known as medical auditors, they review the data to ensure the accuracy of the record as well as assess the quality of patient care. Medical reviewers must complete at least a 2-year associate's degree through a technical school or community college.

Medical auditor: Examines and analyzes accounting records to determine financial status of an establishment and prepares financial reports concerning operating procedures. Usually works with payer auditors to resolve any billing discrepancies. Medical auditors typically have a nursing and finance background and understand charge description masters (CDMs) within a provider organization.

Medical documentation auditor: Ensures accurate and complete documentation through compliance and encounter audits and clinician feedback. Provides documentation feedback to clinicians from Evaluation & Management (E&M), CPT, and ICD-9 audits conducted by using all state, federal, and third-party payer regulatory standards for both inpatient and outpatient groups.

Medical coding auditor: Specifically focuses on auditing and reviewing diagnosis and procedure codes assigned to an episode of care. This person's background may be as a health information management individual or clinician with a certification in coding.

Internal auditor: An independent, objective consultant designed to add value and improve an organization's operations. The internal auditor helps an organization accomplish its objectives by bringing a systematic, disciplined approach to evaluate and improve the effectiveness of risk management, control, and governance processes.[21]

Medical data auditor: Participates on a revenue integrity team to provide gap analysis (identify gaps from future required state), gap management (assurance that gaps identified are implemented), denial management (corrective action on revenue cycle breakdowns), and revenue integrity audits (business analytics and business process). Individuals are skilled in people, process, and technology applications.

Please note that the medical data auditor is viewed as an evolving hybrid intended to manage the rapidly changing dynamics of processes associated with business and clinical intelligence derived from clinical systems. The medical data auditor continues to maintain current practices and keeps pace with any changes that occur on the financial side of healthcare delivery.

Revenue Integrity Management Today

Beyond the efforts of various professional development organizations such as HFMA that assist healthcare professionals, other industries are tackling the issue of revenue management through a range of organizational support systems. For example, support within the hospitality industry is extensive. The goal of the Revenue Management Society is "to provide a forum to define and promote best practice in the use of revenue and yield management techniques, through discussion and communication between the key users of these techniques within the Travel, Transportation and Leisure industries."[22] Another organization, Hospitality Finance, Revenue and IT Professionals (HOSPA), a nonprofit educational organization, is an association dedicated to the hospitality industry and focuses on finance, revenue management, and IT professionals. The British Association of Hospitality Accountants (BAHA), which was formed in 1969, recognized the need to have revenue management as its own discipline with the development of appropriate practice standards.[23]

Circling back to revenue management in healthcare, the need for the highly specialized skill set of a CRO may be necessary for the C-suite to stay one step ahead of government mandates. This chapter presents the subtle point of market shifts forcing changes in revenue models for both payers and providers of healthcare services. What is the revenue growth focus of a CRO in healthcare?

The CRO needs to first operationalize the current ACA-mandated regulations that will affect his or her business revenue model. The CRO needs to be prepared for unexpected legislative mandates that will modify and shift the incentives of his or her revenue model. This revenue model shifting will occur within both public and private payers' businesses, and the CRO will most likely be the revenue architect of an organization. Key attributes of a CRO[24] will ultimately include being the market maker (liquidity) working inside the C-suite sanctuary to communicate the organization's vision. The CRO's leadership within the organization is critical to communicating the short- and long-term revenue growth strategy for the organization. Other attributes of this leadership function are excellent business acumen and being a wise arbiter of key functions throughout the revenue cycle.

Data analytics are driving business decisions. The quality and integrity of that data are critical to the success of that organization and directly mapped to the CIO or CDO. Critical functions and management roles are shifting from the "gut" reaction types to "measurable data-driven metrics types," whose recommendations or decisions are based on sound business and clinical intelligence.

Author's Note: No matter the current or emerging role, we revert back to the driving theme of this book—that all information roles are increasingly dependent on data.

Balancing Act

The most significant balancing act is incorporating electronic healthcare delivery systems that focus on clinical management while at the same time keeping pace with industry financial issues and changing revenue models. Some may hope that health IT operates like a field of dreams—"If you build it, they will come." However, it appears that with the ongoing extensions of required mandates, the "field" will not manifest itself for at least another 5–10 years. If you build and validate with a competent revenue integrity team, the healthcare organization will minimize the aftermath of rapid changes that occur during this journey. If an organization constructs and attempts to validate a process with the wrong team, it will demonstrate Darwin's theory of survival of the fittest in real time—it will simply cease to exist.

The healthcare market is on a fast pace with the goal of developing industry-wide electronic health records, and this is closely followed by implementation of meaningful use criteria. For example, eligible professional staff that operate under meaningful use criteria stage 1 must prove that they have met 18 objectives when documenting patient care. Eligible hospitals must meet a total of 16 objectives.[25] The execution of this first task ensures that compliance with the meaningful use criteria has been fully implemented and properly documented. These efforts rely heavily on a properly constructed and comprehensive electronic health record system that is friendly to the end user. The second task educates the clinical staff to use and apply the criteria when documenting patient care.

Finally, experienced medical data auditors must validate the appropriate use of these criteria by reviewing the documentation within the electronic record. From personal experience, this process is extremely labor-intensive and requires experienced staff solely dedicated to resolving issues. As a medical data auditor, I have witnessed the cerebral light switch "clicked on" clinically, but totally switched off financially, where neither of the two shall cross paths.

Under these conditions, the situation would be characterized as critical, and a process needs to be created quickly to identify the damaged parts at a personnel, process, or technology level (or all of the above) to determine why the light went out. The emerging role of the MDA is still in the discovery phase and is an underutilized resource for managing both the CIO objectives, considering electronic health record system technology, and the need to maintain and provide assurance that the advanced technology does not interfere with the organization's revenue stream integrity.

Author's Note: Data analytics are driving business decisions. The quality and integrity of that data are critical to the success of that organization and directly mapped to the CIO or CDO.

Key Market Barriers to Overcome[26]

The biggest barrier to overcome in healthcare today is the separation of market conflicts and perverse incentives. To many who study the industry, this is a "fundamental fatal flaw." Today healthcare fails to effectively separate patient management from the financial versus clinical perspective. Hopefully, the development of enhanced metrics and sophisticated data analytics (made simple) will help to sustain progress toward the end goal of better patient care. Nevertheless, clinical data points supporting clinical decisions must be made independent of financial data points supporting financial decisions. What does this look like in the data?

> **Option 1:** A payer plan pays 80% of the cost associated with chemotherapy, with a mortality rate of 50%, and at a less expensive per dose cost.
>
> **Option 2:** A payer plan pays 50% of chemotherapy, with a mortality rate of 80%; however, the cost per dose is higher.

The claim data notes that 95% of patients were offered and received chemotherapy option 1 and were never presented with option 2. The crux of the matter? Data supports option 2, increasing the patient's life span.

This is an example of conflict of interests and perverse incentives. Once the patient dies, so do the costs associated with that care episode. Are we offering the patient all clinical options separate from the financial implications of each?

Role of Revenue Integrity Management

The role and responsibilities associated with revenue integrity management have risen to new levels in this fast-paced industry and require a much stricter form of vigilant oversight in patient care documentation domains, as well as meeting the obligations of financial compliance requirements. This role serves as a gatekeeper in facilitating and keeping an organization's financial health in check while the CIO, CDO, and other information roles continue to implement technology initiatives. Although Table 8.2 references several auditing roles, the medical data auditor is a new hybrid and critical to merging the gap between finance and IT. As stated earlier, professionals operating in this arena must be skilled in the interpersonal, process, and technology assessments to be successful. They need to apply their operational experience, multidiscipline subject matter expertise, medical auditing, compliance, and revenue cycle management to facilitate organizational objectives. The MDAs (hospitality finance, revenue, and IT professionals) should bridge the data needs and data efforts of IT, finance, and departmental disciplines throughout the organization.

Final Thought

Have you conducted a human capital assessment of your organization? Do you have the "right people doing the right job" to ensure successful implementation, adoption, and leverage of new technology? It is important to leverage all of your human capital assets. Chapter 9 provides additional considerations for information management roles.

CFO Perspective

Technological advances in healthcare, including electronic health record implementation and related technologically incentivized revenue streams, present a double-edged sword to the healthcare industry. While the patient care benefits of an integrated system are universally agreed upon and the revenue upsides peak provider's interests, the shortfalls in technology infrastructure, inadequate technology staffing and lack of vetted organizational models make a venture into the new technological era a dangerous and challenging venture in many ways. Rebecca Busch identifies many of these risks and challenges, most notably the evolution of new, but necessary hybrid management roles that join clinical and financial technology in a new and different way.

Kevin Flynn
Chief Financial Officer, Associates in Nephrology, SC, Chicago, Illinois

References

1. Revenue, http://dictionary.reference.com/browse/revenue (accessed October 1, 2014).
2. History of Revenue Administration, 2012, http://www.gib.gov.tr/index.php?id=468 (accessed October 1, 2014).
3. Carlson, R.H., A Brief History of Property Tax, 2005, http://www.historyoftheancientworld. com/2013/04/a-brief-history-of-property-tax/ (accessed October 1, 2014).
4. Integrity, http://dictionary.reference.com/browse/integrity (accessed October 1, 2014).
5. Management, http://dictionary.reference.com/browse/management (accessed October 1, 2014).
6. Post-Acute Care Blog, 2012, http://www.healthtech.net/post-acute-care-blog/bid/114719/a-brief-history-of-electronic-health-records-ehrs/ (accessed October 1, 2014).
7. http://www.whitehouse.gov/issues/ (accessed October 1, 2014).
8. DeSalvo, K., and Lewis, L., Office of the National Coordinator Update, 2014, http://www.healthit. gov/buzz-blog/from-the-onc-desk/office-national-coordinator-update/ (accessed October 28, 2014).
9. Centers for Medicare and Medicaid Services (CMS), Transform and Modernize the Health Care System through Efficient Public Programs, 2007, http://www.cms.gov/MissionVisionGoals/ Downloads/CMSStrategicActionPlan06-09_061023a.pdf (accessed October 1, 2014).
10. Text of Obama Speech on the Economy, 2014, http://www.cnbc.com/id/28559492 (accessed December 18, 2014).
11. Obama, B., Remarks of President Barack Obama—As Prepared for Delivery, 2009, http://www. whitehouse.gov/the_press_office/Remarks-of-President-Barack-Obama-Address-to-Joint-Session-of-Congress/ (accessed December 2014).
12. Accountable Care Organizations (ACO), 2013, https://www.cms.gov/Medicare/Medicare-Fee-for-Service-Payment/ACO/index.html?redirect=/ACO/ (accessed December 2014).
13. Meaningful Use, 2014, http://www.hitechanswers.net/ehr-adoption-2/meaningful-use/ (accessed October 2014).
14. Read the Law, 2012, http://www.hhs.gov/healthcare/rights/law/index.html (accessed October 2014).
15. Health IT Legislation, 2010, http://healthit.gov/policy-researchers-implementers/health-it-legislation (accessed October 2014).
16. Meaningful Use.
17. Ibid.
18. Electronic Health Records, 2014, http://www.himss.org/library/ehr/ (accessed October 2014).
19. Electronic Health Records Overview, 2006, http://www.himss.org/files/HIMSSorg/content/files/ Code%20180%20MITRE%20Key%20Components%20of%20an%20EHR.pdf (accessed October 2014).
20. Medical Business Associates, Inc., http://mbaaudit.com/ (accessed October 2014).
21. Institute of Internal Auditors, 2014, https://na.theiia.org/Pages/IIAHome.aspx (accessed October 2014).
22. Revenue Management Society, 2008, https://www.linkedin.com/groups?gid=128419 (accessed October 1, 2014).

23. Hospitality Finance, Revenue and IT Professionals, http://hospa.org/en/ (accessed October 1, 2014).
24. Savitz, E., The CEO's New Secret Weapon: The Chief Revenue Officer, *Forbes*, March 13, 2012, http://www.forbes.com/sites/ciocentral/2012/03/13/the-ceos-new-secret-weapon-the-chief-revenue-officer/ (accessed October 1, 2014).
25. 2014 Definition Stage 1 of Meaningful Use, 2014, http://www.cms.gov/Regulations-and-Guidance/Legislation/EHRIncentivePrograms/Meaningful_Use.html (accessed October 6, 2014).
26. Busch, R., *Electronic Health Records: An Audit and Internal Control Guide* (New York: John Wiley & Sons, 2008).

Chapter 9

Integration of
Information Roles

The energy of the mind is the essence of life.

—**Aristotle**
Greek philosopher and scientist

This chapter will introduce the concept of information; the attributes, considerations, risks, and opportunities associated with the subject of information; and how users cognitively process information within the human brain, interact with others, and communicate within a business environment. In Chapter 4, the discussion centered on the development of new C-suite positions or, in the absence of these newly created roles, the paradigm shift in executive responsibilities. In this chapter, we take a deeper look into the roles and responsibilities of the new C-suite brand we call information executive. This (hospitality finance, revenue, and IT professionals) fast-paced technology and data-driven healthcare market has created the need for subgroups of information and equivalent subject matter expertise within the overall organization, including its leadership.

A Bit of Human Anatomy and History

An information root or core, its development, processing, storage, and task execution, is analogous to how the brain functions as part of the human anatomy. It is complex, not fully understood, and constantly abstracting, processing, and adapting. As a precursor to a discussion on how information is evolving in this advanced technology age, we need to examine the granddaddy of all processors—the human brain. The interworking of the brain, comparable to the aforementioned C-suite information executive, is similar to that of a committee of experts. All of the brain parts work together, but each part possesses its own distinctive properties.

As with C-suite information executives, the brain's communication hierarchy resembles diverse levels of responsibility, known as forebrain, midbrain, and hindbrain. Each must execute specific functions while calling upon and interacting with successive units or levels of other parts of the brain. These team players are known as the cerebellum and cerebrum; to characterize the brain as the most complex system known to humankind would be an understatement, so we'll just say that with respect to hemispheres and lobes, one coordinates movements, and the other, intellectual activities. When you plan an event, imagine an outcome, use reasoning to argue an issue, or walk down a set of stairs, these two lobes do much of the work, acting as short-term storage sites, allowing one idea to be held in the mind's short-term storage while other ideas are being considered in real time.[1]

Every minute of every day, executives can be bombarded with information, and that information is constantly changing, evolving throughout their business environment. We have billions of cells in our brain that send and receive signals influencing everything from the linear facts cycling within a stream of information to the intuitive emotions we feel contemplating thoughts. Understanding how the brain functions provides insight into how information can be effectively captured and managed. Consider the concept "left brain, right brain" in terms of separate thought processes or distinct styles, each with a particular talent, one being analytical, linear, logical, and all about the facts, and the other offering creativity, imagination, and intuition. All this engineered genius is necessary to harmonize how information is received and perceived, applied and managed.

For a parallel view, in the same way that the brain shapes information, information shapes the business environment. For example, what triggers certain moods, behavior, and thinking? Here are a few fun facts on the brain:

- The first known writing about the brain was found in ancient Sumeria around 4000 BC. The anonymous writer describes the euphoric, mind-altering feeling caused by eating poppies.[2]
- The newest part of the cerebral cortex in terms of evolution is the neocortex ("new bark"), which scientists believe is responsible for the development of human intelligence.[3]
- The human brain consists of approximately 100 billion neurons (which is as many cells as there are stars in the Milky Way). As a comparison, an octopus has 300,000 neurons, a honeybee has 950,000, and a jellyfish has no brain at all.[4]
- While awake, a human brain can generate enough energy to power a light bulb (between 10 and 23 watts).[5]
- The human brain can process information as fast as 268 miles per hour. Information travels to the brain at different speeds because neurons are built differently.[6]
- Contrary to the popular belief that humans use just 10% of their brain capacity, humans actually use virtually every part of the brain, and most of the brain is active all the time. Experts estimate that in a lifetime, a human brain may retain 1 quadrillion separate bits of information.[7]
- The human brain has around 100,000 miles of blood vessels.[8]
- There are more than 100,000 chemical reactions happening in the human brain every second.[9]

Understanding how the brain processes information (a framework) is similar to what an effective data business strategy requires. Within a framework, there is a complete understanding of all of the organization's functions, information content, data pathways (input and output), and data application. That being said, what is information? How is it defined? Let's start with an overall definition of information.

The following is a full breakdown of the term:

1. The communication or reception of knowledge or intelligence
2. Knowledge obtained from investigation, study, or instruction; intelligence, news, facts, data inherent in, and communicated by, one of two or more alternative sequences or arrangements of something (as nucleotides in DNA or binary digits in a computer program) that produce specific effects; a signal or character (as in a communication system or computer) representing data; something (as a message, experimental data, or a picture) that justifies change in a construct (as a plan or theory) that represents physical or mental experience or another construct; a quantitative measure of the content of information; specifically, a numerical quantity that measures the uncertainty in the outcome of an experiment to be performed
3. The act of informing against a person
4. A formal accusation of a crime made by a prosecuting officer as distinguished from an indictment presented by a grand jury[10]

Other common terms allied with information are *data* and *facts*. In this context, information will be viewed as data and associated with the communication or reception of knowledge or business and clinical intelligence. Different types of data exist for our examination or analysis and are categorized accordingly. Business information, or data, is defined as

> data that is (1) accurate and timely, (2) specific and organized for a purpose, (3) presented within a context that gives it meaning and relevance, and (4) can lead to an increase in understanding and decrease in uncertainty. Information is valuable because it can affect behavior, a decision, or an outcome. For example, if a manager is told his or her company's net profit decreased in the past month, he or she may use this information or data as a reason to reduce financial spending for the next month. A piece of information or data is considered valueless if, after receiving it, things remain unchanged.[11]

In the spirit of a manager or his or her organization influencing the behavior of its workforce, another layer of brain function must be understood and requires a brief understanding of two other processing components of the brain: fast thinking (instinctive and subconscious, using less brain power) and slow thinking (conscious, which uses more brain power). These brain functions parallel those systems that we design and apply within our own work environment. It always helps to understand how we react to information tossed at us and how it is perceived. For example, let's take the following fun fact: there are more than 100,000 chemical reactions happening in the human brain every second.[12] This is a lot of work. The brain will intuitively rely on using less brainpower (system 1, fast thinking) to get to a conclusion more often than using more brainpower (system 2, slow thinking) simply to conserve energy.[13] Let's take the following question: How many animals of each kind did Moses take on the ark?

System 1, less effort, unconsciously makes an association of Moses within a biblical context and immediately starts to answer the question of how many animals without the involvement of system 2, which would take notice and say, "Wait! It wasn't Moses—it was Noah." In a different context, look at a reaction to crossing the street—you see a speeding car and stop. The mind does not immediately calculate rate of speed, distance, and impact. The brain has learned in most instances that walking in front of a speeding car could result in one's demise. System 1 creates context without the individual realizing it and relies on prior experience. Therefore, people more often than not will simply stop at the sight of a speeding car, which is referred to as priming. For example, if you see the word *wash*, how would you complete SO_P? System 1 would trigger SOAP. If the word *eat* was displayed, you would most likely complete SO_P as SOUP. The words *wash* and *eat* have priming effects that emanate from system 1. System 2 may think it is in charge, but it is system 1 that influences rapid reaction or the instant reflex decision. System 1 provides a context for a quick decision and is the initial response. It is human nature. One last brain test: solve for *x*.

$$11 \times 11 = 4$$

$$22 \times 22 = 16$$

$$33 \times 33 = x$$

How does this apply to healthcare on a day-to-day basis? Clinical decisions regarding patient care are dependent on the health professional involved in providing that care. This example illustrates how a series of steps, a response to information, and the brain's natural way of thinking prevented a positive outcome:

- A 21-year-old post–eye surgery patient is in the intensive care unit.
- He is restless and begins to become combative.
- The first course of action is to obtain additional data.
- A stat blood oxygen level is ordered.
- The results associated with this test are recorded on a typical medical record document and are delivered to the patient's bedside. Results are normal. It is assumed that the patient is in pain, although the cause of it is unclear.
- Blood is pressure increasing, pulse is increasing, the skin is pale, and the fingertips are bluish.
- The patient is given morphine for pain.
- The patient relaxes and then begins to gasp.
- He goes into a full cardiac arrest; his heart rate accelerates and then stops.
- The patient expires.

What did a post–forensic review of care disclose? The nurse and doctor initiated lab work to rule out issues with oxygenation. Although the physical symptoms noted hypoxia, the provider continued to react to normal blood work (data). System 1 was properly functioning, and reaction to the immediacy of incoming data was flat, straight, and normal. The truth of the matter disclosed that the lab indicated the wrong bed number for the results. The patient's blood levels were abnormal, and the introduction of morphine compromised this patient's ability to effectively receive oxygen. The patient arrested and died, in essence suffocating as a result of the introduction of morphine.

The provider (lab) was only conscious of the blood work results and not the name of the patient on the document. A somber lethal example will often provide clarity on the impact of not having the right information at the right time. Creating systems to manage data to get it right the first and every time will minimize or eliminate the potential to prevent these types of events from occurring. Now compound this with the need to manage costs, fundamental shifts in the healthcare market delivery system of wellness management, as opposed to illness management, and ongoing legislative changes such as the Affordable Care Act. This short list has created the need for information (data) subgroups and corresponding subject matter experts who must be resident within the organization, and its leadership must fully appreciate the power of information at their fingertips or, more likely, just out of reach. Thus, the evolution or emergence of a range of new roles is created.

Author's Note: Consider how the brain processes information versus how man-made technology processes information. They both impact every aspect of an organization's operation. The complexity of information has developed the need for segmented skill sets and expertise.

Integration of Leadership Roles

Throughout the industry or profession of business and specifically in healthcare, the executive suite falls into three basic categories: traditional roles with expanded responsibilities, true information roles, and executive subject matter expertise support roles.

Traditional Roles

Chief executive officer (CEO): The highest-ranking executive in a company whose primary responsibilities include developing and implementing high-level strategies, making corporate decisions, managing operations and resources, and acting as the communications focal point between corporate operations and the board of directors. In many cases, the CEO will sit either on the board or in the chair position.

Chief operating officer (COO): The senior manager responsible for managing the company's day-to-day operations and reporting to the CEO.

Chief financial officer (CFO): The senior manager responsible for overseeing the company's financial activities. The CFO's duties include financial planning and monitoring cash flow, analyzing the company's financial strengths and weaknesses, and recommending options. The CFO is similar to a treasurer or controller in that he or she is responsible for overseeing the accounting and finance departments, and ensures that the company's financial reporting system is accurate and timely.

Chief compliance officer (CCO): The individual responsible for ensuring that the company complies with regulatory requirements and internal policies. A compliance officer may review and set standards for outside communications by requiring disclaimers in emails, or may examine facilities to ensure that they are accessible and safe. Compliance officers may also design or update internal policies to mitigate the risk of the company breaking laws and regulations, as well as spearhead internal audits.

Chief marketing officer (CMO): This role has experienced significant change, and in many cases, it has been removed from the C-suite floor. That aside, this individual is responsible for corporate branding, advertising, marketing channels, customer outreach, and all other marketing-related issues. The CMO is still considered part of the top management tier with responsibilities that basically cut across all company product lines and geographic regions.

The following are categorized as emerging information roles that are triggered by a big data environment and the need for technology innovation, and increasing security issues that result from technology transfer, storage, and privacy:

Chief information officer (CIO): The job title commonly assigned to the individual responsible for information technology and computer systems that support enterprise goals.

Chief information security officer (CISO): Manages the information security domain and is primarily responsible for securing anything related to digital information. The CISO and chief security officer (CSO) roles may be interchangeable, but CISOs may also handle the corporation's physical security requirements.

Chief medical information officer (CMIO): Serves as the bridge between the medical and IT departments at a healthcare organization. This individual may also be referred to as the director of medical informatics or health informatics.

Chief nursing information officer (CNIO): Provides operational oversight of electronic health record (EHR) system design and implementation, staffing, education, change management, and performance improvement.

In addition to specific information roles, additional core competencies are being embedded into organizations. These roles are impacted by the need for information management and data analytics support to an organization. These roles are illustrated as follows:

Chief technology officer (CTO): Individual within an organization who has ultimate responsibility for all technology policy and related matters, such as research and development (R&D).

Chief data officer (CDO): Corporate officer responsible for enterprise-wide governance and utilization of information as an asset, via data processing, analysis, data mining, information trading, and other means.

Chief strategy officer (CSO): Executive charged with helping formulate, facilitate, and communicate the overall strategy of an organization, usually a large corporation.

Chief experience officer (CXO): Executive who ensures positive interactions with an organization's external customers. The job title of chief experience officer is increasingly replacing that of chief customer officer in retail and entertainment industries and chief activity officer in healthcare and travel.

Chief clinical transformation officer (CCTO): Tends to report to the CEO of the health system. He or she acts as the administrative leader across the broad array of transformation initiatives, but often shares joint responsibility for clinical transformation with a high-profile physician leader.

Chief population health manager (CPHM): Manages the full continuum of healthcare services across a defined population.

Chief revenue officer (CRO): Responsible for all activities that generate revenue. In most companies, the CRO is tasked with primary or shared responsibility for operations, sales, corporate development, and marketing, pricing, and revenue management since these functions extend across multiple teams in most companies.

These roles are highlighted in Figure 9.1 by title and segmented into three layers (traditional, information, and support leadership). Information (*i*) is the driver in developing the second and third tiers; Figure 9.2 segments the second and third tiers as well and lists the core competencies need of each role. Each role and functional area has unique data points that are generated and processed. Regardless, all the information generated from these organizational segments does need

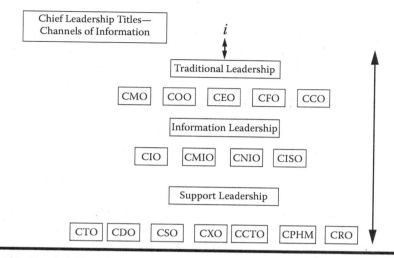

Figure 9.1 Chief leadership titles.

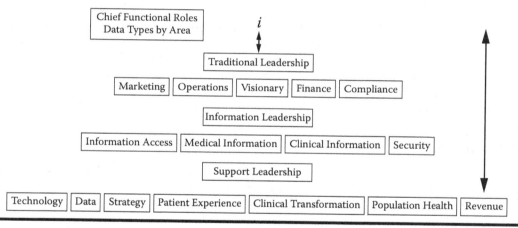

Figure 9.2 Chief leadership data types by functional role.

to be aggregated. The data aggregation should parallel the data strategy for the organization. That integration can be effective by breaking down leadership focal points, as illustrated in Figure 9.2.

Management Role Integration

In a rapidly changing, high-volume, complex environment, transitioning your organization from an environment of reactive management teams to one of proactive management teams can be overwhelming and at times seemingly hopeless, depending on resources, time, talent, and most importantly, attitude or desire to succeed. The first step is to take an inventory of the organization's human capital.

Creating a leadership organization chart as illustrated in Figure 9.1 is a great start. The previously discussed interactive, iterative, and reiterating behavioral (IIRB) model can be applied here. First, identify all the players—in this case, titles and roles involved in the organization, including any vacant leadership positions. Second, identify industry requirements. For example, a compliance officer may have different job requirements relevant to your industry segment and may not need to be connected at the senior leadership level. Third, note the information continuum within each leadership role and identify all the people, processes, and technologies utilized to manage their respective areas, which in some industries is termed a desk audit. The damage or consequence continuum of the IIRB model involves conducting a risk assessment within each department that identifies gaps or vulnerabilities. Finally, incorporate controls for all mandated legislative requirements, such as Health Insurance Portability and Accountability Act (HIPAA) security requirements for protected health information.

A functional and core competency assessment will parallel the respective leadership areas. These data type requirements driving information (*i*) are illustrated in Figure 9.2. The focus of this book is the development of new information or data roles that drive tier 1 leadership decision making. The essential elements that drive technology innovation have created the need in many organizations to incorporate a dedicated team or teams to focus on this important mission. Incorporating a chief data officer and implementing data strategies to guide all information users to become "most effective" data end users is taking on its own course to administer big data. Clinical intelligence is needed to drive business activities associated with the patient experience, population health management, and clinical transformation. An interesting area that needs additional attention is revenue management that includes actionable business intelligence. This has not hit healthcare's C-suite domain as rapidly as other industries, in particular, our publicly (taxpayer) subsidized systems. However, with the Affordable Care Act driving changes in revenue models for both payers and providers, it is an area that will ultimately demand greater attention.

Balancing Act

Acceptance of new business and clinical models commingled with the implementation of new technologies will be front and center, and providers will need to continue to manage patients in a transitional environment. Asking clinical staff to incorporate and sustain training into their daily routine while actively engaging in patient care will add to conflicting priorities in an already strained environment.

Key Market Barriers to Overcome

Technology adoption will come with a price; however, management's challenge will be the ability to "work through the noise" and continue to move forward. Even as I write, I pause to read an email blast alert, "We have received reports that the electronic prescribing system is down. FOR THE NEXT 24 HOURS YOUR PATIENT'S PRESCRIPTIONS WILL HAVE TO BE MANUALLY WRITTEN AND ORDERED." I pause at the implication—how many patients will not receive their medication on time, if at all? Then I get another email: "ALERT: OVERNIGHT ALL PATIENTS WERE INADVERTENTLY DISCHARGED. PLEASE BE PATIENT AS WE REINSTATE AND CONFIRM ADMITTED PATIENTS." We are entering a new era of crisis management.

Author's Note: The executive suite falls into three basic categories: traditional roles with expanded responsibilities, true information roles, and executive subject matter expertise support roles.

Role of Revenue Integrity Management

Health information technology adoption is progressing collectively as a market with legislated requirements that emerged under HIPAA that require electronic implementation and the adoption of changes to billing processes known as administrative simplification. Our government continues to move the market in the direction of electronic adoption, in addition to implementing uniform data points. This can be observed in the uniform technology adoption by defining parameters of meaningful use data. All providers will be required to collect the prescribed data in order to qualify for the incentive or avoid penalties. Throughout this process, revenue integrity management will morph into various other forms of attack and sophisticated accountability methods, but it will still be critical to remain focused on the process of assurance (am I doing the right thing and getting paid for it?).

Final Thought

Remember that the energy of the mind is the essence of life. Reflect on an earlier brain fun fact: while awake, a human brain can generate enough energy to power a lightbulb (between 10 and 23 watts).[14] Imagine what an organization can do with the collection of productive brains focused on one mission? In this chapter, we see how information is processed from an individual perspective to that of an entire organization, which is the collection of its individuals. Are all your brains working together? Chapter 10 provides a practical application to identify and reunite the functional segregation of an organization's "brain" network.

CDO Perspective

As Rebecca aptly points out, the executive leadership roles are becoming increasingly integrated. In many organizations and industries, they are driven nearly to the point of consolidation. Yet, each role offers a significant contribution and provides a unique value proposition. The integrity of each role and its contribution must be respected and protected.

This is especially pronounced in the healthcare industry. As the industry embraces the challenges of triple aim (i.e., improved patient care experience, improved population health, and reduced cost), the collaboration of the information executive team is critical. Any single point of failure will not only defer realization of the triple aim; it may have catastrophic results for the patient.

The question you must face is "How will you and your team respond to the challenge?" In addition to establishing a multidisciplinary strategy, the team members must interact seamlessly and operate as a single entity. Much like a human organ can't survive independently, the team must operate as a single organism. This requires shared perspectives, goals, strategies, and mutual respect. It's also critical for these values to be embraced by the entire organization. What steps are you undertaking to lead your peers, team, and entire enterprise through these challenges?

—James Brenza
Chief Data Officer, InXite Health, Delaware, Ohio

Endnotes

1. Brain Basics: Know Your Brain, 2014, http://www.ninds.nih.gov/disorders/brain_basics/know_your_brain.htm#intro (accessed October 2014).
2. Turkington, C., and Harris, J., *The Encyclopedia of the Brain and Brain Disorders*, 1st ed. (Facts On File, 1996).
3. Stephen, J., *The Odd Brain: Mysteries of Our Weird and Wonderful Brains Explained*, 1st ed. (Andrews McMeel Publishing, Kansas City, MO, 2006).
4. Chudler, E., Brain Facts and Figures, 2011, http://faculty.washington.edu/chudler/facts.html (accessed October 2014).
5. Newquist, H., Kasnot, K., and Brace, E., *The Great Brain Book: An Inside Look at the Inside of Your Head* (Scholastic Nonfiction, New York, 2005).
6. Turkington and Harris, *The Encyclopedia of the Brain*.
7. Wolpert, S., African Americans and Caucasians Have Similar Emotional Brain Activity When Seeing African Americans, UCLA Psychologists Find, 2005, http://newsroom.ucla.edu/releases/African-Americans-and-Caucasians-6127?RelNum=6127 (accessed October 2014).
8. Turkington and Harris, *The Encyclopedia of the Brain*.
9. Ibid.
10. Information, http://www.merriam-webster.com/dictionary/information%20 (accessed October 2014).
11. Information, http://www.businessdictionary.com/definition/information.html#ixzz3GthWlRzz (accessed October 2014).
12. Top 10 Facts about Human Brain, http://degreed.com/blog/top-10-facts-human-brain/ (accessed August 2014).
13. Kahneman, D., *Thinking, Fast and Slow* (Farrar, Straus & Giroux, 2011).
14. Newquist et al., *The Great Brain Book*.

Chapter 10

Redefining Workflows

The sculptor produces the beautiful statue by chipping away such parts of the marble block as are not needed—it is a process of elimination.

—Elbert Hubbard
American writer

Chapter 10 introduces the concept of a workflow—what it is and, from a historical perspective, how an effective understanding of workflow is crucial to an organization's ability to determine its present state. The development or use of a workflow schematic diagram is critical to understanding any existing system or when considering the introduction or modification of a new technology or process.

Within the healthcare arena, the chief information officer (CIO) should be providing leadership direction for the development, mapping, and analysis of workflow concerning all processes related to information technology. Any process or system review including audits must include a detailed layered workflow "map" of the personnel, processes, authorities, budgeting, and so forth. Furthermore, posttechnology implementation workflows must be analyzed to ensure that all IT applications truly meet organizational needs, as opposed to just the needs of IT for the sake of IT.

With the passing of the Affordable Care Act (ACA) legislation and ongoing electronic healthcare record requirements, the healthcare community is experiencing change at breakneck speed. This is increasing the demand for experienced medical data auditors (MDAs) to keep pace with complex health-related information documentation that forms the backbone for revenue integrity efforts.

This new internal medical data auditor hybrid role is effectively bridging IT, finance, and operations through the development and utilization of analytical workflow tools. That being said, for the many institutions in the healthcare industry that lack a chief data officer (CDO) or, for that matter, a CIO, the multidisciplined MDA team continues to be the go-to department or team that efficiently and effectively conducts workflow mapping and process auditing and ultimately defines both current and future states to determine work priorities. This chapter presents a case study that highlights the work of an MDA team under the direction of a CIO and will clearly define how this highly specialized role was utilized within a provider setting to support the revenue integrity mission.

A Bit of History

What is workflow? It is "the series of activities necessary to complete a task."[1] In reality, the concept of workflow or the order in which tasks are done has been in existence since the emergence of mankind. Hunting, starting a fire, food preparation, and who eats or does not involve some sort of workflow process: someone observes, analyzes, calculates, decides, and takes action, and there you have a workflow.

Beyond the basic tactics, techniques, and procedures employed to hunt the woolly mammoth, it is the tool kit that the hunter employs that has evolved. From a business perspective, workflow can be defined as "the demonstration of a business process in whole or part, during which documents, information or tasks are communicated from one participant to another and demand action according to a set of procedural rules."[2]

Within a business environment, workflow documentation involves a methodological approach to identifying every department, hierarchical lines of communication, authority, budgeting process, and so forth, and then schematically mapping the findings (workflow) in such a way as to identify the "left foot–right foot" ebb and flow, or the order in which daily operations are conducted. The workflow mapping process must identify all personnel in the organization, policies, procedures, any automated steps driven by software tools, and all business rules that direct or cause an action to be taken.

Workflow mapping attempts to identify or make sense of what is actually happening, as opposed to what is supposed to be happening. Hard-core investigative workflow mapping is similar to a formal audit in that the process involves validating by observing and direct testing that procedures are in fact being followed as documented. With respect to documenting any automated process, workflow software can be something as simple as an Excel workbook checklist or as complex as an electronic health record (EHR) system.

In the context of pure software, workflow can be defined as the bits and bytes of "any functionality that automates the flow of information based on some level of pre-defined rules."[3] Regardless of the types (manual or automated) of steps identified within any business processes, all independent and dependent functions and their relationship to the operation, whether formal or informal, must be identified and mapped. Business process management (BPM) requires accurate workflow documentation and business process modeling. These attributes are illustrated in the revenue integrity management function presented in this chapter's case study. The interactive, iterative, and reiterating behavioral (IIRB) model's adaption of mapping workflows (Figure 10.1) to subsequently define or redefine them includes identification of the following:

- People—involved with the business process and its management; desk audit involving all manual processes
- Benchmark—reference; the business process defined and management
- Information—the technologies in place and its management; movement of all data points and any supporting processes; automated processes
- Consequences, risks, and damages—when business functions break down or are obstructed; direct and indirect monetary impact
- Roadblocks—preventing business process from functioning; decreasing transparency
- Rules—any laws impacting the business function; compliance requirements

Two additional concepts or capture points have been integrated into the discovery phase of identifying the business workflow process: efficiency and quality. In modern history, the use of workflows can be found in the studies of Henry Laurence Gantt (1861–1919), an American

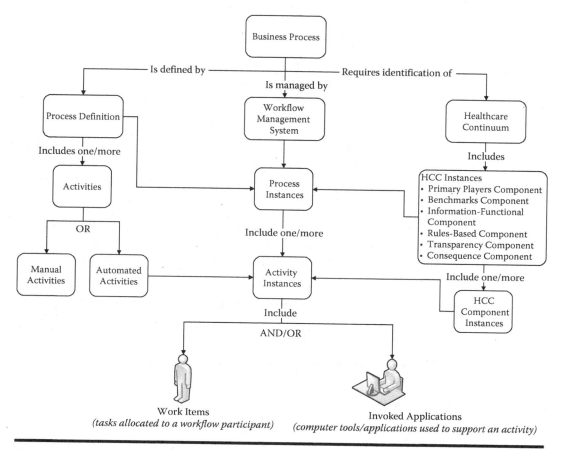

Figure 10.1   IIRB model adaption of business process mapping.

mechanical engineer and consultant who is known for developing the Gantt chart defined as the "type of bar-chart that shows both the scheduled and completed work over a period. A time scale is given on the chart's horizontal axis and each activity is shown as a separate horizontal rectangle (bar) whose length is proportional to the time required (or taken) for the activity's completion. In project planning, these charts show start and finish dates, critical and noncritical activities, slack time, and predecessor–successor relationships."[4]

The Gantt chart was utilized on major projects such as the construction of the Hoover Dam and U.S. Interstate highway system. Gantt reinforced the use of workflow mapping to effectively manage projects.

During this same time period in history, Frederick Winslow Taylor (March 20, 1856–March 21, 1915), an American mechanical engineer, studied and published on the subject of efficiency within business processes. Taylor published his theories on efficiency technique in his book *The Principles of Scientific Management*[5] and is considered the father of scientific management and one of the first management consultants. This era began with the use of workflows to organize major projects (Gantt), followed by the development of efficiencies in workflows (Taylor).

As technology progressed in manufacturing, keeping pace with ongoing inventions, new tools to facilitate efficient office work environments and the need to develop and manage filing systems increased dramatically. The need to manage information—the physical movement and storage of large amounts of data—increased after the end of World War II. The use of workflow management evolved to produce metrics when assessing quality in addition to assessing organization and efficiency. The advent of computers, software programs, and new applications introduced the need for workflows to segment people, process, and technology as a component of workflow identification, followed by redefining those workflows in a new environment.

All of this innovation required massive data storage capacity and a means to access it. The late 1990s witnessed a proliferation of workflow software products. Technology continued to advance in software functionality, enhanced programming of business rule engines, policy and compliance management tools, vulnerability and risk assessment programs, and modeling tools. This has had significant consequences for CIOs in the context of growing IT budgets, skill sets, and the evolution of core competencies specific to the business of information management. It also established the logic driving the proliferation of information roles to manage big data.

Today, workflow management bridges the gap between people and the current operational automated data points. An effective business process management (BPM) must allow for quick adaptation and measurement of required future states, in addition to incorporating ongoing efficiencies and improvements to current workflow. A solid BPM is a critical best practice within any CIO management function.

Author's Note: Workflow management bridges the gap between people and the current operational automated data points.

Redefining Workflows

This case study occurs at a safety net hospital and incorporates the use of a hybrid medical data audit (MDA) team integrated with the CIO function to address all people, process, and technology issues inhibiting data points that impact both clinical and business intelligence. The medical data auditor is a hybrid of a more common role often referred to as a medical audit specialist or medical auditor.

Organizations such as the American Association of Medical Audit Specialists are dedicated to establishing practice standards for professionals who specifically audit for healthcare reimbursement. The activities that a medical auditor typically engages in "include but are not limited to hospital bill audit, compliance, healthcare internal audit, utilization review, case management, risk management, health information management, quality improvement, workmen's compensation, representatives from health plans, insurance carriers, fiscal intermediaries, government and regulatory bodies, and healthcare consulting agencies."[6]

In addition, coding subject matter experts are in the process of developing practice standards for the medical audit profession. As an illustration, the American Academy of Professional Coders (AAPC) has focused on the review of coding and documentation guidelines to improve its membership's revenue cycle training and credentials documentation for a professional medical auditor.[7] The MDA illustrated in this case study is an evolution of the traditional medical auditor specifically focused on reconciling reimbursement to documented services within an organization. The MDA includes traditional revenue cycle and revenue integrity, in addition to informatics, data, business analytics, internal controls, and business process analytics. All of these skill sets are utilized and applied in this case study.

Case Study

Cardiology will be the clinical area depicted in this case study. The initial concern was that certain critical patient data was not passing through a series of defined workflows that involved multiple persons responsible for capturing, storing, and transmitting information, in addition to multiple software platforms failing to translate critical data into a patient support or reliable financial output. In addition, the organization failed to develop a unified process for patient registration or standard charge capture criteria. For example, one department could structure charge capture based on developing physician orderables versus automated charges driven by the clinical electronic healthcare record. These inconsistencies in workflow standards preclude optimal efficiency management and change controls within information systems management. They also create significant challenges with respect to follow-up data analytics after the delivery of services. Under these conditions, the CIO established and implemented a revenue integrity team that consisted of medical data auditors to determine a baseline current state and capture all missing information to achieve the desired future state, followed by the development of a mitigation strategy to prevent future occurrences.

RIT Demonstration

The revenue integrity team (RIT) provided MDAs who were skilled in people, process, and technology assessments. The need for MDAs was in response to complex market changes in managing extensive payer contracts (reductions in reimbursement), an increased number of work streams becoming cross-disciplined, accountable care organizations (ACOs), population health management, and the ongoing changing landscape to use data more strategically. MDAs apply their operational experience, multidiscipline subject matter expertise, medical auditing, compliance, and revenue cycle management skills to identifying issues and correcting problems with the purpose of facilitating the accomplishment of organizational objectives. In doing so, the MDAs bridge the data needs and overall efforts of IT, finance, and departmental disciplines throughout the organization.

RIT Illustrative Focus

The cardiac catheterization laboratory procedure within the cardiology department was audited for a period of 1 month. The sample identified a volume of 3.2 procedures per day for a 1-month period; the clinic's use of four different software programs to capture, store, and transmit patient data was contributing to lost or fragmented data workflows. The software sources included a clinic-based electronic storage system, a financial system, a health information management (HIM) program, and an electronic health record system. Identified registration issues prevented accurate capture of all patients who were processed within cardiology for the audit time period.

RIT within the Domain of the CIO?

The question initially raised was, why is IT managing a revenue integrity team and not finance? The medical data auditor is a hybrid of several roles and functions: IT, business analyst, internal audit, compliance, case management, medical audit, data scientist, third-party defense, revenue integrity, and revenue cycle management. RITs incorporate highly specialized clinical and allied health staff professionals trained in audit, finance, compliance, risk management, business analytics, and data science–type functions.

Charge capture and resource utilization are critical components that impact an organization's cost accounting of healthcare services rendered. Collaboration between clinical, business, and supporting departments such as health information management services is required to sustain or improve the charge capture process. This case study considers a cyclical process of defining and redefining workflows that impact the revenue integrity of the organization. The key attributes to consider are defining the business flow and addressing efficiency, quality, and revenue integrity, which require identifying the people, process, and technology associated with each business function.

The RIT initially facilitated charge capture and applied utilization analytics to ensure compliance with private payer contracts and Medicare and Medicaid, and legislative requirements such as the Affordable Care Act (ACA). Assimilating current requirements being followed and the development of risk assessment tools, along with issue mitigation, provided solutions for the provider's clinical operations. The traditional revenue model of fee-for-service healthcare requires a robust cost accounting system. The RIT documented all current workflow that drove revenue, and then identified a future state position.

As a result of the RIT, changes were made within the organization, and the MDA provided pre-, concurrent, and postimplementation audits. In the context of reimbursement considering the traditional revenue model of the past, providers received additional reimbursement for documented high-cost outlier patients. The current and ongoing legislative mandates have and will continue to change the revenue model for healthcare in that under Medicare and Medicaid, providers will be penalized for those same high-cost outliers. The typical compliance audit involves validating provider fees against a defined set of quality outcome documentation requirements or validating charges against documentation that defines quality metrics. However, these existing "fee schedules" are being replaced with quality metrics.

In the future, the compliance audit will be redefined to become auditing quality metrics that characterize patient outcomes against reimbursement. Additional auditor subject matter expertise skill sets will be required in order to be effective with this type of review. The quality of performance metrics will dictate payments, thus paying for performance. Outliers in the future will not result in additional payment to the provider, but instead the potential for financial penalties. Future compliance audits will involve validating the outcome of the quality metric for validation of reimbursement.

Case Study Background

In this case study, redefining workflows is demonstrated by assessing and capturing data points from a people, process, and technology (PPT) perspective: who we are, what we do, and what we use to improve what we do.

In the case study illustration for the cardiology department, the RIT identified the workflow within the clinical operations of the department. They did this by following the provider audit gap template process shown in Table 6.7.

- ◼ **The gap:** First analyze the problem causing the revenue insufficiencies and data flow disconnects. Three important gaps must be identified:
  - Improving reimbursements—the gap between what you are billing and the revenue to which you are entitled

- Increasing operational efficiency—the gap between current processes or systems and industry best practices to ensure your clinical and financial departments are in alignment and running efficiently
- Minimizing risk—the gap between your current cost of noncompliance and a reduction in recurring compliance exposure, take-backs, and underpayments
■ Critical operational questions or resources that may be requested by the MDA are
  - Itemized listing of missing charges or revenue capture.
  - What is the billing error rate for the unit? Identify net and absolute error rates, overcharges, undercharges, and unbilled charges.
  - What is the root cause of each error type?
  - What is the root cause of interphase issues between identified clinical and financial systems?
  - What denial patterns exist by type—internal systems and external systems (e.g., the payer system)?

Additional considerations involved in developing the cardiology workflow process are included in Table 10.1.

Revenue integrity management was operationalized to meet the demands of federal and state reimbursements and to maintain compliance of federal and state agencies on proper claim submissions.

Author's Note: The payer industry has been auditing providers for decades. The savings materialized from these audits has funded budgets to maintain ongoing integrity audit programs within government-sponsored programs. The concept of self-funding for program integrity is expected to continue by auditing for waste, fraud, and abuse of the new government initiatives.

So managing—and streamlining—the revenue cycle process demands a review of the people, process, and fragmented technology that currently exist in these individual workflow silos scattered across the country to connect and identify where data is stored and how it moves from one

Table 10.1 Review of Audit Scope

Scope of care given: What is the service? Who is the provider?
What are the respective electronic systems (clinic-based electronic storage system, financial system, HIM program, electronic health record system, etc.)?
Is the clinical staff coding accurately?
How is system performance maintained by IT staff?
Can results be mapped from point of care through posting of payment and validation of patient records?
Are services accurately coded and classified based on patient need, services provided, and payer requirements?
How is data collected, recorded, and stored to support the claims?

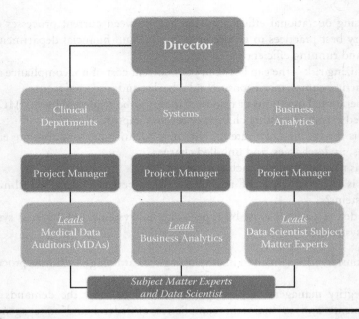

Figure 10.2   Hybrid roles of the RIT (data management team).

location to the next. In healthcare, it's not unusual when progressing through this review process to see that some of the information or data is moving forward electronically, while other packets of information are moving around on paper. Clinical documentation in the majority of departments is mired in a hybrid of hard-copy and digital media, so the challenges required to harness all those bits and bytes, faxes and photocopies, and subsequently coding that information for EMR's sake, require extremely capable and motivated professionals dedicated to precision outcomes. To survive the dynamic challenges of this complex environment requires a diverse set of skills that may be found by combining several types of roles within the RIT. Figure 10.2 provides an overview of the multidiscipline team applied in this case study, in addition to other integrated skill sets, such as business analytics, systems, and clinical operations.

The statement of work for the cardiology RIT project was first initiated by confirming the statement of work, creating a documentation file to document the statement of work, and defining the metrics to measure the results of the gap initiative. After the gap was conducted, procedures were constructed to mitigate all identified issues or problems. The case study further describes the metrics applied, which included benchmarking the services provided with the services captured via documentation. All variances were addressed as part of gap identification, followed by gap mitigation processes and procedures being put in place. A postreassessment was conducted to ensure that the changes remained intact.

The statement of work specifically targeted several workflows within the cardiology department, including registration analysis, process analysis for charge capture, documentation integrity, charge analysis findings and recommendations, charge description master (CDM) analysis, an illustrative supply example (pacemaker analysis), exception report analysis, and denial analysis. The departmental goal specifically addressed accuracy of revenue and compliance. The workflows that were confirmed and validated to impact revenue integrity included registration review, process analysis, documentation integrity, charge integrity, CDM integrity, systems mapping review, exception report, and denial analysis. Redefining workflows in a hospital system is achieved by

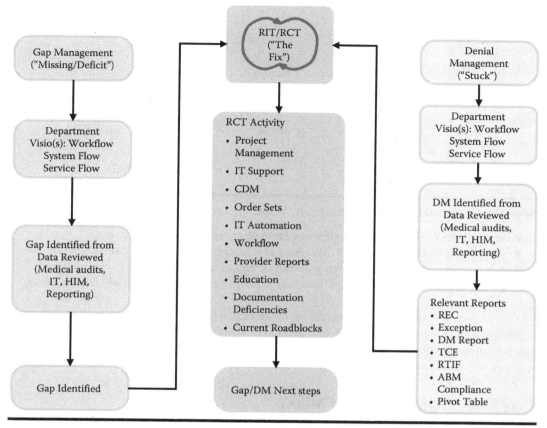

Figure 10.3   RIT medical data audit methodology (behavioral assessment tool).

assembling the right team members to do the right jobs. The team composition that was most effective in this case study is highlighted in Figure 10.2.

The methodology applied by the RIT is noted in Figure 10.3. The methodology incorporates strategic value, project direction, business process integration, and remediation expertise. Once a gap is identified, the next task is to develop a process that will bridge the gap. All too often, providers are left in a position with a gap report and no recommendation for improvement or mechanism to fix the issue. The RIT (Figure 10.2) provides that active ongoing mitigation mechanism illustrated in Figure 10.3. The process is contemporaneous and cyclical and begins by identifying and analyzing the gap, which is labeled as the missing data. The missing data is addressed by developing a gap management process. At the same time, it is important to identify what is denied because in this case, the activity is not missing but just "stuck." The etiology of the denied claim is addressed by developing a mitigation strategy and developing a denial management process to execute the mitigation of that denial—the fix. The fix is a blended overlapping of management process with gap initiatives. The process must be monitored, measured, and then reassessed. Figure 10.4 provides an overview of the workflow for the RIT.

Revenue integrity target goals include achieving quality of operational efficiency, compliance, and legitimate reimbursement. This practice standard is supported within the medical audit and internal audit literature. Key market issues to overcome by providers include

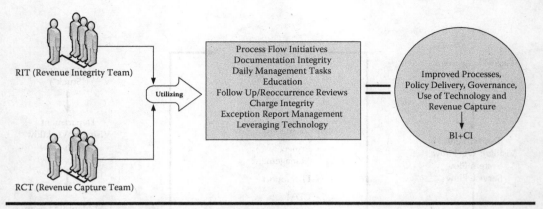

Figure 10.4 Workflow of RIT (data integrity team).

- Variability of cash flow and insufficient net revenue to support operations
- Data and communication silos that obstruct efficiency throughout the revenue cycle
- Adverse financial costs associated with noncompliance and adaption of new initiatives
- Insufficient and underdeveloped resources to adapt to new legislated payer requirements

The cardiology case study confirms that providers must have a plan of attack and, more importantly, a qualified team of subject matter experts to implement and monitor the plan to ensure that process improvements are executed. In this case study, the RIT identified the revenue problems, applied the fix, and continued to educate the staff and monitor improvement.

Case Study Highlight: Use of MDAs

MDAs were unable to validate total sample cases for the month because clinical documentation and image capture, along with EMR and billing systems, were neither fully integrated nor interfaced. Processes used to determine the gap included registration workflow documentation, analysis of the business process, review of documentation, charge and CDM integrity, systems mapping validation, validation of claims-on-hold algorithms, and validation of denial management report work lists. Figure 10.5 documents the cardiology current workflow state.

Case Study Highlight: The Gap

An initial gap was identified: charge capture gaps occurred as a result of charge description master (CDM) deficiencies, clinical documentation deficiencies, inadequate (or lacking) processes, and policy issues that required clarification of enforcement.

- Cardiology was not charging for all services rendered.
- 18% of bills were submitted with incorrect cardiology charges.
- 24% of bills were submitted without a procedure charge.
- Only 5% of bills were submitted with correct procedure charges.
- The CDM identified items to be charged; however, processes and procedures were not in place to capture and initiate charging.
- The physician performing the lab procedure failed to sign off on the medical record document.

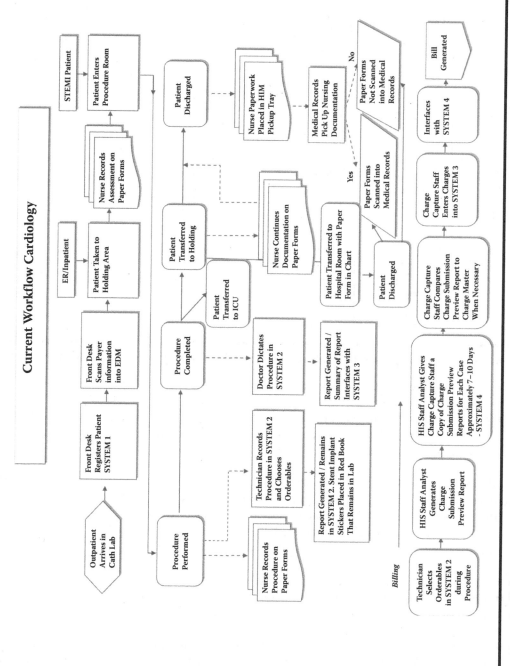

Figure 10.5 Cardiology current workflow state.

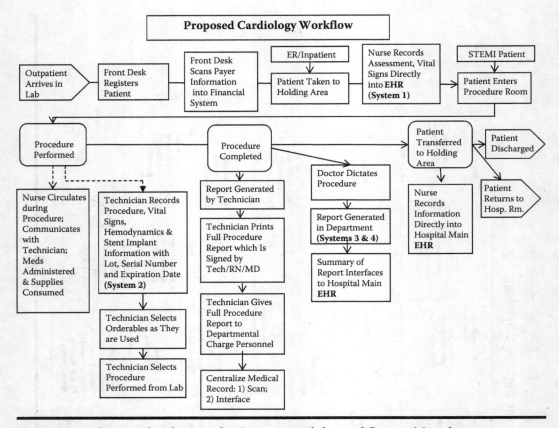

Figure 10.6 The completed RIT evaluation proposed the workflow revision shown.

- Hard-copy procedure reports were unavailable to staff as a reference guide to properly complete the quick reference sheet for charging purposes.
- EKGs performed throughout the institution were not appearing on the hospital bill because they were stuck in the department computer (software-driven) reporting system, waiting for a physician to read and sign the reports.

All findings were reviewed and adjustments to workflows were proposed in addition to CDM and documentation updates. Proposed workflows are highlighted in Figure 10.6.

The MDA also conducted a line-item audit and documented the charge routing and services systemwide. Table 10.2 identifies the base gap with respect to charge capture.

The following recommendations were initiated:

- Implement a new interdepartmental charge capture process.
- Implement line-item procedure billing for inpatients.
- Have MDAs perform concurrent reviews and educate department staff.
- Implement CDM changes.
- Prepare hard-copy procedure report to use in charge capture.
- Have intraoperative documentation be performed solely in the cardiac catheterization EHR.
- Enter preoperative and postoperative documentation into the main hospital EHR.

Table 10.2   Demonstrated Targeted Charges with Workflow Improvements

Focused Sampling: Original Gap Findings			
Revenue Code	*Revenue Code Description*	*Missed Charges*	*Overbilled*
250	Pharmacy (general)	$71,991.28	$29,830.32
270	Med/surg supplies & devices (general)	$17,328.00	$0.00
278	Med/surg supplies & devices (other implants)	$558,144.00	$0.00
305	Lab—clinical (hematology)	$324.00	$0.00
323	Radiology—diagnostic (arteriography)	$8,599.28	$0.00
480	Cardiology (general)	$43,180.10	$0.00
481	Cardiac catheter lab	$2,423,558.52	$134,965.02
	Total	**$3,123,125.18**	**$164,795.34**

- Prepare a hard-copy procedure report to follow all patients.
- Include a full copy of the procedure in the medical record.
- Include a full copy of the stent or implant information in the medical record.
- Bill for contrast on all procedures.
- Implement an interface between various cardiology systems for automation of information transfer (long term).

A workflow diagram was prepared to validate the integrity of charge capture processes. The ideal situation would be to consolidate all systems into one. In the interim, however, recommendations were proposed to define what workflow requirements were needed to make the current systems work. It is not uncommon to create interim fixes, provide feedback to support overall strategic planning, and make recommendations as to what technological solutions best enable data to be processed more efficiently. This interim process is illustrated in Figure 10.7 and facilitated by the MDA conducting a pre-, concurrent, and postaudit.

The following are MDA activities that facilitate smooth workflow transitions:

- Through user interviews and observation of current registration, care delivery, and documentation processes via the customer's EHR systems and charge description master (CDM), MDAs can identify and document opportunities for improving operational functions, including charge capture processes. MDAs also review diagnosis code documentation chosen by the customer to improve accuracy, efficiency, and timeliness of bill generation, improving the organization's accounts receivables.
- Complete and interactive demonstrations (workflow diagrams) are created by the MDAs with the assistance of medical nurse auditors to identify and test missed but legitimate revenue opportunities.
- MDAs review customer's CDM for accuracy and completeness with respect to technical fee billing in ambulatory clinics.

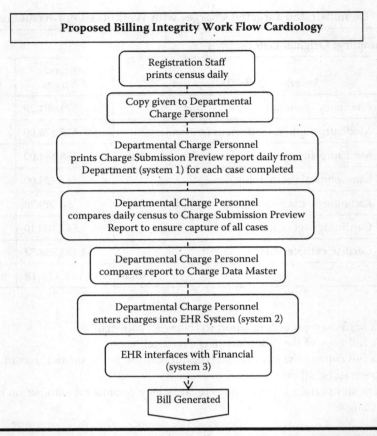

Proposed Billing Integrity Work Flow Cardiology

Registration Staff
prints census daily

Copy given to Departmental
Charge Personnel

Departmental Charge Personnel
prints Charge Submission Preview report daily from
Department (system 1) for each case completed

Departmental Charge Personnel
compares daily census to Charge Submission Preview
Report to ensure capture of all cases

Departmental Charge Personnel
compares report to Charge Data Master

Departmental Charge Personnel
enters charges into EHR System (system 2)

EHR interfaces with Financial
(system 3)

Bill Generated

Figure 10.7   Demonstrated workflow improvements for billing using current technology.

- MDAs assign and meet the teams, and they
  - Identify the appropriate RIT for the selected department.
  - Identify the appropriate revenue capture team (RCT) by department. The department RCT works with the RIT to review charge capture processes, policy, technology, and clinical issues relative to revenue integrity.
  - Review gap findings with the RCT in respective departments as requested by the customer.
  - Meet with selected clinical and administrative support to confirm their understanding of identified problems.
  - Communicate goals and benefits of RIT and how quality of care can be improved.
  - Review, document, and present findings on an ongoing basis.

In context with the methodology depicted in Figure 10.3, the fix requires a set of defined tasks, illustrated in Figure 10.8, and includes registration, compliance requirements, education of clinical and business staff, charge integrity validation, validation of charge systems mapping, review of accounts held up (discharged but not final billed [DNFB]), clinical documentation, denial reason codes, all processes, and a final CDM review. The fix in essence begins a process to fix any gaps, problems, or inhibiting factors that are slowing revenue flow.

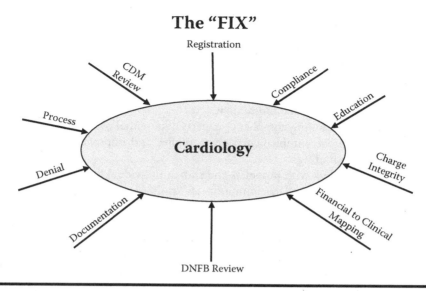

Figure 10.8 Resources involved in the fix for cardiology.

The fix will ensure proper pricing, charging, coding, and billing and keep up with payer requirements. Validation includes identification of the disruption in communication flow—an assessment of engagement at all levels, from management to the front line.

Questions to ponder: Has adequate corporate governance been established to ensure accountability? Are all applicable users provided access to the tools required to ensure the integrity of the work functions they are responsible for completing? A review of policy and procedures is also important to ensure that they reflect appropriate efficiencies. A final check should include validation of all payer contracts being built into the financial system.

Case Study Highlight: The Tasks

A series of tasks were executed to ensure facility and physician revenue integrity. The MDA actively participated in policy and process change. The MDA also reviewed the workflow documentation with each user and validated the IT process as it pertained to each specific issue or problem that was identified. The MDA had full participation in the orientation briefings pertaining to all known issues and problems. Furthermore, the MDA worked with the business users to implement solutions and ensure cooperative efforts to achieve goals.

The identified metrics measured improvement in charge capture processes and documentation of associated diagnosis codes chosen by the customer to improve efficiency and timeliness of bill generation. The case study reflected the alignment of financial and clinical processes as well as identified high-risk areas. The results were defined and measured and provided mitigation and support to the implementation of the current technology and overcoming system underutilization.

Author's Note: The case study was redacted and modified to provide anonymity.

Case Study Highlight: The Fix

The following is an illustrative listing of specific to-do tasks:

Plan the fix:
- Customer will provide final authentication in selecting or correcting customer's selection of any billing codes for reimbursement.
- Notify customer's billing compliance experts of potential overbilling and take action.
- Reaffirm new process implementation to resolve and improve upon the initial list of ambulatory gap findings.
- Document and work with providers and staff at individual level to address issues.
- Identify errors as critical data communicates (transfers) between disparate systems across entire revenue cycle (manual and automated).
- Identify missing or invalid data.
- Create daily exception report and management summaries that identify issues and errors and resolution procedures within the charge capture process.
- Develop and implement corrective actions necessary to decrease error volumes.
- Initiate new processes, policies, and so forth.

Untangle the technology:
- Provide technological and business support services to increase efficiency and use of other customer IT systems to improve the charge capture process.
- Implement and modify interfaces to improve the throughput of data between systems.
- Identify, document, and automate systems that eliminate the need for manual review and audit processes.
- Develop reports and audit tools to support review processes and provide appropriate management reporting.
- Manually transpose documented services and supplies into charges using systems specific to customer departments.
- Document and correct charges that fail to transfer from clinical to billing systems.
- Conduct software systems review that supplies revenue capture.

Schedule the day-to-day:
- Create or review daily summaries of all exceptions and rejections to resolve issues and errors with the charge capture process.
- Initiate new processes and policies to control deficiencies.

Educate—best practices:
- Provide clinical staff with a clear understanding of how they affect the billing and collection tasks.
- Explain how revenue integrity operations positively affect an increase in quality patient care.
- Communicate the downrange consequences or impact that inaccurate charging and billing practices have on the hospital's liability, financial health, and patient satisfaction.
- Identify, create, and provide feedback on new processes to solve charge issues and continue monitoring.
- Demonstrate ways to sustain charge capture success via periodic meetings with clinical teams.

Case Study Highlight: Results

Results were achieved by forming a committee consisting of the RIT and client or customer staff to implement a process for charge capture. The RIT shared the initial gap findings.

- The RIT initiated a departmental charge capture process and supplied the client with workflow diagrams of both the current and the anticipated future state for charge capture. Procedure codes and charge item descriptions were provided to update the CDM.
- Relevant procedure codes that were outdated or missing were supplied, ensuring the integrity of the CDM for the department.
- A quick reference sheet with procedural names, procedure codes, and required supplies was developed. The staff became knowledgeable on all listed procedures and billing regimens. A workflow diagram was created that identified the process and staff responsible for accurate charge capture (Figures 10.2 and 10.4). An audit of the clinical documentation of the procedure was performed. The audit confirmed that a procedure cannot be billed without a physician signature.
- A process was created and documented to ensure receipt of physician signatures and implemented in the future state workflow diagram.
- It was recommended that all system-specific clinical documents generated within independent departments be forwarded to health information management (HIM), where they can be aggregated in the hospital's independent electronic medical record center.
- It was recommended that pre- and postdocumentation stored within the departments' separate systems be included in the primary medical record database. In fact, any patient documentation generated within the department, including stent and implant information, must be aggregated and routed to the hospital's central electronic record system.
- Finally, the RIT created a workflow that ensured procedure reports are directed to the appropriate doctor for review and signature.

The charge capture results from addressing these gaps are illustrated in Figure 10.9.

Case Study Highlight: Follow-Up

After initial results were documented, the MDA worked with the RIT to focus on follow-up reassessments. The RIT follow-up and recurrence review in departments, as prioritized and selected by the customer, included

- Assessing and reassessing new processes implemented to resolve and improve upon the initial list of issues from the ambulatory gap analysis findings
- Recognizing, documenting, and reporting any problematic recurrences and issues associated with inconsistent performance to customer leadership
- Providing final authentication in selecting or correcting any billing codes for reimbursement
- Documenting and working with providers and staff at an individual level to address issues appropriately through communication, education, and if possible, observable reconciliation with the appropriate parties until improvement is made
- Reporting improvements, or lack thereof, to appropriate customer's administration

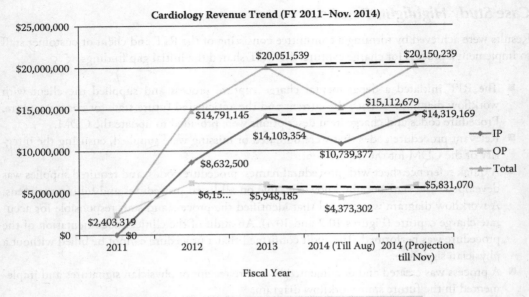

Figure 10.9 Cardiology case study impact.

The case study continues with an illustration of a shift in focus within cardiology. The case study highlighted the work involved with gap analytics, followed by gap management to fix the identified deficit. This ongoing case study discussion within cardiology illustrates the impact of the MDA when involved in denial management mitigation. The billing statements were sent and subsequently denied because billing codes were submitted with the requisite charges missing. In other words, if a procedure code is submitted for "pacemaker," the bill must include the charges for a pacemaker. If it doesn't, the claim is denied.

Case Study Highlight: Metrics

A listing of accounts was provided on denied claims. Upon review, RIT staff determined that pacemakers were missing from the bill. The MDA applied the work steps previously identified, and a root cause analysis determined that the "pacemaker charge" from the CDM was not coded correctly. It was incorrectly correlated with a pacemaker pad costing $400.00. The failure was not processing the correct procedure charge "pacemaker" for a price of $9000.00. Pacemaker cases were not being charged for the actual generator or leads, which were high dollar amounts. The team updated work-flow documentation and implemented a revised charge process. In their workflow, the MDA team

- Initially crosswalked the clinical documentation to the CDM and then to the financial system.
- Performed an analysis of medical record integrity, charge process, staff knowledge, and CDM review and integrity.

- Conducted a data analysis of the registration process that determined encounter type and recommendations to change district codes.
- Conducted a review of the on-hold report (outpatient exception report) recognizing trends in the cardiology area.
- Analyzed denials to identify upstream trends.
- Repeated a CDM review to ensure all current charges were present.
- Conducted a follow-up analysis and workflow documentation review.
- Provided staff education opportunities.

The role of the MDA, as illustrated in the cardiology case study, was effective in analyzing gap and denial management activities.

Key Market Barriers to Overcome

The key market barrier here is obvious—corrupt data. Data quality and assurance of its integrity are directly proportional to the organization's ability to effectuate documentation of current workflow state. A future workflow state cannot be defined without proper documentation of the current workflow state. It would be synonymous to grabbing a map to determine your route of travel without knowing where you are presently located. At a minimum, the management of big data requires a highly specialized multidisciplined team with defined core competencies. These core competencies are discussed in Chapter 12.

Author's Note: Be mindful of land mines that may include individuals within operations who have a perceived attachment to a process that may generate unseen obstructive behavior toward change.

The team should be launched under the direction of the CIO. Depending on the complexity of the organization and the current state of technology, the functions of MDAs may evolve as a department in and of itself headed by a CDO. As of this writing, I still sit in meetings during which professionals implore, "Just tell me what data it is I need to capture." The answer is typically characterized by the quick retort, "A scavenger hunt to identify and exploit all of the data silos secreted within these very walls." This struggle exemplifies the need for a formal data strategy not only within your specific organization but also across the healthcare continuum.

At a recent conference, I sat in a session entitled "Emerging CMIO." It was a shoptalk of chief medical information officers (CMIOs) and how they were utilized within their respective organizations. One particular theme was apparent: they were given the title based on their specific background in informatics, and their roles varied significantly. Their job descriptions ranged from a "figurehead" to one of strong collaboration with clinicians in the design and selection of an electronic health record system.

This is putting the "cart before the horse" because without solid tools and methodologies in place or at their disposal, the C-suite information officers will find themselves constantly stumbling over the cart. Let the horse drive the cart, in essence; the RIT discussed in this book is the horse. As discussed throughout this book, today's information is vast, has many faces, and takes many forms. In the healthcare industry, our technology can be complicated and processes unnerving; however, utilizing the systematic methodologies of a core RIT places the horse in front of the cart, supporting the ever-evolving roles and responsibilities of the CIO, CDO, and CMIO.

Although this case study provides a simple and direct application of the MDA and RIT methodology, the team also concurrently addressed acute needs within the organization. For example, the infrastructure for addressing meaningful use verification was integrated into the team's operational doctrine. The cross-functional team that included nurses with diverse clinical backgrounds and members with operational backgrounds throughout the entire revenue cycle were asked to quickly transition and respond to an acute C-suite directive resulting from a new set of compliance rules that had to be implemented stat. Since the team was already immersed in departmental work requirements, they were able to apply the workflow methodology, assemble a process within 48 hours, and execute a strategy to obtain physician signature proxies on a timely basis. During the process, the team discovered that a group of physicians did not meet the documentation criteria.

The team moved to update the workflow and then executed an education program for these physicians to help them attain their goals. The team responded to structured work plans and is in place to respond to acute needs within the organization. This is not an ordinary team. The team is a conduit to breakdown market barriers that result from lack of data, underutilized data, unknown data, and the lack of data reporting. The MDA team was effective in the cardiology case study. In addition, their availability as a critical data response team was pivotal to meeting other needs of the organization.

Final Thought

Do you currently utilize any type of medical auditor? How well does your revenue integrity initiative integrate the role of a medical data auditor? Chapter 11 provides a perspective on ideal core competencies for evolving into a data-driven organization.

Director of Nursing Informatics Commentary

The case study provided clearly indicates the need for documenting actual and desired workflows. Particularly noteworthy were the examples uncovered by the medical data audit team of the significant amount of lost revenue when the wrong items were charged, as in the pacemaker example. The audits also revealed tremendous missed charges and overcharges, which now can be rectified by putting unified processes into place.

—**Susan K. Newbold**
Director, Nursing Informatics Boot Camp, Franklin, Tennessee

Endnotes

1. Rouse, M., Workflow, http://searchcio.techtarget.com/definition/workflow (accessed October 2014).
2. Workflow Management Coalition, 1996, http://www.aiai.ed.ac.uk/project/wfmc/ARCHIVE/DOCS/glossary/glossary.html (accessed October 2014).

3. Higgins, J., Workflow Software: What's It All About? 2010, http://www.cpapracticeadvisor.com/article/10263154/workflow-software-whats-it-all-about (accessed October 2014).
4. Gantt Chart, http://www.businessdictionary.com/definition/Gantt-chart.html#ixzz3HJ3h4koG (accessed October 2014).
5. Taylor, F.W., *The Principles of Scientific Management* (Sioux Falls, SD: NuVision Publications, 2007).
6. The Voice of the Medical Audit Community, 2013, http://www.aamas.org/index.html (accessed October 2014).
7. Certified Professional Medical Auditor (CPMA˚), 2014, https://www.aapc.com/certification/cpma.aspx (accessed October2014).

Chapter 11

Evolving to a Data-Driven Organization

> Creative destruction is the process of organizational mutation that incessantly revolutionizes the economics from within....
>
> **—Paraphrased from Joseph Shumpeter's theory of economic innovation and business cycle**

"Innovation requires creative destruction"; so as healthcare organizations move forward to get their digital domains in order, existing data pipelines and information silos will become obsolete and patient intelligence will be "distributable." Evolving to a data (information)-driven organization will impact how health organizations collect, aggregate, store, analyze, and manage data and all of its applications. This chapter brings to light a number of concepts and considerations, or tactics, techniques, and procedures (TTPs), that define how we may evolve into a data-driven organization. TTPs require a bare-bones understanding of data in its rawest form.

To fully appreciate data as an asset requires the ability to isolate and then aggregate all the bits and pieces we call data or information into an understandable or user-friendly format: order from chaos. The interactive, iterative, and reiterating behavioral (IIRB) assessment model is one tool that enhances one's knowledge or understanding of an organization's data point–current state path toward any information future state. Creating a fluid data-driven future state without highly experienced and knowledgeable leadership coordination that is augmented by highly specialized, dedicated, and motivated teams of information and process integrity personnel will be synonymous to going to war without a rifle or ammunition.

Never attempt an assault on an enemy position without overwhelming numbers of highly trained, informed, motivated, and well-armed personnel. You need the right person for the right job, and all orders must be clear, concise, and direct. In our industry (healthcare), "all relevant data" is the objective to be assaulted, and the personnel trained to carry out this mission are highly trained and experienced revenue integrity teams with the right tools for the job.

How will data pipelines be identified? Who will manage data aggregation, and who will interpret and define the interdependent and intradependent relationships of all existing data points? And last but not least, who will define the organization's data strategy? The ultimate aggregator of an individual's health information should be the patient. A patient-centric environment requires the central portion or relevant core of aggregated data points regarding one's health to be available and controlled by the patient.

As organizations continue to ramp up their respective data warehouses and analytic capabilities, one more issue should be considered: the use of the word *patient*. The archaic definition of the word *patient* is "one who suffers or is a victim." A more modern day definition is that of a "person who is under medical care or treatment." Regardless, a shift from *patient* to perhaps *individual* or *personal health* would better represent the objective. A shift from patient-centric to individual health management would promote the intentions of population health management objectives.

Consider population health represented by the need to conduct human capital assessments and create contributions toward one's human capital. As organizations begin to develop their respective in-house data strategies, the issue of comprehensive patient access to their healthcare data must be deliberated in order to allow patients to effectively advocate for themselves on a real-time basis.

A Bit of History

In Chapter 10, the work of Frederick Taylor, which focused on the business of analytics and time management, was discussed. Henry Ford used business analytics to maximize efficiencies of assembly line labor. The introduction in the 1960s of computer and software decision support systems and technology that involved building model-driven decision support systems, followed by theory developments in the 1970s, greatly enhanced the use of analytics. The 1980s witnessed numerous developments of financial planning systems and spreadsheet-like decision support tools that opened the way to the development of data warehouses to support large-scale information decision support systems. The 1990s represent the era of knowledge-driven decision support systems that helped foster the use of web-based tools.[1]

Historical milestones date back to 1945, when Vannevar Bush proposed the idea of Memex, a hypothetical proto-hypertext system to store all of one's books, records, and communications. The 1950s saw Massachusetts Institute of Technology (MIT) projects that included man-made computers and the development of programing languages to support decision systems at formal organizations such as the Association of Information Systems (AIS) in 2001.

Health informatics trends and evolving practice standards can be found within the Healthcare Information and Management Systems Society (HIMSS), founded in 1961 (originally as Hospital Management Systems Society [HMSS], changing to HIMSS in 1986). Further specialized, HIMSS analytics "supports improved decision making for healthcare organizations, healthcare IT companies and consulting firms by delivering high quality data and analytical expertise."[2] With regard to government-sponsored initiatives, the Office of the National Coordinator for Health Information Technology (ONC) "is at the forefront of the administration's health IT efforts and is a resource to the entire health system to support the adoption of health information technology and the promotion of nationwide health information exchange. ONC is organizationally located within the Office of the Secretary for the U.S. Department of Health and Human Services (HHS)."[3] The ONC maintains a public resource to stay current on health information technology for both professionals and consumers at HealthIT.gov. A data-driven organization will first build the architecture (data strategy) to electronically capture data elements. Once the house is built, the appropriate team should be engaged and developed. A process to sift and abstract intelligence will drive the future of that organization. Chapter 12 will focus specifically on the chief data officer (CDO) role and the supporting infrastructure.

Author's Note: The root cause of all errors, gaps, and failed milestones at some point circles back to a data point that was unknown, misunderstood, misplaced, ignored, or just simply not processed.

Data: The Core Asset

What is data? Words such as *information*, *captured results*, *statistics*, *numbers*, and *records* come to mind. Furthermore, healthcare providers have been known to be egregious developers and hoarders of compiled data silos. Concerning our health records, all types of databases and formats exist, ranging from the more complex "digitally stored" medium to hard-copy documents randomly stuffed in file folders. Considering the concept of e-health, think of data in terms of either defined or undefined information. Defined data is information that has an assigned meaning or significance.

The requirement to define significance or meaning is the first step in assigning value to an intelligence asset or data point. Undefined information is data that appears without any assigned meaning or significance and may represent hidden nuggets of gold or obstructive land mines; however, both defined and undefined information generates new discoveries and understanding. A comprehensive understanding of data and its purpose provides the framework for developing an appropriate data strategy for an organization. This understanding is critical when conducting audits of any electronic, hard-copy, or hybrid-based data stores, including all exchanges of information between supporting communication systems. Therefore, as logic would dictate, a comprehensive data dictionary is essential to the success of any effective health information data aggregator. The medical data auditor can be characterized as a layered hybrid of the traditional internal data audit role model.

The Institute of Internal Auditors defines an *internal audit* as follows:

> Internal auditing is an independent, objective assurance and consulting activity designed to add value and improve an organization's operations. Auditing helps an organization accomplish its objectives by bringing a systematic, disciplined approach to evaluate and improve the effectiveness of risk management, control, and governance processes.[4]

With respect to data aggregation and integrity, the internal audit process provides reasonable assurance that the organization's data infrastructure is intact and that the organization is executing a sound data strategy. Internal audits should include a validation of internal control mechanisms that ensure all established policies and procedures are followed when interacting with defined data sets. Consider the following explanation of internal control and its relation to information systems provided by the U.S. Office of Management and Budget:

> Internal Control—organization, policies, and procedures—are tools to help program and financial managers achieve results and safeguard the integrity of their programs.... Control activities include policies, procedures and mechanisms in place to help ensure that agency objectives are met. Several examples include: proper segregation of duties (separate personnel with authority to authorize a transaction, process the transaction, and review the transaction), physical controls over assets (limited access to inventories

or equipment), proper authorization, and appropriate documentation and access to that documentation. Internal control also needs to be in place over information systems—general and application control. General control applies to all information systems such as the mainframe, network and end-user environments, and includes agency-wide security program planning, management, control over data center operations, system software acquisition and maintenance. Application control should be designed to ensure that transactions are properly authorized and processed accurately and that the data is valid and complete.[5]

Author's Note: An *error* results from the wrong data, at the wrong time, resulting in the wrong decision. *Fraud* occurs when the right data is utilized at the right time (point of vulnerability) to execute the right illicit transaction.

Controls should be established at an application's interface to verify inputs and outputs, such as edit checks. General and application controls over information systems are interrelated; both are needed to ensure complete and accurate information processing. Due to the rapid changes in information technology, controls must also adjust to remain effective.[6] Medical data auditors (MDAs), therefore, should ask several questions when reviewing a health system operation, such as

- What controls are in place to collect and manage all relevant forms of health and business information created during the course of patient care?
- What tests can be conducted to ensure data integrity and provide assurance that a breach has not occurred?
- Does the system incorporate adequate controls to prevent unauthorized data use and ensure that authorized users have appropriate levels of access?

Today, industry leaders are developing market standards and products for capturing, storing, managing, and securing electronic health information. The advent of practice standards and requirements has placed an emphasis on data content and requires organizations to systematically develop comprehensive data libraries to maintain overall continuity.

Data Library: Inventory of Data Assets

The data library consists of all data activities that define the collection and organization of any new or existing information. Checklist 11.1 illustrates the flow of data activities that will help identify and document all relevant data components.

Author's Note: Checklist 11.1 provides suggestions. Your organization should adapt those attributes critical to the data strategy.

The first task involving data audits is to identify the subject matter of interest and all related factors that impact the organization. For example, data should be defined its type (electronic

Checklist 11.1 Audit Activities Data Library Checklist

☐ Accessibility	☐ Map
☐ Accuracy	☐ Mine
☐ Action	☐ Modeling
☐ Analysis	☐ Next response
☐ Application	☐ Output
☐ Atomicity	☐ Partition
☐ Audit	☐ Precision
☐ Authentication	☐ Redefine
☐ Comprehensiveness	☐ Relevancy
☐ Consequence	☐ Response
☐ Consistency	☐ Solution
☐ Definition	☐ Source
☐ Durability	☐ Testing
☐ Existence	☐ Timeliness
☐ Identification	☐ Use
☐ Implementation	☐ Value
☐ Isolation	☐ Warehousing

Source: Busch, R. *Electronic Health Records: An Audit and Control Guide*, New York, Wiley & Sons, 2008.[7]

format versus nonelectronic), location, housing, definition, utilization, and end users and by any all-unique data attributes. The following example illustrates the process of identifying data elements associated with one isolated operational component, the processing of a service claim.

- Facilities such as hospitals and clinics submit claims electronically on form UB-04 (universal billing form developed in 2004). This form contains up to 86 potential data fields, which are defined by the universal billing committee.
- A provider typically populates data (inserts information) in portion to these 86 potential fields and transmits the UB-04 to a third-party administrator (TPA) or insurance company.
- The TPA or insurance company then decides which provider data elements it will accept for processing.
- Depending on the corresponding data elements the TPA stores on file or unilaterally accepts or rejects, an employer plan may be further limited by what data the payer acknowledges or accepts.
- Determining what and why a market player has dropped a particular data element is important in the identification of internal controls on both sides.
- Market players must distinguish between the common data attributes of electronic and paper submissions.

In the paper world, the original UB-04 claim (evidentiary file) document passes through the claim submission process without any content disturbance. However, an electronic claim document allows for any number of opportunities for personnel in the document's chain of custody to unilaterally change, introduce, or delete data for various reasons. Identifying altered content or the absence of data by omission is a key audit function and significantly impacts data validity, reliability, or comprehensive claim assurance.

The MDA will identify, define, and label all data elements, and subsequently document specific use criteria to determine corresponding linkage or eliminate data if appropriate to the condition and authorization. MDAs record and track all deleted, redefined, or introduced data subject to further validation and audit. If a data element's definition fails to reflect its application or use, then the MDA must expand the definition. In defining the source of each data element, the MDA must include all prior transitions of that data. If MDAs download insurance company healthcare claims on behalf of employers, then they must note the appropriate data transactions, which may look similar to the following chain:

(1) Provider → (2) Company *ABC* clearinghouse → (3) Insurance company *DEF* →
(4) PPO network *GHI* → (5) Insurance company *DEF* → (6 and 7) Vendor check and explanation of benefits (EOB) printing → Insurance company *DEF* → (8) Insured → (9) Employer plan sponsor → (10) Insurance company *DEF*

In this illustration, data values are not limited to monetary considerations. Data also includes values that characterize process flow and contractual or operational issues.

Author's Note: Data as an asset requires the ability to isolate and then aggregate [it] … into … [a] user-friendly format: order from chaos.

Another Approach on the Scavenger Hunt for Data

An audit was being conducted within a new, state-of-the-art specialty hospital that allegedly functioned in a fully integrated interoperable electronic environment. The first stop was in the emergency room (ER). ER data processing or information capture began with patient registration, including the documentation of services provided; however, a problem was discovered concerning the all-electronic environment when trying to walk the patient to the intensive care unit (ICU).

The MDA team quickly determined that the registration system lacked the virtual capability to electronically discharge patients from the ER and admit them electronically to the ICU. The MDA team identified that ER staff were routing hard-copy documents to the ICU staff, which subsequently input the patients' information into the system electronically to admit them. MDAs must identify and understand a wide variety of local norms, ritual actions, idiosyncrasies, and basic "missing links" within the audit environment, which is followed by detailed workflow documentation critical to isolating potential process gaps. Once the MDA team discovers missing data, they should subsequently add the necessary data fields to the data library and then redefine the workflow process and documentation.

In this case, the facility inadvertently limited the virtual interoperability between the ER and the ICU. The development team that created this specific electronic environment did not identify, anticipate, or fully understand the provider's operational environment, including workflow or database end-user requirements. System developers created a roadblock or failed to understand a key element in interoperability by making decisions without an understanding of data use or data end users. Critical to the process is proper documentation of current and future state workflow by creating data maps to determine, among other things, virtual and manual data uses and data end users.

Data mapping must be tested by first documenting the anticipated data points and then tracking those data points through all operational data processes. If the facility had "acceptance" tested the system's ability to electronically transition patients (data points) from one location (ER) to another (ICU) with a data map, then developers would have identified a breach in interoperability prior to taking ownership.

As an interesting aside, during this audit engagement it was determined that the investment group that developed and constructed the facility were physicians. In addition, at no point had any of the physician investment group members considered a morgue in their facility plans, and they were completely caught off guard following the facility's first adverse outcome—a deceased patient. A functional data-map test and workflow certification would have captured this electronic and physical disruption in the flow of critical data.

A comprehensive well-defined data library determines the basis upon which an organization can effectively mine intelligent information or data. To illustrate, consider as a concept the scientific study of matter. Traditionally, matter can be looked at as mass that occupies space. Captured or aggregated data could be considered equivalent to mass in the physical world in that it occupies space within some technological environment.

Scientists recently began exploring the concept of black matter, which, simply defined, is "all the mass in the universe that we cannot see." Furthermore, and somewhat daunting, scientists believe that most matter in the universe is black matter. Consider our ability to utilize digitally aggregated health data as the basis for an opportunity to efficiently locate and determine the identity of healthcare's black matter data. An electronic versus hard-copy storage system housing trillions of data has the capability to generate multitudes of intelligence products that were previously unattainable for the healthcare community to use and analyze. In other words, strategically aggregated data presents the opportunity to shed light on virtual black matter data.

Mining data to generate intelligence is the greatest value proposition in a technology-driven aggregated health data environment. Creating a well-structured data library will provide opportunities for the understanding and application of data not previously within reach of the healthcare community. Significant implications stemming from an increase in access to data intelligence include the ability to reduce cost, increase quality of care, and thwart the ethically challenged from thriving in this current segmented marketplace. Data mining based on a solid electronic infrastructure of defined data elements opens the door to derive intelligence from large amounts of quality information and comprehensive analytical data models.

Data Intelligence

As a nurse practitioner, one of the hospitals I worked at developed a data model for infection rates that identified a high rate of postbypass patients on one specific unit and gradually discovered a pattern that linked one particular surgeon with an unusually high postoperative infection rate. The hospital initiated a study that collected and analyzed data from all applicable medical records. Each medical record was manually reviewed to compile all relevant documentation, after which the information was subject to analysis to determine findings and then retested to validate conclusions forthwith. This process, audit, or self-assessment took 1 year to eventually isolate the conditions resulting in high rates of infection in postbypass patients.

More to the point, the inquiry identified high rates of infection linked to one individual, as opposed to many individuals, causing the condition to manifest. A corrective action plan was developed to mitigate this specific condition or individual, as opposed to the entire institution. Armed with an electronic database under these same conditions, the probability of discovery would have increased exponentially and in a fraction of the time.

Technology initiatives in healthcare are mobilizing providers to develop the capability to enable the healthcare community to collect, process, understand, and respond to data in an instant. Technology tools will promote data output that the community can reasonably rely on; however, in some cases, data output may produce inconclusive information. When inconclusive data outputs occur, the proper response is to redefine the prior steps or perhaps reevaluate the original premise or presenting issue.

In the previous example, once the institution was armed with the clinical intelligence necessary to address the unusually high postoperative infection rates, the hospital was able to implement a response, which in this case was to remove the surgeon's surgical privileges pending treatment of his own infectious condition (surprise). The hospital could have also responded by including better monitoring of etiology for postoperative infections or evaluation of employee and staff health policies.

The concept of collecting patient outcomes by provider now exists, but measuring this information by specific staff members is an innovative path forward to developing data aggregation and the applied technology (software) that can communicate the intelligence product to all stakeholders. Technology-driven aggregation data centers will eventually enable decision makers to assimilate and process data in a more efficient and timely manner. The virtual world provides the opportunity to collect and analyze outcomes and produce intelligence information at each measurable level and subsequently feed on success to move the healthcare community forward.

New Data Assets

Data, whether in electronic or manual form, is constantly evolving to meet increased demands for speed, accessibility, and comprehension. MDAs and those that manage an organization's data strategy must keep in mind that although increasing the speed at which information arrives helps to deliver results more rapidly, it can also produce hazardous results and at rates considered alarming. In a healthcare setting, the speed of receiving, processing, and reacting to an abnormal laboratory test can generate an adverse outcome to the patient. In the payer world, if 1000 fraudulent claims are processed per minute, then money (capital) could potentially vaporize long before an error is realized. Checklist 11.2 highlights some of the data management concepts involved in the processing of new data.

Checklist 11.2   New Data Management Processing Concept Checklist

☐ Deductive	☐ Inductive
☐ Hidden patterns	☐ Neural network
☐ Information	☐ Predictive

Source: Busch, R. *Electronic Health Records: An Audit and Control Guide*, New York, Wiley & Sons, 2008.[7]

As new data develops from a data library, results may fall into neural networks. Neural networks help identify hidden patterns that are not normally seen with unstructured and undefined data. Data libraries help end users to understand the reasoning behind any predictive or deductive model analysis. Neural networks provide specific information that can be broken down into clusters, and clusters in turn can be further broken down into neurons. Therefore, neurons are basically derived from original data elements. This data directs the transmission of an intermediate response to the information. This process is cyclical: data output leads to the center point of data components, a further breakdown of the elements, and finally, the development of a data algorithm. For example, in the provider setting, a neural network may consist of the elements that cause a specific medical error. Any relevant processed data can be used to prevent this error from recurring.

In the business office, a neural network may consist of the elements that cause a certain type of denial of payment. Processed data can therefore be used to produce recognizable characteristics of a denial type in order to correct and address the issue internally and on the individual claim. A very simple algorithm could be developed to prevent the error in the future, and in turn, the denial could involve a neural network with a list of operational attributes that created the denial. The provider may program an algorithm to seek out errors to mitigate this condition before the claim is ever submitted, and the center point would generate an exception or error report that demands additional intervention and review.

More New Data: Ultimate Data Aggregators

The ongoing creation of new data generates even more data outputs and opportunity for data analysis (see Checklist 11.3). Technology-driven data aggregators will ultimately drive change in healthcare. For example, measuring and documenting adverse outcomes to medications can help providers make adjustments to treatment protocols and improve outcomes. New data will improve the quality and efficiency of healthcare delivery, in addition to empowering the users with information that will impact day-to-day decisions.

Processed Data: The Start of Mining for Intelligence

The generation of an anomaly or innovation is the result of analyzing processed data. Processed data, as illustrated in Checklist 11.4, develops new clusters, neurons, and subsequent etiologies.

Checklist 11.3   More New Data Checklist

□ Analysis	□ Innovation
□ Intelligence	□ Output

Source: Busch, R. *Electronic Health Records: An Audit and Control Guide*, New York, Wiley & Sons, 2008.[7]

Checklist 11.4   Processed Data Checklist

□ Clustering	□ Innovation
□ Etiology	□ Neurons

Checklist 11.5   Categories of Data Activity Checklist

☐ Algorithm	☐ Hierarchies
☐ Analytics	☐ Intelligence
☐ Content	☐ Language
☐ Business intelligence (BI)	☐ Natural
☐ Clinical intelligence (CI)	☐ Machine learning
☐ Assets	☐ Master data management
☐ Center points	☐ Operational data
☐ Components	☐ Outputs
☐ Elements	☐ Taxonomies

Source: Busch, R. *Electronic Health Records: An Audit and Control Guide*, New York, Wiley & Sons, 2008.[7]

Etiology provides the cause and effect of certain sets of data elements. By segmenting clusters by subject matter, neurons acting as the decision tree for processing data elements derive intelligence and lead toward understanding the etiology of anomalies.

Data Warehouse: The Route to a Data-Driven Organization

Organizations typically wrestle with multiple internal and external data warehouses or silos as they move forward in the aggregation or merging of company information. Data warehouses or "segregated silos" are large stores of data accumulated from a wide range of sources and used to guide management decisions. Data warehouses are considered home for all of the information that has been captured and stored for current or future use. Without these massive storage domains (warehouses), companies would have black holes of scattered, meaningless, and unusable information—similar to a carton of eggs. Without the carton, the eggs are a real pain to organize, transport, or store. Checklist 11.5 lists categories of data captured and stored in a data warehouse.

Key Market Barriers to Overcome

One of the many (significant) barriers to overcome in developing a data warehouse is avoiding what is referred to as a data avalanche. What does this mean? Think of a massive avalanche of snow (big data) cascading down a mountain, gathering more speed, snow, and debris as it heads south. By the time it reaches the bottom, its mass and velocity have the potential to destroy anything in its path. Big data has the potential to act in a similar fashion in that an overwhelming amount of information in a multitude of formats can simply overwhelm your capability or capacity to effectively define and acquire what you are looking for.

To provide context, consider this big data factoid: 90% of all data produced throughout human history has been created in the last 2 years.[11] Given these extraordinary compound information growth rates and increased velocity at which data is delivered, corporations will have to anticipate which specific data sets to capture and store and which to bury in a mass of useless information debris. If an organization were to store all the information relevant to any specific interest without a defined capture strategy, data structure, and volume limits, a data avalanche condition would potentially threaten to overwhelm even the most robust storage medium (architecture).

The ability to move from isolated, disconnected data silo environments to a formal strategic plan is the first step. Organizations "must choose which information to analyze before it even enters the data architecture."[12] A strategic plan must include three fundamental changes in managing data. Step 1 includes data acquisition structure, storage requirements, and data disposal strategy. Once a strategic plan has been adopted, step 2 is the development of a corporate or enterprise information governance policy and implementation plan that must come from the C-suite. If the CEO fails to support the new data strategy, then accountability for overall data integrity will not filter down throughout the rank and file. The third step is operationalizing your corporation's data assets to serve the community of end users.

Once these milestones have been achieved, optimization of data is now subject to the knowledge, skills, and abilities of the subject matter expert (SME) developing algorithms to siphon (extract) actionable intelligence from the noisy "big health information" data warehouse. Therefore, algorithms are defined as the process mechanisms or set of rules to be followed in calculations or other problem-solving operations, especially by a computer. In effect, software is developed by constructing a set of rules to make something happen and then providing a simple front end for users to steer the machine.

The effective use of algorithms (roadmap to capture a clear picture) is a skill set that, when properly thought out and applied, will lead an organization to evolve into a true data-driven environment. Theoretically, the goal would be to ask your database any question and get the answer. The algorithmic challenge is to formulate the right question in a fashion that the computer and database understand. The ability to develop an effective operational intelligence database will be directly proportional to the ability of management to communicate, develop, or construct the correct questions or define specific instructions in the algorithmic dialogue. Subjecting internal control mechanisms into the data testing process allows for reasonable assurance of data integrity in the financial, operational, and service sectors of a technology-driven data-aggregated environment. The rapid growth of information requires a fundamental shift in how organizations manage it.

Preparing for the Future

The American Health Information Management Association (AHIMA) is developing practice standards for information governance.[13] The framework is referenced as Information Governance Principles for Healthcare and designed to help organizations improve information governance. The framework presents eight principles:

1. **Accountability:** Appointment of an accountable member in a leadership position to oversee the program
2. **Availability:** Assurance of information that is timely, accurate, and efficient
3. **Compliance:** Assurance of compliance with any applicable laws and regulations
4. **Disposition:** Securely disposing of data that is no longer necessary
5. **Integrity:** Managing all information to ensure authenticity and reliability
6. **Protection:** Implementing protections from breach, corruption, and loss of information

7. **Retention:** Ensuring data is kept for appropriate length of time, depending on legal and regulatory requirements

8. **Transparency:** Publicly documenting all information governance processes and actions in a verifiable way.[14]

This book focused on considerations resulting from the introduction and impact of big data. They range from changes in information management to technology use and managing revenue to practice standards and ultimately new emerging functions and leadership roles. Figure 11.3 provides an overview of a strategic data aggregation approach with the goal to convert data to a measured asset with infinite output possibilities. Recall Chapter 9 listing chief leadership roles and subject matter expertise. Review Figure 11.1's leadership roles in comparison to the functional roles in Figure 11.2. Now cross-reference the subject matter expertise of the leadership roles in Figure 11.2. The CDO should consider all the functional needs among internal and external partners.

A data aggregation strategic plan needs to incorporate and filter all the data from the respective operations. This strategy involves the ability to operationalize the plan. Figure 11.3 represents a

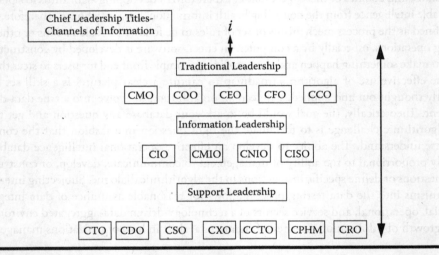

Figure 11.1   Leadership roles: traditional, informational, and support.

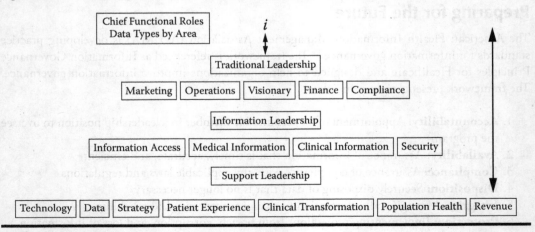

Figure 11.2   Subject and data type by leadership role.

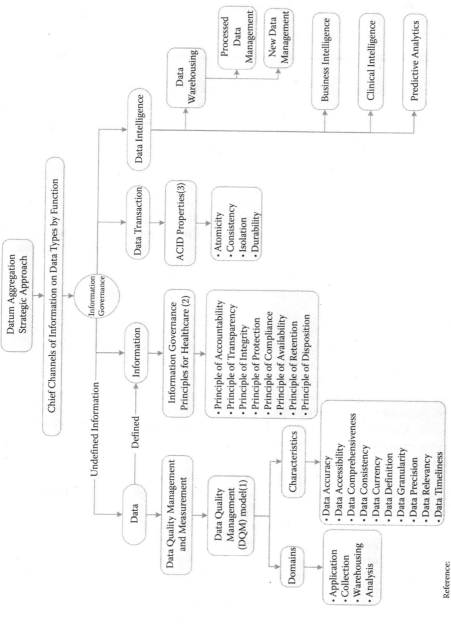

Figure 11.3   Compilation of a data aggregation strategic approach.

compilation of proposed practice standards and key components that should be addressed prior to an organization mobilizing its efforts.

Author's Note: Has your organization implemented data policies and standards that define practices that are "must," "shall," and "may" with respect to documentation and capture of data assets?

This chapter's explanation of data behaviors and elements provides auditors with the necessary checklists to review data within an organization and develop, execute, and maintain an effective data strategy for that organization. Chapter 12 provides a suggestion as to the information governance and support roles to manage this process.

Final Thought

It's all about the data. A data inventory plan is a critical precursor to the development of a data strategy. Delineate all data types, and then segment and tag the data as unstructured (does not have defined or consistent value), semistructured (silos within internal and external platforms—semiaccessible), and structured (defined, available in active and inactive states).

CDO Perspective

Adopting a data-driven culture is particularly challenging for established organizations that grew up in an era where the decision-making process was necessarily more subjective. The cultural change almost always requires significant modification of deeply-ingrained institutional expectations and practices, and long-standing perspectives on the assessment and management of risk, growth, and profitability often need to be revisited. Accordingly, becoming a data-driven organization is as much an exercise in change management as in information management, and failure to recognize this duality portends failure.

Organizations considering this transition should be prepared for change across every domain. Technical and operational components will almost certainly require modernization, both from an infrastructural and from a human resource perspective. Most organizations find this process difficult and labor-intensive, yet ultimately more palatable than the requisite changes in leadership styles and management practices. A truly data-driven culture is incompatible with decision-making processes that favor "executive judgment" or "institutional knowledge." A leadership team that is unable to embrace the new culture and set an example of change is also incapable of marshalling the organization through this evolution. Conversely, leaders who see a tangible path to value associated with this transition and are willing to rise to manage the change aspects may well be rewarded with improvements in efficiency and value that were previously thought unattainable.

The stakes are high in this game. Outcomes will be proportional to investments in the process of becoming a data-driven organization, but only if those investments are equal parts conceptual, cultural, monetary and operational. Incomplete commitment will produce the worst possible outcome: an organization that talks about being data-driven, yet defends a cult of personality around its leaders. Conversely, dedicated effort and willingness to evolve will result in an organization that is better able to compete in the modern business environment.

—Dr. Nicholas Marko
Chief Data Officer, Geisinger Health System, Danville, Pennsylvania

References

1. Power, D.J., A Brief History of Decision Support Systems, http://dssresources.com/history/dsshistory.html (accessed November 2014).
2. HIMSS Analytics Supports Improved Decision Making for Healthcare Organizations, Healthcare IT Companies and Consulting Firms by Delivering High Quality Data and Analytical Expertise, 2014, http://www.himssanalytics.org/home/index.aspx (accessed November 2014).
3. About ONC. 2014. http://www.healthit.gov/newsroom/about-onc (accessed November 2014).
4. Standards & Guidance—International Professional Practices Framework (IPPF)', 2014, https://na.theiia.org/standards-guidance/Pages/Standards-and-Guidance-IPPF.aspx (accessed November 2014).
5. OMB Circular A-123: Management's Responsibility for Internal Control; Memorandum to the Chief Financial Officers, Chief Operation Officers, Chief Information Officers, and Program Managers, December 2004, http://www.whitehouse.gov/omb/circulars_a123_rev (accessed November 2014).
6. Circulars, http://www.whitehouse.gov/omb/circulars_default (accessed November 2014).
7. Busch, R., *Electronic Health Records: An Audit and Internal Control Guide* (New York: John Wiley & Sons, 2008).
8. Ibid.
9. Ibid.
10. Ibid.
11. Putman, S., Changing a Key Assumption to Manage the Big Data Avalanche, http://blogs.sas.com/content/datamanagement/2013/06/26/changing-a-key-assumption-to-manage-the-big-data-avalanche/ (accessed November 2014).
12. Ibid.
13. AHIMA Issues Health Care Information Governance Framework, 2014, http://www.ihealthbeat.org/articles/2014/10/2/ahima-issues-health-care-information-governance-framework (accessed November 2014).
14. Ibid.

Chapter 12

Defining the Role of the Chief Data Officer

The chief danger in life is that you may take too many precautions.

—**Alfred Adler**
Austrian medical doctor, psychotherapist

If you agree that managing data is critical to maximizing profitability, patient care, regulatory compliance, and overall strategy, then you might also reach the conclusion that there is room in the C-suite for another executive with a pure focus on how to manage and exploit data. Chapter 11 discussed emerging standards from the American Health Information Management Association (AHIMA) on information governance. However, if you are going to have a chief data officer (CDO), you also need to consider formally defining data governance within your organization to supplement the perspective and evolving role of a CDO.

Data Governance

According to the Encarta Dictionary,[1] *governance* is defined as "having authority over something, controlling or restraining something, having influence over or being the law for something." Translating that to data governance, it means having authority over data, controlling or restraining data, having influence over or being the law for data. Author and consultant Danette McGilvray defines data governance as "the organization and implementation of policies, procedures, structures, roles, and responsibilities that outline and enforce rules of engagement, decision rights, and accountabilities for the effective management of information assets."

McGilvray further notes that data governance ensures that the appropriate people representing business processes, data, and technology are involved in the decisions that affect them, which includes escalation and resolution of issues, implementing changes, and communicating resulting actions.[2]

A Bit of History

For as long as data has existed, organizations have assigned personnel to utilize and manage the information for the benefit of the company. The pure existence of data has not changed; it's all around us—everywhere. However, the ability to access, manipulate, analyze, and exploit big data is a recent development that some industries have conquered, lighting a pathway for others, and then, of course, there are those who continue to stare at data like a deer in the headlights. According to the *MIS Quarterly Executive* article by Lee et al., the first CDO was established at Capital One in 2003. Hospitals, like banks, have a repository of valuable data, which can be utilized to not only improve profitability, but also make a remarkable contribution to the quality of life for millions of individuals. CDOs are just starting to emerge in the healthcare industry and, in many cases, are struggling to determine the logical step-off point from cover to attack this immense beast. Eugene Kolker holds one of the rare CDO titles in healthcare, having first taken the position at Seattle Children's Hospital in 2007. IBM has called the chief data officer the "new hero of big data and analytics."[3]

The *Healthcare IT News* article "Chief Data Officers Come to Healthcare"[4] discusses how "historically, data strategy has resided within IT." However, the changing dynamics of both clinical delivery and financial reimbursement models has elevated the importance of data as something that is "necessary and integral to business strategy and execution,"[5] writes Chris Nott, chief technology officer for big data and analytics at IBM UK. CDO Kolker explains, "Our deal is trying to leverage data as a strategic institutional asset. It's not about technology. It's not IT. It's about how to transform data into information, how to transform information into better-informed decisions."[6]

Kolker has 25 years of extensive experience in data analysis, predictive analytics, and algorithm development. Seattle Children's Hospital's data strategy has three parts, according to Kolker. The first one is the science, analytics, and modeling of data. The second aims to use the CDO to build the service internally. "Within our own walls, we act as internal consultants," says Kolker. "And that has worked, for the past few years, really well. For those who don't hire a CDO, you can use an external service provider as CDO, for example, cdoanalytics.org." The third component, he says, "is people skills, social skills. That's extremely important." He uses data scientists to mine hidden opportunities within the hospital's five dozen subspecialties and numerous other services, including inpatient, outpatient, and emergency. As stated in earlier chapters, the key is using your people, process, and technology (PPT) in the spirit of collaboration to work toward a "shared vision, clearly articulated goals with measurable outcomes." Kolker adds that it is not enough "to take a problem and just go in your room and solve it." It is critical to work with different stakeholders "to understand what their needs are, to recalibrate to see whether this is where we're going together." Right now, his hospital is focused on utilizing benchmarking to improve quality and safety. A hospital should optimize its data strategy with a multidisciplinary team of practitioners, leaders, managers, and a staff of data experts. Kolker continues, "It's critical to work with different stakeholders to understand what their needs are, and recalibrate towards a common goal." He emphasized that with collaboration comes the critical need to have the right people for the right job. Kolker stated that right now his hospital is focused on utilizing benchmarking to improve quality and safety.

> People talk about technology, and we need to have it … data science, analytics? Absolutely. Business practices? Definitely. But still the major focus is people—who are going to make decisions or not, perform interventions or not. Our whole focus is to help people make better, data-driven decisions.

"CDOs have various reporting lines including to the Chief Technology Officer (CTO), Chief Information Officer (CIO), Chief Executive Officer (CEO), Chief Marketing Officer (CMO) or the Chief Strategy Officer (CSO)."[7] Even though organizations have made some strides to address data-related issues, they continue to arise and heighten concerns, which has led a growing number of organizations to establish enterprise-level, executive-rank CDOs. Despite the arguments that traditional lower-echelon, data-centric managers and data governance mechanisms can deliver the same results as a CDO, there are critical differences between data managers and CDOs:

- CDOs will build an organizational capability to sustain the entire organization.
- CDOs are responsible for communication and collaboration with internal and external partners and stakeholders.
- CDOs establish, exercise, and are accountable for leadership in resolving data problems.

In essence, CDOs do not replace data managers or data governance practices, but rather provide leadership to managers of data and improve efficiency through the introduction of vital organizational data to executive- and officer-level staff.

Author's Note: The ability to access, manipulate, analyze, and exploit big data is a recent development that some industries have conquered, … [while others] continue to stare at [it] like a deer in the headlights.

First CDO

Capital One appointed Cathryne Clay Doss as its first CDO in 2003.[8] Subsequent to that, the CDO position slowly started to develop, as large public institutions, including U.S. federal and state governments and the U.S. military, recognized the need for someone to manage overall data processing. The private sector has followed the U.S. government's lead in this area at a rapid pace, and today more and more companies have implemented the CDO position. According to an article published by David Laverty of the executive recruiting firm Russell Reynolds, 50% of Fortune 500 companies will employ a CDO by 2015.[9]

To Whom Does the CDO Report?

According to a *MIS Quarterly Executive* article by Lee et al., of all of the CDOs interviewed for it, 30% report directly to the CEO, 20% to the chief operations officer (COO), and 18% to the chief financial officer (CFO); others report to the CIO, CTO, chief medical officer (CMO), or chief risk management officer (CRMO).[10]

Role and Responsibilities of the CDO

Peter Aiken, president of DAMA and cofounding director of Data Blueprint, stated in an article published by Rob Karel, "The CDO's sole focus is data—how to manage data as an asset and convert it into tangible business value. And as assets go, data is our sole non-degrading, non-depletable, durable, strategic asset."[11] The chief data officer is responsible for managing data, improving data quality, and monitoring online access effectiveness. However, the CDO's responsibilities may vary between organizations, depending on a candidate's breadth of subject matter expertise and leadership capabilities that are overlaid on top of an organization's needs.[12]

In an article published by Larissa T. Moss, "The Role of Chief Data Officer in the 21st Century," Dr. Anne Marie Smith, principal consultant at Alabama Yankee Systems, LLC, summarizes the qualifications for a CDO position as follows:[13]

- Bachelor's degree in finance, business, computer science, or other relevant field
- Fifteen-plus years of relevant data management experience, including architecting data management solutions and designing/developing data governance policies/standards
- Strong project leadership and management skills to lead organizational change to effectively meet strategic and tactical goals
- Strong written and verbal communications skills required; must be equally comfortable discussing the enterprise information management (EIM) strategic perspective with executives and implementation details with operational staff and IT
- Organizational/political agility with the ability to drive large, cross-functional data management programs involving coordination with multiple stakeholders
- Ability to help define and articulate the enterprise data management strategic vision and translate it into tactical implementable steps
- Solid knowledge of the organization's industry and its challenges in the use of data and information
- Certification in data management and understanding of the various technologies of data management within an organization
- Strategic decision-making skills with a high degree of latitude

According to the cubic framework outlined in Lee et al.'s article, three key dimensions were identified to provide a better understanding of the CDO roles:[14]

1. *Collaboration direction (inward versus outward)*—The collaboration direction captures the focus of the CDO's engagement, either inside or outside of the organization. Collaborating inward means focusing on internal business processes associated with internal business stakeholders. In contrast, collaborating outward implies that the CDO's focus is on stakeholders in the external value chain and environment, such as customers, partners, suppliers, or non-profit regulatory entities. Initiatives led by internally-focused CDOs typically include developing data quality assessment methods or mechanisms; cataloguing data products, sources, and standards; creating processes for managing metadata or master data; engaging in information product mapping; and establishing data governance structures. These initiatives seek to deliver consistent data inside the organization and to address root causes of various data quality issues. Streamlining the internal business process associated with key data flows takes cross-functional cooperation, and it can yield efficient and effective business operations. The CDO's success in these initiatives depends heavily on ability to effectively lead the relevant internal stakeholders and map out the transformation journey. In contrast, outwardly-focused CDOs strive to persuade and collaborate with external partners. For example, an outwardly-focused CDO of a global manufacturing company led a business process-embedded "global unique product identification" initiative, geared towards

improved collaboration with external global partners. Outward CDOs may also focus on external report submission activities, particularly if the company has experienced an external embarrassment or a sizable disaster, such as being exposed by poor-quality reports.

2. *Data space (traditional versus big data)*—"The data space that a CDO focuses on can either be transactional data, typically in relational databases, or the newer and more diverse big data." Because traditional data is the strength of an organization, and without a strong foundation the organization's most basic capabilities are impaired, many CDOs focus on it. On the other hand, big data CDOs help provide the leadership necessary to adapt to and manage the analysis of big data and the implementation of insights from these analyses.

3. *Value impact (service versus strategy)*—The CDO's role can focus on improving services or on exploring new strategic opportunities for an organization. This dimension reflects the impact desired from a CDO. In many cases, the CDO role is a direct response to the on-going need for an executive's oversight and accountability to improve existing functions of the organization. Increasingly, however, CDOs are sought who can add strategic value to their organization by taking advantage of new tools such as data aggregators or other data products based on digital streaming data. These CDOs are also exploring ways to develop new market niches, or transform the company in order to develop smarter products and services.

Based on the three dimensions described above, Lee et al. identified eight different role profiles for CDOs:

1. *Coordinator: Inward/Traditional Data/Service*—The coordinator CDO manages enterprise data resources and sets up a framework that optimizes collaboration across internal business units (inward). This allows for the delivery of high quality data to data consumers in the organization for their business purposes, thereby improving business performance (service). The coordinator works with traditional data, such as customer information and other transactional data (traditional data).

2. *Reporter: Outward/Traditional Data/Service*—In heavily regulated industries, such as finance and healthcare, an emerging trend in the CDO role is a focus on enterprise data to fulfill external reporting and compliance requirements. Like the coordinator, the reporter CDO fulfills a business obligation (service) through the delivery of consistent transactional data (traditional data). However, the reporter's ultimate goal is high quality enterprise data service delivery for external reporting purposes (outward).

   Similarly, reporter CDOs are often found in financial service organizations and work with compliance or risk management entities to fulfill external reporting requirements. Reporting CDOs are typically established when a company experiences difficulties in report production in addition to playing an important role in data integration from information silos of recently merged companies required for external reporting purposes.

3. *Architect: Inward/Traditional Data/Strategy*—An architect CDO's direction and data space are the same as the coordinator CDO (inward, traditional), but the value impact is focused on using data or internal business processes to develop new opportunities for the organization (strategy).

4. *Ambassador: Outward/Traditional Data/Strategy*—An ambassador CDO promotes the development of inter-enterprise data policy for business strategy and external collaboration (outward, strategy) and focuses on traditional data (traditional). For example, the CDO in a financial services institution defined common datasets for risk management. He promoted

a set of data standards and data assessment measures for financial data exchange among peer financial institutions.

5. *Analyst: Inward/Big Data/Service*—The analyst CDO resembles the coordinator, except that he or she focuses on improving internal business performance by exploiting big data, thus requiring different data management and data analysis capabilities. The need for an analyst CDO often emerges after an organization hires data analysts or data scientists but does not designate an executive leader to provide an enterprise perspective to their efforts.

6. *Marketer: Outward/Big Data/Service*—The marketer CDO develops relationships with external data partners and stakeholders to improve externally provided data services using big data. CDOs in data product companies are often marketer CDOs. They develop working relationships with retailers, financial institutions, and transportation companies that are purchasing their company's data.

7. *Developer: Inward/Big Data/Strategy*—The developer CDO navigates and negotiates with internal enterprise divisions in order to develop new opportunities for the organization to exploit big data.

8. *Experimenter: Outward/Big Data/Strategy*—The experimenter CDO engages with external collaborators, such as suppliers and industry peers, to explore new, unidentified markets and products based on insights from big data. Through strong collaborative relationships across industries, the experimenter CDO maintains access to various sources of data and uses them for creating new markets and identifying innovative strategies for organizational growth.[15]

The cubic framework outlined in Lee et al.'s article can also be used to identify the role and need for a CDO in an organization. These steps are

1. Assess current status of your organization's data-related business practices (based on the three dimensions of the CDO cube).
2. Determine the CDO role profile needed for your organization (based on the eight roles described), and whether an executive-level CDO is required to fulfill these needs.
3. Strategize the likely path for the CDO based on a projection of organizational future needs.[16]

CDO Role in Healthcare

The chief data officer (CDO) is responsible for enterprise-wide governance and utilization of data as an asset. This includes creating, maintaining, and coordinating all elements related to data strategy. The CDO will work with all areas (both clinical and business) that create, collect, or use (or could use) data. The CDO will be responsible for all stakeholders' efficient use of data, using external sources to augment information needs. The CDO must have a strong understanding of data's role in all business operations, including, but not limited to, clinical areas, marketing, finance, IT, and legal.

Furthermore, the CDO should seek out opportunities to utilize data to increase enterprise value. This can include increasing revenue by finding new uses for data and decreasing costs by streamlining processes. The CDO will lead our information-centric organization to be more efficient in our ability to deliver high-quality use of data. Ultimately, what should not be forgotten in this process is that data use is all about the patient. As Kolker commented in a recent interview, "By some accounts we are a decade or so behind other cottage industries in part because innovations in healthcare have a higher bar. Rightly so, because we are talking about people's lives, not about how people click. The right click can change a life, the wrong one can take a life."

Recognizing that data quality is an integral part of all business processes, every job requires attention to data quality, reporting data defects, determining the root causes, improving the affected data quality processes to eliminate the root causes, and monitoring improvements. The CDO develops and maintains methodologies and best practices related to a consistent data governance and stewardship program; these include

- Ensuring that data created within all functional areas (including both clinical and business areas) is maintained in a central area for efficient use.
- Ensuring data quality and integrity, including the creation of a process for stakeholders to express concerns related to data integrity.
- Rationalizing and standardizing systems, technologies, or other tools used for information management throughout the organization.
- Establishing and enforcing standards, processes, frameworks, tools, and best practices for process modeling, semantic modeling, and logical physical data modeling.

The CDO is responsible for managing the resolution of data problems or weaknesses. As a result, an effective CDO needs to have the support of senior leadership and an effective governance program to ensure success. The CDO and departmental support will often act as internal consultants for departments in the area of data strategy or those seeking support on data analytics. The use of medical data auditors (MDAs) was illustrated in examples throughout this book. Further, this role may be involved in conducting a regular review of emerging technologies to assess their relevance and viability in solving ongoing information management challenges. It is important that an organization CDO work closely and in tandem with other information leaders within the organization. Specifically, the CDO should be working with the CIO and chief information security officer (CISO) in setting standards for regulatory compliance, data policy, data security, and data retention.

Recommended CDO Qualifications

- 20+ years of industry experience in multiple functional areas of hospital administration
- Strong understanding and experience with a complex IT organization
- Strong understanding and experience with complex data analytics
- External consulting experience and hospital administration experience
- Experience in managing multiple stakeholders within a matrix organization
- Experience in managing and building multifunctional teams
- Track record of successful transformational change within complex organizations
- Strong written and verbal communication skills

Considerations

Ideally, the best person for this position has a successful track record accomplishing the goal of a typical CDO. As the role of a CDO is not yet common in healthcare, it may make sense to consider candidates (and even seek out candidates) who have achieved similar goals in other industries. The CDO will need a strong multifunctional team to ensure that all areas of expertise needed in the CDO organization possess the requisite knowledge, skills, and abilities (KSAs). Augmenting the CDO's team with third-party consultants may be necessary for the short or long term. The use of medical data auditors was illustrated in examples throughout this book. The ability to lead, inspire, and manage teams will also be critical for the success of this role.

Transforming an organization that is not data-driven to a data-centric organization information end user may also require that the CDO's first 90 days be focused on creating a baseline of all technology and data being used within the enterprise. The CDO will need to build a team to manage ongoing operations and put together a plan for an initial assessment of current operations.

CDO Organization

When building a CDO organization, you might consider starting with a skeleton team that does an initial evaluation. This team must consist of members who have experience in all areas of both clinical and hospital administration. This trained cross-functional team must include experts in workflow documentation, clinical processes, administrative processes, and data and trend analysis. Indirect support may include information architects, data analysts, and business modelers. The hybrid role of MDA is an evolution of the medical auditor in the revenue cycle and internal audit.

Medical data auditor: This individual may be a clinician or clinical operations expert who has been cross-trained in medical auditing, internal audit, and revenue cycle. Further, as illustrated in various examples throughout this book, he or she may also include the skills sets highlighted below.

Workflow documentation specialist: The primary role of this individual is to document workflow for both clinical and administrative processes within the hospital. The workflow documentation specialist will interview relevant hospital staff and observe hospital staff in documenting workflow. The workflow documentation specialist will liaison with nurse auditors and administrative auditors to validate and recommend improvements for workflow.

Nurse and clinical auditors: These individuals are experienced healthcare providers who will first assist in documenting baseline clinical procedures. They will work with the team to improve operations from both a clinical and a financial perspective. These auditors will test and validate the workflow.

Hospital administrative auditors: These auditors are experienced hospital administrative operational support roles with deep operational knowledge, such as registration, medical records, billing, and coding. These individuals will first assist in documenting baseline administrative procedures and then work to improve operations from both a clinical and a financial perspective. These auditors will also test and validate the workflow.

Data scientists: These individuals will work with the team to identify trends and potential problem areas that warrant further research. Data scientists are well versed in data analysis and statistics. They will be involved in identifying areas for improvement in both clinical and administrative processes. Once an area is identified as a potential problem, the data scientist will work with the nurse and administrative auditors to suggest areas to test. If a problem exists, the auditors will provide recommendations to improve the process. Once recommendations are tested and validated, the processes will be implemented and updated.

Key Barriers to Overcome

The CDO will need to have sufficient staffing and training. The simple truth is that no hospital to date has optimized the use of its data. For this reason, it will be difficult for experienced staff and trained personnel to execute the mission of the CDO organization. The initial team embedded within the hospital will be pioneers developing the methodologies and training their future peers.

The CDO will need to develop effective communication and cooperation with all functional department heads and staff. It is critical to ensure that proper reporting and financial incentives are in place to encourage people to work together. The CDO may face political challenges in having the role viewed as a threat to boundaries. Individuals previously responsible for activities may now fall under the domain of the CDO. Others may have difficulty letting go of authority. The CDO may also face pushback from stakeholders who do not want known data integrity issues (that should have been resolved) to be exposed. The CDO must provide value to stakeholders and be accountable to business unit leaders to facilitate the use and analysis of data. Department heads and all other stakeholders will be responsible for following policies and procedures set forth by the CDO's office. Clear lines of authority and responsibility, metrics, and incentives will need to be in place to ensure that power struggles are minimized and that the unit heads work together in the hospital's best interest.

Where will the budget for the CDO office come from? Clearly there will be a reallocation of assets throughout the organization to facilitate these initiatives. Initially, there will be an investment to support the CDO's office; however, in the near future, the combination of gains in revenue and cost-saving measures should more than compensate for the cost of this new office.

Author's Note: The CDO formally entered into healthcare from a policy perspective with the introduction of CMS's first chief data officer (CDO) in November 2014. The Office of Enterprise Data and Analytics (OEDA), which is led by Niall Brennan, the agency's first chief data officer (CDO), is tasked with implementing efforts in data collection and dissemination. It will be interesting to observe this role as it develops within the healthcare industry.

Final Thought

Data can be a very powerful asset. The best return on investment can be achieved by having a strong data strategy. Advanced predicative analytics can improve quality of care to identify high-risk patients and initiate strategies to minimize adverse outcomes. Data and data analytics can also be used to identify areas that increase revenue by locating patterns of missed billing opportunities and uncovering areas of inefficient processes, which can improve the bottom line. The data chief has the opportunity to evolve his or her organization to meet the demands for intelligent data–driven actions. The magnitude, volume, depth, and scope of data cannot be fully realized if it is not organized and accessible to the right people, at the right time, for the right reasons.

CDO Perspective

Data and analytics enhance our understanding of health and healthcare to take on a triple aim of improved outcomes, reduced costs, and better access. Seattle Children's CDOAnalytics has a multidisciplinary team that works closely with business, clinical, and IT leaders. The team combines best consulting practices and business processes with data analytics in a way that is applicable to problems from the operating room to the boardroom (cdoanalytics.org). For example, CDOAnalytics has developed an approach to identify medically complex patients at the point of care, thus improving patient care coordination and reducing costs. Other examples include A/B comparison modeling for key decision making, leveraging benchmarking to improve care and safety, and optimizing priorities for business development. Yet, analytics alone will not be sufficient to make significant progress in healthcare, because it will remain people-intensive. Expectations for the future need to take into account the changes required in people's behaviors and lifestyles to improve long-term health outcomes, as well as the degree of organizational readiness necessary to capitalize on these changes. From any angle you look at it—data, analytics, technology, operations, strategy, society, or business—it's all about people.

—**Eugene Kolker**
Chief Data Officer, Seattle Children's Research Institute, Seattle, Washington

References

1. Pallardy, R., Encarta, *Encyclopædia Britannica*, 2014, http://www.britannica.com/EBchecked/topic/186436/Encarta (accessed December 2014).
2. McGilvray, D., *Executing Data Quality Projects: Ten Steps to Quality Data and Trusted Information (TM)* (Burlington, MA: Morgan Kaufmann, 2008).
3. Miliard, M., Chief Data Officers Come to Healthcare, 2014, http://www.healthcareitnews.com/news/chief-data-officers-come-healthcare (accessed November 10, 2014).
4. Ibid.
5. Ibid.
6. Ibid.
7. Wikipedia, Chief Data Officer, 2014, http://en.wikipedia.org/wiki/Chief_data_officer (accessed December 2014).
8. Karel, R., Will the Real Chief Data Officer Please Stand Up? 2014, http://www.informatica.com/us/potential-at-work/information-leaders/will-the-real-chief-data-officer-please-stand-up.aspx#fbid=3t4PuMw2-ex (accessed December 2014).
9. Laverty, D., Building a Smarter Planet: A Smarter Planet Blog, 2014, http://asmarterplanet.com/blog/2014/02/chief-data-officer.html (accessed December 2014).
10. Lee, Y., Madnick, S., Wang, F., Wang, R., and Zhang, H., A Cubic Framework for the Chief Data Officer (CDO): Succeeding in a World of Big Data, 2014, http://www.mitcdoiq.org/wp-content/uploads/2014/01/Lee-et-al.-A-Cubic-Framework-for-the-CDO-MISQE-Forthcoming-2014-copy.pdf (accessed December 2014).
11. Karel, Will the Real Chief Data Officer Please Stand Up?
12. CDO Position Description, https://project-open-data.cio.gov/cdo/ (accessed December 2014).
13. Moss, L., The Role of Chief Data Officer in the 21st Century, 2014, http://www.cutter.com/content-and-analysis/resource-centers/business-intelligence/sample-our-research/biar1302.html (accessed December 2014).
14. Lee et al., A Cubic Framework for the Chief Data Officer (CDO).
15. Ibid.
16. Ibid.

Appendix I: C-Suite Acronyms

Chief clinical transformation officer	CCTO
Chief compliance officer	CCO
Chief data officer	CDO
Chief executive officer	CEO
Chief experience officer	CXO
Chief financial officer	CFO
Chief information officer	CIO
Chief information security officer	CISO
Chief marketing officer	CMO
Chief medical information officer	CMIO
Chief nursing information officer	CNIO
Chief operating officer	COO
Chief population health manager	CPHM
Chief revenue officer	CRO
Chief security officer	CSO
Chief strategy officer	CSO
Chief technology officer	CTO

Appendix II: Datum Asset Strategy: Incorporating Key Points within the Book

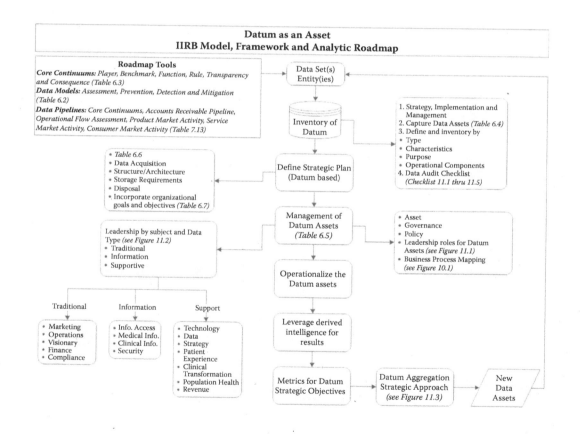

Datum as an Asset
IIRB Model, Framework and Analytic Roadmap

Roadmap Tools
Core Continuums: Player, Benchmark, Function, Rule, Transparency and Consequence (Table 6.3)
Data Models: Assessment, Prevention, Detection and Mitigation (Table 6.2)
Data Pipelines: Core Continuums, Accounts Receivable Pipeline, Operational Flow Assessment, Product Market Activity, Service Market Activity, Consumer Market Activity (Table 7.13)

Data Set(s) Entity(ies)

Inventory of Datum

1. Strategy, Implementation and Management
2. Capture Data Assets *(Table 6.4)*
3. Define and inventory by
   • Type
   • Characteristics
   • Purpose
   • Operational Components
4. Data Audit Checklist
   (Checklist 11.1 thru 11.5)

• Table 6.6
• Data Acquisition
• Structure/Architecture
• Storage Requirements
• Disposal
• Incorporate organizational goals and objectives *(Table 6.7)*

Define Strategic Plan (Datum based)

Management of Datum Assets *(Table 6.5)*

• Asset
• Governance
• Policy
• Leadership roles for Datum Assets *(see Figure 11.1)*
• Business Process Mapping *(see Figure 10.1)*

Leadership by subject and Data Type *(see Figure 11.2)*
• Traditional
• Information
• Supportive

Operationalize the Datum assets

Leverage derived intelligence for results

Traditional
• Marketing
• Operations
• Visionary
• Finance
• Compliance

Information
• Info. Access
• Medical Info.
• Clinical Info.
• Security

Support
• Technology
• Data
• Strategy
• Patient Experience
• Clinical Transformation
• Population Health
• Revenue

Metrics for Datum Strategic Objectives

Datum Aggregation Strategic Approach *(see Figure 11.3)*

New Data Assets

Appendix III: Human Capital Workflow

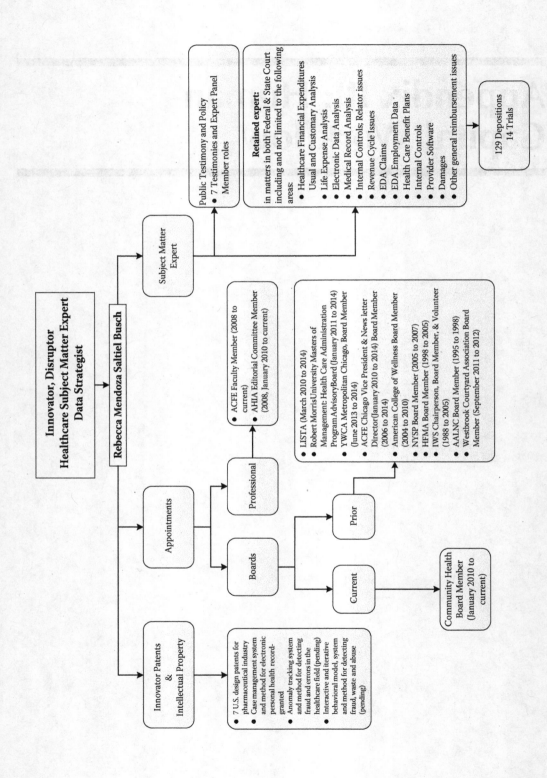

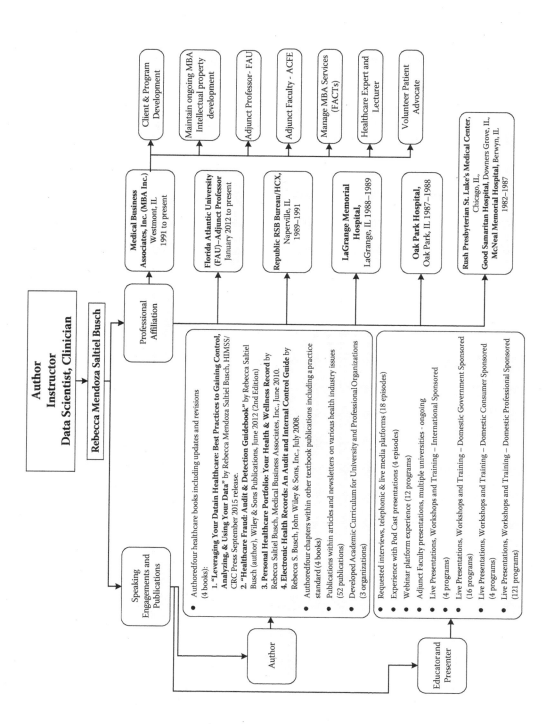

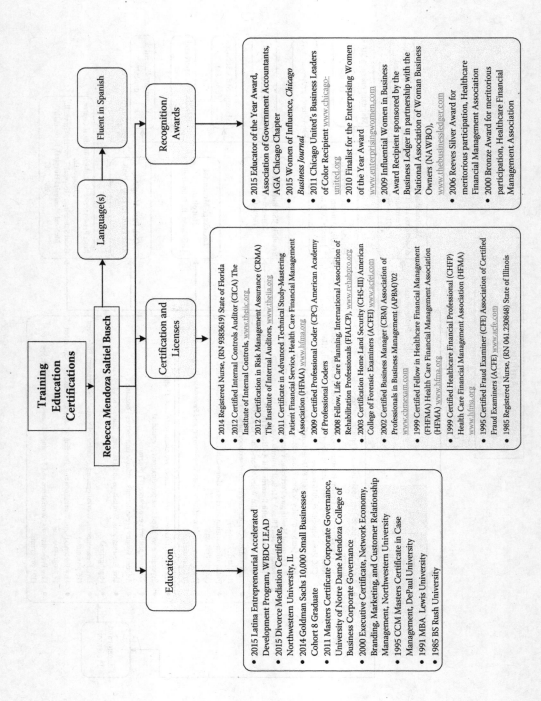

Training Education Certifications

Rebecca Mendoza Saltiel Busch

Language(s)

- Fluent in Spanish

Education

- 2015 Latina Entrepreneurial Accelerated Development Program, WBDC LEAD
- 2015 Divorce Mediation Certificate, Northwestern University, IL
- 2014 Goldman Sachs 10,000 Small Businesses Cohort 8 Graduate
- 2011 Masters Certificate Corporate Governance, University of Notre Dame Mendoza College of Business Corporate Governance
- 2000 Executive Certificate, Network Economy, Branding, Marketing, and Customer Relationship Management, Northwestern University
- 1995 CCM Masters Certificate in Case Management, DePaul University
- 1991 MBA Lewis University
- 1985 BS Rush University

Certification and Licenses

- 2014 Registered Nurse, (RN 9383619) State of Florida
- 2012 Certified Internal Controls Auditor (CICA) The Institute of Internal Controls, www.theiic.org
- 2012 Certification in Risk Management Assurance (CRMA) The Institute of Internal Auditors, www.theiia.org
- 2011 Certificate in Advanced Technical Study-Mastering Patient Financial Service, Health Care Financial Management Association (HFMA) www.hfma.org
- 2009 Certified Professional Coder (CPC) American Academy of Professional Coders
- 2008 Fellow, Life Care Planning, International Association of Rehabilitation Professionals (FIALCP), www.rehabpro.org
- 2003 Certification Home Land Security (CHS-III) American College of Forensic Examiners (ACFEI) www.acfei.com
- 2002 Certified Business Manager (CBM) Association of Professionals in Business Management (APBM)'02 www.cbmexam.com
- 1999 Certified Fellow in Healthcare Financial Management (FHFMA) Health Care Financial Management Association (HFMA) www.hfma.org
- 1999 Certified Healthcare Financial Professional (CHFP) Health Care Financial Management Association (HFMA) www.hfma.org
- 1995 Certified Fraud Examiner (CFE) Association of Certified Fraud Examiners (ACFE) www.acfe.com
- 1985 Registered Nurse, (RN 041.230848) State of Illinois

Recognition/Awards

- 2015 Educator of the Year Award, Association of Government Accountants, AGA Chicago Chapter
- 2015 Women of Influence, *Chicago Business Journal*
- 2011 Chicago United's Business Leaders of Color Recipient www.chicago-united.org
- 2010 Finalist for the Enterprising Women of the Year Award www.enterprisingwomen.com
- 2009 Influential Women in Business Award Recipient sponsored by the Business Ledger in partnership with the National Association of Woman Business Owners (NAWBO), www.thebusinessledger.com
- 2006 Reeves Silver Award for meritorious participation, Healthcare Financial Management Association
- 2000 Bronze Award for meritorious participation, Healthcare Financial Management Association

Index

K

Knowledge, skills, and abilities (KSAs), 112, 195
KSAs, *see* Knowledge, skills, and abilities

L

"Leadership ecosystem," 67
LHWCA, *see* Longshore and Harbor Workers'
    Compensation Act
Longshore and Harbor Workers' Compensation Act
    (LHWCA), 4

M

Management of information systems (MIS), 39
MDA, *see* Medical data auditor
Medicaid program, funding provided by, 130
Medical data auditor (MDA), 195
    case study, 160
    questions asked by, 176
    redefining workflows, 151
    revenue integrity management, 127, 134
Medicare reimbursement cuts, 69
Mental Health Parity Act, 12
Merchant Marine Act (the Jones Act)
MIS, *see* Management of information systems

N

Need-gap analysis, 97
Newborns' and Mothers' Health Protection Act, 13
Next-generation firewalls (NGFWs), 71
NGFWs, *see* Next-generation firewalls
Nippur Tablet No. 3191, 4

O

OEDA, *see* Office of Enterprise Data and Analytics
OFA, *see* Operational flow assessment
Office of Enterprise Data and Analytics (OEDA), 197
Omnibus Consolidated and Emergency Supplemental
    Appropriations Act, 14
"One-trick-pony" IT geeks, 41
Operational flow assessment (OFA), 105
Outsourcing, 59

P

Patient financial services (PFS), 51–64
    CRO perspective, 63
    HFMA's MAP Keys in revenue cycle management,
        54–58
        aged A/R, 55, 57
        bad debt, 56
        case mix index, 56
        cash collections, 56

charity care, 56
cost to collect, 56
diagnosis-related group, 56
final billed not submitted to payer, 55
net days in A/R, 55
net income or loss per primary full-time employee
    physician, 57
net income or loss per specialty FTE physician, 58
percent of patient schedule occupied, 56
physician practice management, 56–58
point-of-service cash collections, 55
practice cash collection percentage, 58
practice net days in A/R, 58
primary physician practice operating margin
    ratio, 57
professional services denial percentage, 5
proper claim submission, 57
registration process, 57
scheduling process, 56
specialty physician practice operating margin
    ratio, 57
subtopical areas, 55–56
total charge lag days, 57
total specialty physician compensation as a
    percentage of net revenue, 58
uncompensated care, 56
uninsured discount, 56
history, 52–53
    attributes of financial management, evolution
        of, 52
    efficiency of workflow, 52
    organizations, 53
hybrid roles of, 53–54
    example, 53
    hospital accounting departments, 53
    need for comprehensive skills sets, 54
    patient advocate, 54
    registration functions, 53
key market barriers to overcome, 58–60
    code expansion, 59
    narrow network phenomenon, 59
    outsourcing, 59
    revenue cycle management, 58
operational concept, 51
price transparency, 51
role of data and revenue integrity management,
    60–63
    changes in today's market, 61
    digital continuity, management of, 63
    issues versus problems, 62
    self-assessment issues, 61
    senior information risk owner, 62
    senior responsible owner, 62
state of denial management today, 119
state of patient financial services today, 54
Patient Protection and Affordable Care Act, 132, *see also*
    Affordable Care Act